THE
CHARMED
CIRCLE

Theology For The Head, Heart, Hands and Feet

Robert Masson

Sheed & Ward

For Erin

Sheed & Ward™ is a service of National Catholic
Reporter Publishing, Inc.

Library of Congress Catalog Card Number: 86-61358

ISBN: 0-934134-40-5

Published by: Sheed & Ward
　　　　　　　115 E. Armour Blvd. P.O. Box 414292
　　　　　　　Kansas City, MO 64141-0281

To order, call: (800) 821-7926

Contents

PREFACE

Lest the reader be caught off guard, a few words about this book's *circle* of understanding are in order — especially since a focal notion in it is the image of Christian faith as a *circle* in which the followers of Jesus live. It should be noted that I am using this image in a variety of ways and approach it on several different levels.

In the first place, I am alluding to the sort of thing we have in mind in expressions which refer to a person's "circle of understanding," or to one's "circle of friends," "social circles" or "political circles." On the one hand, this sort of image is apt for describing the way religious doctrines, stories and rituals come together to form a more or less comprehensive worldview or circle of understanding. On the other hand, it calls to mind the way one's thinking, feeling and acting are interrelated, at least ideally, within a specific circle of belief. From yet another perspective, the image is apt for calling attention to the social and communal character of Christianity; faith is not just a matter of intellectual assent to ideas or doctrines. Rather it means taking a stand within a circle of people and for a community of belief and action.

A quite distinct level of meaning is suggested if we recall our use of expressions which warn about the dangers of "circular reasoning" and "vicious circles," about narrow social or political cliques referred to as "closed circles" or about wrong headed ideas or evil people spoken of as "bad circles to get caught up in." For skeptics, and for the skeptic within believers, Christianity can seem problematic and circular in these negative senses.

Both the positive and negative connotations are brought together in the image of a sorcerer's magic or charmed circle which casts its spell around people or things to either protect them or curse them. It is my premise in the pages which follow that although to the sceptic Christianity appears a charmed circle of bewitchment, superstition and hypocrisy, it is, at least when authentic, a graced circle — a circle whose charm is liberating, saving and humanizing.

This book aims to contribute to the ongoing task (for the initiated as well as the uninitiated) of breaking into the heart of this circle to show how it is graced, and in hopes of appropriating its saving and humanizing truth. This aim could also be described from the other side, as it were, as an effort to break out of the false spells and inauthentic circles which enslave and dehumanize us.

The book's argument is introductory, then, in the sense that it intends to help break into the Christian circle. This is not, however, an elementary book. Some of the ideas with which it wrestles are in fact quite subtle because the truly basic and fundamental questions about ourselves and about the meaning of our lives are not simple questions. Nor is God just another being in our world or alongside our world who can be grasped or contained in our concepts. When we speak of God, language is pushed to its limits. Thus, to comprehend this God-talk requires at times that we push towards the limits of our understanding and imagination. Moreover, when Christians propose that we can understand God and the meaning of human life in terms of Jesus and the "spirit" he shares with us, *all* that we know of that man, of ourselves, of our history and of our world is at issue.

It is true that in many ways this faith in Jesus as the "Christ" professes a profoundly simple truth, but it is not a simplistic truth, nor will simplistic analyses do it justice. To speak of such matters requires more than one sort of discourse and more than one kind and level of difficulty. There are, for example, fundamental questions of interpretation, subtle philosophical issues, difficult conceptual matters, historical details, textual problems and nuances of language and literary style that simply cannot be avoided. Consequently, the reader may find that although some chapters of this book will move along quite easily, other chapters will require much slower and more careful attention. Chapters 8 and 12 are particularly challenging. No doubt, the college student working through these more difficult sections will find their instructors' guidance helpful. The book, however, was not written for professors. I hope theologians will find what I have to say here of interest and worth some attention. Nevertheless, the primary audience I have in mind is ordinary people who are intrigued and puzzled by the particular circle of faith Jesus has inspired, but who have not had much opportunity to pursue this interest seriously or deeply.

While I ask the reader occasionally to negotiate somewhat difficult terrain, I also have striven to provide all the information necessary to follow the argument's path. I have only covered essential ground and I have not tried to make things more difficult than they had to be. This has meant not developing a number of themes as fully as I would have liked, especially in the last two parts of the book which are more intimations about the implications of its central thesis than elaborations of these. Thus the argument moves in successively more substantial steps towards the central chapters from which point it then suggests just some of the further directions which need to be pursued once one has broken into the circle of faith. I have attempted to help the reader further by making the questions which guide the argument and the images which mark its trail as explicit as possible.

It should be kept in mind, though, that these questions, arguments and images are merely devices for getting us to an objective. They themselves are not the point. As in most conversations, the point is what gets said "in between" the questions, "behind" the argument and "in front of" the images. Insight, understanding and appreciation are conveyed and won through language, and would be impossible without it, but our actual appropriation of what is in mind goes beyond the words. That is to say, just hearing the words or reading them does not mean that we have really broken into their meaning or that their truth has actually grasped us. Rather, the point of our conversations is usually not the words but to reach another person, a new perspective, a different relationship or an elusive reality which in effect goes beyond or transcends what is said, or in many cases what can be said. "Getting the point" requires that we attend most carefully to the drift of the conversation but it also requires that we not get so caught up in our words or be so limited to them that we end up missing what was really meant. This relation of our words and concepts to what they express is something like the optical illusion produced when you stare at a pattern of colored blocks arranged in parallel and equidistant rows. As you stare at the blocks, dancing spots appear at the intersecting corners. If you try to look directly at any of those dancing spots, however, they immediately disappear.

So it is with much of our conversation, and so it is with theological discourse. Attending to a particular line of questioning, argument or imagery is necessary and essential, but the subject matter and point of our talk transcends these and calls for something more of us. At its heart, authentic Christian theology is a call for ongoing conversion and transformation in our very way of understanding things, in our values, and in all our activities. It requires that our minds be stretched, our hearts be turned around and our lives be concretely transformed so that our hands and feet, as it were, embody humanity more authentically.

Many have helped in my own efforts to break into the theological circle. The influence of a number of these dialogue partners will be obvious in the text, but there are other silent voices for whose inspiration and wisdom I am most indebted. My thinking, of course, has been much influenced by the questions and observations of my students at Loyola College in Baltimore and at Marquette University. I am also grateful for the comments and suggestions of my graduate students and assistants at Marquette, especially Dr. William McInerny, Dr. Roberto Goizueta, Rev. Clark Hyde, Ms. Maura Stetson, Rev. Russel Stommel and most particularly Rev. Richard Steele. The book would never have gotten off the ground or taken the direction it follows without the invaluable lessons I learned from my colleagues at Loyola a number of years ago: Sr. Sharon M. Burns, R.S.M., Rev. William Davish, S.J., Rev. Walt McCauley, S.J., Sr. Mary Aquin O'Neill, R.S.M., Dr. Webster Patterson and our Chairman and mentor in those days, Felix Malmberg, S.J. I am most grateful for the suggestions and encouragement of those who generously read earlier versions of the manuscript, namely Dr Lawrence Cunningham, Dr Ronald Feenstra, Sr. Barbara Finan, O.P., Dr. John Hogan, Dr Paul Misner, Rev. Leo O'Donnovan, S.J., Dr. John Schmitt and Dr. Andrew Tallon. My efforts were significantly helped by the assistance of a summer grant from Marquette University, for which I am most grateful, and by the support of my colleagues here, especially Rev. William J. Kelly, S.J. and Rev. Philip Rossi, S.J. Robert Heyer and Sheed & Ward, of course, deserve the credit and have my appreciation for getting this book in print. Needless to say, I have also counted heavily on the support of my family: Grace, Evelyn, Erin and Clare. Finally, in a less direct but still very fundamental way, I am indebted to the inspiration of my friends at St. Agnes/Holy Angels, to our ministers and to our Bishop Richard J. Sklba and Archbishop Rembert G. Weakland.

1. Introduction

For many of us today, Christianity is like a "charmed circle," cut off by its spell from the other circles in which we live and work. Some find themselves very much on the outside of this circle of understanding. To them, and perhaps to many on the inside as well, Christian theology and preaching seem to speak in an alien tongue. Although the language is familiar, its real cash value for everday life is far from obvious. Indeed, often it seems calculated to mystify rather than clarify. It is necessary to provide those who face this predicament with tools to break the circle's spell, so its meaning can be understood and its truth can be appropriated. That, very broadly speaking, is my objective here.

The book is divided into five parts. The first chapter of each part explores, with the help of representative interrogators, the sort of objections entailed in describing the Christian circle of understanding as charmed or bewitched. As these objections are developed, it will become clear that the Christian vision can be problematic at several different levels. There are, first of all, the difficulties of the head encountered by those who cannot understand or make sense of Christian talk, piety or practice. Then, there are the questions of the heart, which trouble those who profess to understand but who are not moved to believe. Finally, there is the scandal of the hands and feet which affects those who profess to understand and even to be moved by Christianity, but who cannot live it. This would also seem to be the difficulty of those who protest that the Christian circle of understanding is not reflected in practice in the "real" world, or even in the practice of believers themselves. There can be little doubt that Christians who go through the motions, but without real understanding or belief, appear to validate these suspicions of bewitchment, superstition and hypocrisy.

In light of such difficulties it will become clear that Christianity is intelligible, credible and authentic — its circle complete

1

— only when it is embodied in the whole person: head, heart, hands and feet. The organization of the book is thus focused around the problem of bewitchment in Part I, the difficulties of the head in Part II, the questions of the heart in Part III, the scandal of the hands and feet in Part IV, and the integrity of the circle as whole in Part V. That focus also provides a structure for exploring: the circle's general contours in I; its horizon (the concept of God) in II; its center (Jesus as God's humanity) in III; its vector (discipleship) in IV; and, coming full circle, its unity in V. The issue underlying each of these objections and topics, and so each of the book's parts, is the relationship between the human and the divine. How is it possible to speak meaningfully of God in the first place?(I) Is the divine anything more than a projection of our own humanity?(II) How could God become human as Christians claim?(III) Doesn't the worship of God distract from the real needs of humanity?(IV) In the final analysis, aren't the Christian vision and humanism opposed?(V)

I am convinced that these problems of the head, heart, hands and feet are quite genuine, and not easily resolved. I don't for a moment think that this little book can argue them away. Nor can I claim that my thoughts on these issues emerge from neutral ground. I write here as a Catholic theologian informed by particular currents within that very rich tradition. Most of those with whom we will be in dialogue are also Christian. Even our skeptical interrogators were shaped in large measure by Christianity. But it is my hope that the reader will nevertheless find here a conversation that takes seriously the questions of those who are not Christian or who find Christianity problematic to one degree or another. The objective is not to formulate an argument that will compel skeptics into the circle of belief. My more modest objective is first, to show how it is possible to break into the Christian circle; and second, to show from that vantage point what the contours of the circle look like. It is my hope that this endeavor will be helpful, first of all, to those who already dwell, or wish to dwell, within the circle of faith. But I also hope this conversation will have something to offer those who cannot enter this circle, or who enter it at other points and thus see it quite differently.

If we take the bewitchment of theological and religious language as our point of departure, then it can be expected that any attempt to summarize the conclusion towards which the book moves will itself come across as quite problematic. It is far easier to name the questions, than it is to name the destination. On the other hand, it is difficult to follow a road map if you don't know where you are headed. Consequently, it is necessary to anticipate the book's conclusion in the spirit of the proverbial pedestrian, asked to give directions along a route that is easy to follow if you have already taken it, but nearly impossible to describe if you haven't. The Christian circle, then, at least as this pedestrian theologian sees it, is indeed charmed, but its charm is that of a graced circle rather than a vicious one. Its effect, when authentically incarnated, is liberation, salvation and fulfillment, not bewitchment, superstition or hypocrisy. The heart of Christian understanding, to use language that needs more explanation than believers usually admit, is the conviction that God has become one with humanity in the Spirit of Jesus. Consequently, the divine is revealed in the human, and the truly human is only realized through solidarity with the divine. To be human to the utmost, is to be caught up as sisters and brothers in the circle of God's love, as Father and Mother, divine Brother and shared Spirit.

It remains for the chapters which follow to provide the tools for breaking open such claims, so their meaning can be clarified and their truth assessed.

I. THE CONTOURS OF THE CIRCLE

2. The Problem of Bewitchment

Christianity, I have suggested, is like a charmed circle. Its bewitchment, whether of the head, heart or hands and feet, casts its spell over many. For some, those who we could say are on the outside of the circle, Christianity seems to speak in a foreign tongue. The words and grammatical structure are familiar enough. Most know what "God" is supposed to mean, or what the statement that God has become human in Jesus purports to claim. Most are also aware that God, for orthodox Christians at least, is not literally a creature like us, up somewhere in the heavens, and that God's becoming human is not supposed to have been a metamorphosis from one sort of worldly being to another.

But as soon as one eliminates such obviously mythological conceptions, the meaning of Christian talk becomes much more puzzling. If the supernatural is not literally something above this world, if God's "being" is radically different from ours or from any other creature's, if one cannot point to God or describe God or see God, if Jesus, the Jew from Nazareth, was truly a man like us, not God in the disguise of a "superman," then what does it really mean to claim that God has become human in Jesus? And what relevance does such a claim really have for concrete life? When pushed, most Christians are hard put to say. One gets the impression, even without actually reading books like *The Myth of God Incarnate*, that a good many theologians, if they are honest enough, will admit similar difficulties.[1] To many, certainly to the secular press, the Vatican's crackdown on "liberal" theologians seems a clear acknowledgment that these difficulties are getting out of hand even within the ranks.

5

I am not at all sure that sociological surveys adequately indicate the extent to which such difficulties cast their bewitching
spell over people today. Nor should we expect abundant
theoretical testimonies claiming that Christianity is a charmed
circle. Those outside the circle of faith have little reason to
bother with it. Why should one seek to refute what isn't taken
seriously? Why seek to break into a circle that has no practical
meaning or personal significance? This problem of bewitchment is nevertheless evident in the secularization of our society. It is evident in the ease with which reductionistic
psychological, anthropological and sociological theories of religion are accepted by university students and taken for granted
by their professors. It was evident in the popular response to
phenomena like the "death of God" theology or the "myth of God
incarnate" discussion.[2]

It matters little that relatively few in our society consciously or explicitly oppose religion as such, or that few could
actually articulate, let alone explain, the objections of skeptical
social scientists, philosophers and theologians. Nor does it matter much that movements like the death of God theology were
short-lived. The fact that these movements and theories hit responsive cords in the first place suggests that they manifest a
real, even if for the most part unspoken, suspicion of bewitchment.

I suspect that what I am calling here the problem of bewitchment is significant even among nominal believers. I have
in mind the so-called "unchurched," who hold onto the vestiges
of a generalized belief in God while rejecting doctrinal and
creedal stances, and organized religions. I also am thinking of
the "nominally churched" who participate, but only in a very limited way, in some of the Christian customs of their extended
families. Perhaps we should also include those who search for a
new faith in consciousness movements, in cults and in the religions of the East, because Christianity holds so little meaning for
them.

It is important to emphasize that the fundamental issue
here is not the truth of Christian claims, but their very meaning-

fulness. It is one thing to deny Christianity, it is another to assert that its language is so bewitched that there is no way to break into it. But isn't that often what people in effect claim, when they say Christianity, or at least doctrinal and creedal Christianity, makes little sense to them, or that it is irrelevant to their lives?

This sort of objection was cleverly illustrated in a celebrated parable told by the skeptical analytic philosopher, Antony Flew.[3] A revised and updated version would go something like this. Astronomers discover a new planet in our solar system. Not only has it escaped detection for all this time, it also seems to have conditions ideally suited for life. Numerous unmanned probes are sent to the planet. Although there is ample evidence of plant and lower life forms, no animal life of any kind can be detected. Finally two astronauts are sent to investigate. When they land, they find not only plant life, but they find it most extraordinarily healthy, ecologically balanced and aesthetically configured. One of these explorers immediately concludes that there must be an alien gardener. The other views the phenomenon more skeptically as a happy but chance occurrence. Those back on earth decide that both theories must be put to the test and so send every conceivable device to assist the astronauts' efforts to detect the elusive alien tending its garden. But test after test fails to reveal anyone. When the alien cannot be seen with the usual sorts of instruments, the believer suggests that this life form must be invisible to the naked eye. When the invisible gardener escapes detection by infrared, laser, x-ray and so forth, the believer concludes that the alien must be immaterial. It turns out in the end that the alien cannot be seen, heard or felt at all. There is no direct evidence that it actually tends the garden. The alien does not respond to the astronauts' calls. Not even uprooting the garden elicits a response.

If despite all this, the believer persists in speaking of an alien gardener, the skeptic no doubt would have reason to protest that such talk is quite meaningless. What difference is there between an invisible, intangible, immaterial and eternally elusive alien, and an imaginary alien, or even no alien at

all? What originally sounds like an informative and straightfor-
ward assertion, "There is an alien who tends this garden," turns
out to be quite empty words. It really adds nothing to the observation that one has come upon a most extraordinarily healthy,
ecologically balanced and aesthetically configured clump of
plants.

Flew contended that when an original assertion is thus
qualified so drastically, it is "killed by inches, the death of a
thousand qualifications."[4] This, he claimed, is the danger of
most theological utterances. Words and assertions that seem to
make sense are so qualified that they are no longer truly meaningful. Christians for example, assert that God is love, but apparently nothing can count against such an assertion.

> Someone tells us that God loves us as a father loves
> his children. We are reassured. But then we see a
> child dying of inoperable cancer of the throat. His
> earthly father is driven frantic in his efforts to help,
> but his Heavenly Father reveals no obvious sign of
> concern. Some qualification is made — God's love is
> "not a merely human love" or it is "an inscrutable
> love", perhaps — and then we realize that such suf-
> ferings are quite compatible with the truth of the as-
> sertion that "God loves us as a father (but, of
> course, . . .)." We are reassured again. But then
> perhaps we ask: what is this assurance of God's (ap-
> propriately qualified) love worth, what is this appar-
> ent guarantee really a guarantee against? Just what
> would have to happen not merely (morally and
> wrongly) to tempt but also (logically and rightly) to
> entitle us to say "God does not love us" or even "God
> does not exist"?[5]

Flew, of course, implies that Christians cannot credibly answer
this question. Their assertions, consequently, turn out to be
empty words, charmed linguistic circles.[6]

Analogous objections have been raised about the logical

coherence of Christian assertions. How, for example, skeptics ask, can one coherently claim that God could allow evil, if God is all powerful, all knowing, all loving and all good? Such critics would insist that they are not denying that these attributes could be applied truly to God. Rather, they question whether these attributes can have the meanings which they purport to have, and be combined coherently and meaningfully in the ways believers try to, without becoming empty words.

There are, of course, many such objections. And there are also numerous ways of responding to them. The reason for raising such issues at this point, however, is not to debate them, but to illustrate how Christianity can seem charmed to those who, because of problems like these, find themselves on the outside unable to break into its circle.

We can also speak of a bewitchment that prevents those within the circle from breaking out of it. To one concerned about the crucial social, political and moral dilemmas of contemporary life, Christianity can seem to be a "spiritual ghetto" isolating believers from the unnerving ambiguities and hard facts of life's real conflicts. As long as the faithful stay within their comfortable circle, it, and the rest of life too, are coherent and manageable. From the perspective of the wider world, it can seem, instead, that believers are protected from the outside with easy answers, unchallenged consciences and cheap grace. Rather than embodying a saving truth that liberates the believer to contribute to the humanizing of our world, faith's circle can encompass an idolatrous truth, a truth that makes a god of the believers' self-interest, comfort or power base.

One does not have to look outside the Church to discover this suspicion. The voices within, of third world, minority and feminist theologians are telling enough. Hasn't Christian theology, they protest, frequently served as a justification for exploitative, violent, sexist and racist beliefs and acts which are anything but Christlike? If Christian theology, worship and practice do not make us more sensitive to such injustices and do not commit us to a more humane life and to the struggle for a more humane world, then doesn't that circle bewitch us rather than save us?

If theologians within the circle of faith express such suspicions, is it any wonder that others object to it as charmed? Is it surprising that even within the circle, there are many who having honestly faced its potential for bewitchment, find this fact in itself quite perplexing and, indeed, even experience this confusion as casting a spell over the circle they thought their own?

There is a third kind of bewitchment that deserves notice. It is typical of those who could be pictured straddling the circle of faith, neither clearly outside it nor simply inside it. I have in mind those who are convinced that Christianity offers a saving truth, and who indeed live in a way which seems consistent with such a belief, but who are unable to articulate the reasons for this confidence. It is as if a spell has rendered them speechless and confused. Their bewitchment is rooted in the dramatic theological and religious shifts of recent years. For some, beliefs and rituals that were once cherished have been undermined. Formulations of the faith that formerly seemed persuasive have been denied by theologians and even by their own preachers. Everywhere, what was once taken for granted now seems up for grabs, whether because of changes mandated for Catholics by the Second Vatican Council, or because of the ordination of women in the Episcopal Church, or because of the acceptance of revisionist interpretations of Scripture in many mainline Protestant Churches, or because of the ecumenical discussions and agreements between these Churches. Despite sincere faith, good will and upright lives, such people experience Christianity as a charmed circle. They think they live within its perimeters, but they aren't sure any more. They feel they know what it's about, but cannot find the words to assuage nagging doubts or to vent frustrated convictions.

These difficulties are not limited to those whose faith has been undercut by recent theological and religious shifts. Today, many of those who regard themselves as Christians never had the benefit of adequate theological instruction. Perhaps even more significantly, they did not have the benefit of the implicit cultural and religious formation that once was part of being an Irish Catholic, New England Episcopalian, Bible Belt Baptist or Midwest Lutheran. Instead, they find themselves in a pluralistic, complex and divided world which seems to preclude clear formulations or professions of faith. In their cases too, despite very sincere faith, good will and an upright life, we find believers who are speechless and confused, who experience Christianity as a charmed circle.

Ironically, here in America, many of the very institutions which were created to protect our different faiths often have the effect of undermining them. These institutions reinforce a secular culture, or circle of understanding, in which religious claims and theological language have no real standing.

Richard Fenn has shown, for example, how the "rituals" and "liturgies" of our courts and universities can have that effect.[7] The courts, he explains, in order to protect religious diversity, and respectful of the limits of their own competence, do not usually recognize the relevance of theological arguments or give them any authority. To do so would inevitably entail granting the court itself authority as a religious institution and arbitrator between the conflicting claimants to religious truth. Consequently, the theological arguments of Karen Ann Quinlan's parish priest could have no legal weight in the court charged with determining whether she should be disconnected from life-supporting machinery. Nor could another court recognize the authority of theological or religious claims made in defense of Fr. Daniel Berrigan and the Catonsville Nine, who believed they were compelled by their faith to acts of civil disobedience. Nor, it is often assumed, can the university professor's or student's religious beliefs be regarded as the appropriate basis for examinations or for passing a course.

The court and the university, in their efforts to protect religious diversity and freedom, in effect relativize and disregard faith's authority. The rules of the game require that religious truths be treated as matters of opinion. Theological claims can have no effective standing in such circles. Although witnesses

must swear to their testimony on the Bible, and students of the
Bible must stick to the text, the Bible itself is not usually a valid
"court of appeal" in the court or in the classroom. No belief or
theological position can be treated as truer than any other, with
the effect, often enough, that all beliefs and theological statements seem quite empty.

How, in such contexts, can the Christian faith, or indeed
any faith, seem more than charmed circles alien to the real
world of science, commerce, politics, law and medicine? The
issue is not just academic. Whether it is a problem of the head,
or of the heart, or of the hands and feet — whether one is inside
the circle of faith, on the outside or schizophrenically straddling
its perimeter, there can be no genuine understanding or evalua-
tion of Christianity, until one has managed to break through
these bewitchments into its circle.

Notes

1. Ed. John Hick (London: SCM Press, 1977). See also, *The Truth of God
Incarnate*, ed. Michael Green (Grand Rapids, Michigan: Eerdmans, 1977) and
Incarnation and Myth: The Debate Contniued, ed. Michael Goulder (Grand
Rapids, Michigan: Eerdmans, 1979).

2. For an excellent overview of the death of God theologies see Langdon Gilkey's *Naming the Whirlwind: The Renewal of God Language* (Indianapolis and
New York: The Bobbs Merrill Company, 1969).

3. "Theology and Falsification," in *New Essays in Philosophical Theology*,
ed. Antony Flew and Alasdair Macintyre (New York: Macmillan, 1966 [first published 1955]).

4. Flew, p. 97.

5. Flew, pp. 98-99.

6. This phrase was used by Kai Nielsen in his *Contemporary Critiques of
Religion* (New York: Herder and Herder, 1971), which book, incidentally, is an
excellent illustration of the kind of critiques of religious discourse advanced by
skeptical analytic philosophers.

7. *Liturgies and Trials: The Secularization of Religious Language* (New
York: The Pilgrim Press, 1982).

3. Breaking into the Circle

Breaking into the circle of Christian faith is no simple matter for those on the outside. It is difficult to find a point on its perimeter which does not presuppose knowledge, if not acceptance, of some prior point.

Say, for example, we begin with the question about the meaningfulness of the Christian idea of God. It will soon become apparent that the Christian conception is not simply derived philosophically, from the head as it were, but is dependent on the prior conviction that God is revealed in Jesus the Christ. That conviction is arrived at through conversion and faith, that is to say through the heart. One cannot get an accurate picture of what is in the head, or evaluate its meaningfulness, then, without attending to the prior movement of the heart from which that picture emerges. Thus purely philosophical analyses of the Christian idea of God, such as those advanced by skeptical analytic philosophers and sometimes by believers as well, strikes most lay people as quite sterile and many scholars as quite off the mark. Dogmatic, confessional and devotional conceptions are necessarily presupposed and so must be analyzed too.

The movement of the heart, moreover, is not an abstract matter. It is necessarily something very practical and embodied, a matter of the hands and feet. Hearts are truly turned around and won over in practice and by concrete events. The conviction that Jesus is the Christ, for example, presupposes the historical context and events that led up to his disciples' confession that he was risen. Furthermore, today hearts are turned around to that conviction only when they are won over by the concrete practice of contemporary Christian "witnesses." So one cannot attend to the movement of the heart without engaging the historical events of Christian tradition and the concrete ethical and liturgical practices of Christian communities in which that movement of the heart is grounded. Without this, purely dogmatic, confessional or devotional analyses are hardly potent against suspicions of bewitchment, superstition and hypocrisy.

Engagement with the tangible realities of Christian tradition and practice, however, presupposes the meaningfulness of the Christian's idea of God. To assess the historical accuracy of claims about what happened to Jesus on the third day, or to appreciate the recommendation to live as God's children, or to be won over and turned around by the lives of those who follow such a recommendation, it is necessary, first, to know to some extent what Christians mean by God and be convinced that this idea is meaningful. Consequently, if the concept of God is not philosophically well grounded, historical research cannot in itself prove dogmatic claims, nor can even exceptionally humanitarian deeds compel a religious interpretation.

But the meaningfulness of the Christian idea of God is what was at issue in the first place. So we seem to come full circle. Every crucial and problematic juncture presupposes some other crucial and problematic juncture. There is no neutral point of entry. It seems there is no way to enter except to blindly jump into the circle and succumb to its bewitchment. Even theologians seem caught in this dilemma. Among contemporary Catholics, for example, Walter Kasper argues for a more historical point of departure, insisting that the philosophical starting point of theologians like Karl Rahner is misleading.[1] At the same time, liberation theologians argue for a more ethical and concrete point of departure, to correct the distortions of theologians who begin with philosophy, history or dogma.[2] But then more philosophically oriented theologians like David Tracy have objected to the more practical point of departure of liberation theologians as incomplete and unconvincing.[3] Where does this leave those on the outside trying to break into the Christian understanding, except with further evidence that its circle is charmed?

In many ways it is just as difficult for those within the circle of faith to break out of the bewitchments of idolatry to which we referred in the last chapter. It should not be necessary to review the testimony of history. All too often, the circle in which Christians live has been closed, bigoted, violent and exploitative. What's worse, Christianity itself frequently has been set forth as justification for such aberrations. But this sort of circularity and bewitchment is not unique to Christianity or to religion. There is a circularity to all understanding. What we "know" is conditioned by our culture, language, history, education, personal experience and numerous other presuppositions.

What I see and hear in a discussion of school desegregation and busing, for example, is very much influenced, for good or ill, by my own race, ethnic heritage, education, family situation, economic status and opportunities, neighborhood and so forth. I cannot, as it were, slip out of my skin to achieve objectivity. We are not disembodied ghosts. It is that very skin, the flesh of our culture, education and experience, that enables us to see or hear anything as meaningful in the first place, and that enables us to draw conclusions or see alternatives. Objectivity, then, to the extent that it can be achieved, is reached through recognizing and learning to respect and discern the influence of our intellectual pigmentation on what we see, hear, feel and know.

This circularity of understanding is rooted in the very structure of human existence. The relation of the head, heart, hands and feet is itself already circular. I think, for example, of my own impassioned teenage arguments with my father or intense "discussions" with my daughters. What one understands in such interchanges is very much influenced by what one wants. If you want the car, if your will is really set on it, it is awfully difficult to understand why your father would see things differently. Sometimes you simply won't see his reasoning, no matter how emphatic, insistent or reasonable he is. Parents can be so unsympathetic and stubborn, so "reasonable!" Certainly there are fleeting moments in the heat of such discussions, after the impetuousness of adolescence or the self-righteousness of middle age has already pushed us too far, when we recognize, at least inside, our own stubbornness and lack of objectivity. In more sober moments, we would have to admit that, perhaps from the very beginning, we saw and heard for the most part only what we wanted to see and hear, understood for the most part only what we wanted to understand.

Our understanding, however, also influences the will. Even to speak, as I did, of "arguments" with my father and of "discussions" with my daughters already shows an understanding that is brought to the situation, coloring our interpretation of it, and so setting the context within which choices will be made. The term "discussions," as opposed to "arguments," for example, suggests a father who is cautious about where, how late and with whom he will permit his daughters to go out, not because of his role as an authority figure, but because he believes he knows better than they, what is prudent. Whether accurate or not, that father's self-understanding will influence how he chooses to advise or discipline. Likewise, a daughter may want something different for herself than what her father wishes, because she has come to know role models for women with which he is not familiar, or does not understand, or does not want to understand.

This tug between understanding and will is in turn influenced by the concrete actions that are part of our web of relationships with one another. If an adolescent is secretly experimenting with alcohol or drugs, he or she is going to approach parents on this topic with a very different understanding and will, than if there had been no experimentation. It is just as evident that a parent who drinks will approach this discussion with an understanding and will that is different from one who does not. Our actions (raising our voices or lowering them, slamming the door or leaving cracks open, following directions or giving directions), our roles (parent or child, boss or employee, professional or laborer, owner or renter) and our persona (male or female, believer or skeptic, person of influence or nobody, chauvinist or quiche eater) profoundly affect what we will understand and how we will choose.

Needless to say, there is no way to escape this circularity. It is the very same interrelationship of the head, heart, hands and feet that both enables us to understand, choose and create our different worlds with all their beauty and truth, and also can so bewitch and captivate us, that our sight becomes distorted, our choices warped and our worlds sick. It is no easy task, then, to break out of our own circles of understanding or to break into another's. I take as evidence enough the present state of our world, with its strife among nations, ideologies, religions and families, typified today by the anarchy of Lebanon, or by the arms race between East and West, or by the conflicts in Afghanistan and Central America, or by the starvation on the African continent and much of the third world, or by the accelerating rates of suicide, abortion and divorce in the affluent world. Where is our understanding? Where are our hearts? Where are our hands and feet?

Liberation theologians have described this bewitchment which is manifested in so many different ways as a kind of "ideological captivity."[4] An ideology is, in effect, what I have spoken of as a person's circle of understanding. Used in this broad sense, it means "any system of ideas expressing a particular point of view about reality,"[5] or "the system of goals and means that serves as the necessary backdrop for any human option or line of action."[6] "On this level," Robert McAfee Brown explains,

> everyone has an ideology; it may be a Marxist ideology, a bourgeois ideology, a working-class ideology, a fascist ideology, a communitarian ideology. On this level also we can speak of the ideology of an age or epoch — one era is a time of "the failure of nerve," another of the reassertion of individualism.[7]

Brown points out, however, that ideology is also frequently used in a more pejorative sense to indicate its potential for what I have called bewitchment. Here ideology refers to a "rationalization" or a "bending of the evidence" used to justify one's self-interest or to hide one's true motivation. These positive and negative senses of the term are related, for as we have already noted, the circle of understanding, will and action which gives us access to the world, also carries with it the potential for closing us off from the world or for obscuring our view of it. It is this latter connotation which is usually intended when we call something "ideological." Furthermore, whether from reflections on our personal relations with others, like the description of a heated discussion above, or from observations of the role that ideology has played in political and social conflict, we know that the prevailing tendency of our ideologies is to rationalize the status quo, to justify things as they stand, to protect the perimeters of our comfortable circles and to discount as charmed circles whatever challenges our self-interests. Consequently our ideologies, all our circles of understanding (not just religious circles) are open to suspicion. They cannot, without risk of bewitchment, be simply taken for granted.

The term "ideological captivity" does not refer simply to the fact that we have ideologies, or to the fact that the prejudice of our ideologies is inevitably in favor of our way of seeing the world and doing things, or even to the fact that our ideologies are always open to the suspicion of bewitchment. We cannot, as we noted before, slip out of our ideological skins. We become captivated by our ideologies, bewitched, when we fail to acknowledge these facts and their influence on the way we see things and do things. Consequently, liberation theologians stress the need for an approach to Christianity that will keep us from forgetting this.

Sometimes this approach is described as a hermeneutics of suspicion and engagement. As contemporary philosophers and theologians use the term "hermeneutics" (from the Greek word "to make clear"), it simply means the science of interpreting written texts or historical events. If, as we have already noted, understanding has a circular character, then our interpretation of texts and of events, past and present, will also have a circularity to it. What I see in a story, poem or drama, and how I understand a happening or diagnose its causes and significance, is to a very great extent determined by the presuppositions, or understanding, I bring to them. There is, as they say, a "hermeneutical circle." If we are not to be captivated by our presuppositions, then it is crucial to find ways of raising our suspicions so that the circles which we see and to which we commit ourselves will be truly there and genuinely liberating. The most obvious way to insure this, is to confront our circle of understanding with another significantly different one and to test these against each other and against our concrete experience, to try them out with our hands and feet, as it were. We need to look at our world with a different pair of shoes on, and through a different set of lenses.

For liberation theologians, that different pair of shoes and lenses is the "view from below," the view from the world of society's poor and marginalized. The liberationists have in mind, here, the worlds of the "nobodies" caught between warring sects in Lebanon, or crushed by repressive governments of the left and the right, or the starving in Africa, or the unemployable or barely subsisting in the the wealthy industrial centers of the Northern Hemisphere, or the exploited in the emerging industrial centers of the Southern Hemisphere and Far East. When you look at the Christian scriptures and tradition from such perspectives, they argue, when you really let yourself be engaged by both the Gospel and these worlds of the poor, you will inevitably hear a very different message than Christians in the first world usually seem to hear. If not, the liberation theologian insists, something must be wrong with your perspective. As Brown puts it,

> Any ideology that allows us to juxtapose an outraged recognition that "there is monstrous evil in the world" with the complacent conclusion, "I am satisfied that the world should not basically change," must arouse suspicion. Only out of such suspicion can the chains of ideological captivity be smashed.[8]

That rescue from captivity, he adds, must include reversals in our self-understanding and theology.

To examine this approach further would get us too far ahead of ourselves. Liberation theologians are convinced that bewitchment can only be overcome by a rigorous "circulation" between a number of factors: between our situation and the text of scripture and tradition; between the text and its historical situation; and between our situation and our reading of the text, and the way our situation and our reading looks when tested from a different perspective, namely, that of the poor. Such a process, they hope, will lead to a new interpretation, a new circle of understanding, which in turn must be subjected to a hermeneutics of suspicion and engagement in what hopefully is a continuing movement forward in truth and justice.

But all of this presupposes the meaningfulness and truth of Christian faith in the first place. It presupposes one who believes in God and who accepts the authority of Jesus, the prophets and the Christian community. Furthermore, it also seems to suggest that the "view from below" is the only adequate perspective for interpreting the Christian faith. But if, as I have argued, Christianity itself seems a charmed circle, then these things cannot be taken for granted. To break into the Christian circle, it is necessary to find a method that will also respond to the questions which bother those to one degree or another outside the circle of faith who are unable to break into it, perhaps in part because of their sensitivity to the scandal that there are any poor at all.

The hermeneutical circle with which we are dealing here is wider than that usually considered in liberation theology. We need a more disclosive secret for breaking into it, and a more comprehensive solution, one that will emphasize the head and heart, as well as the hands and feet.

Notes

1. See his *Jesus the Christ*, trans. V. Green (New York: Paulist Press, 1976), pp. 48-59.

2. See, for example, Juan Segundo's description of theology as the "second step" in *The Liberation of Theology*, trans. John Drury (Maryknoll, New York: Orbis Books, 1976), pp.75-81; Leonardo Boff's "Epilogue" to *Jesus Christ Liberator: A Critical Christology for Our Time*, trans. Patrick Hughes (Maryknoll, New York: Orbis Books, 1979), pp. 264-94; or Jon Sobrino's critique of natural theology in *Christology at the Crossroads: A Latin American Approach*, trans. John Drury (Maryknoll, New York: Orbis Books, 1978), pp. 221-35.

3. *Blessed Rage for Order: The New Pluralism in Theology* (New York: The Seabury Press, 1975), pp. 240-50.

4. For an extraordinarily lucid explanation of the term and excellent introduction to liberation theology, see Robert McAfee Brown, *Theology in a New Key: Responding to Liberation Themes* (Philadelphia: The Westminster Press, 1978), pp. 77-88.

5. Brown, p. 78.

6. Segundo, p. 102.

7. Brown, p. 78.

8. Brown, p. 80.

4. The Secret: Theological Anthropology

Although there is no truly neutral point of entry for breaking into the circle of faith, there is a common juncture. That juncture is our very humanity. The circles about which we have been speaking, however diverse and autonomous, however bewitched or enlightened, are nevertheless all *human* spheres of understanding and action. They embody or embodied, for someone, what it means to be human, what counts as authentic, how we should understand ourselves, what we should do with ourselves, how we should relate to one another, how we should come to grips with our worlds, how we should play and celebrate, how we should settle our differences, how we should suffer and die.These circles are the vehicles that both express our humanity and give us humanity. Thus, although our circles may differ quite radically, as indeed our conception and concrete embodiment of humanity may, all nevertheless are responses to correlative needs, to correlative questions. All, at least implicitly and partially, are anthropologies: lived understandings of what it is to be human. The common juncture, then, is the points of correlation between our charmed circles and the lived anthropologies which they articulate.

Admittedly these points of correlation may be difficult to find, may have little in common and may present themselves rather as disjunctions. What one sees as human, another may barely recognize as human, may indeed regard as primitive, savage, beastly, inhuman or even dehumanizing. But the judgment that another circle of understanding is incomplete, hollow or warped is at the same time evidence that a juncture, however discordant and inchoate, exists. However different the questions and the answers of our various circles, their horizons, if not the same, are at least related. Their correlation, then, offers a juncture and so a point of entry for breaking into a circle of understanding different from our own. It will provide the basis for my suggestion that the concept of "theological anthropology," if properly understood, offers a secret key for breaking into the charmed circle of Christian faith.

First, let me explain more exactly what I mean by "anthropology." What I have in mind is not the academic discipline which goes by that name. Nor do I intend exactly the branch of philosophy which is given that title. Nor in the first instance am I even referring to a specialization within theology. Rather, what I have in mind is the prior "lived understanding" of humanity that sometimes gets articulated in our philosophies and theologies, and sometimes is shaped by them. This lived understanding of humanity is at the roots of what scientific, philosophical and theological anthropologies study.

But one does not have to be learned to have an anthropology in this more basic sense. Rather, all of us, whether we know it or not, are already engaged in anthropology. All of us, both individually and corporately, are defining what humanity is and will become. Our humanity is not a given. It cannot be taken for granted. What we are, and what we will become, as persons and as societies, always presents itself as a question.[1] This question is raised concretely by the inhumanity present in every sphere of our lives: the economic, political, social and personal. It is raised for us as individuals and as communities. It is raised in the banal matters of the everyday as well as in the larger conflicts that make the news.

Our history is full of illustrations: the massive inhumanity of Nazis toward the Jews, the dehumanizing network of the Soviet *Gulag Archipelago* described so eloquently by Solzhenitsyn, the murderous upheaval of the Cambodian revolution so movingly portrayed cinematically in the *Killing Fields*, or the decimating exploitation of Native and Black Americans in our own country. Nor should we overlook the illustrations afforded by the common meanness and cruelty of the everyday world, that are not any less dehumanizing just because they are not always so dramatic or so easily documented.

Human history is to a very large extent, on any honest reading, a history of inhumanity. We could find in our dictionaries pages of words which describe this state of affairs: pogrom, genocide, holocaust, terrorism, assassination, extortion, exploitation, violence, cruelty, torture, murder, militarism, nuclear winter, toxic clouds, sexism, extortion, homicide, rape, racism, bigotry, apartheid, persecution, betrayal, unfaithfulness, greed and so forth. We have such an extensive vocabulary for the inhuman, because the books we are writing with our lives, individually and corporately, have required it. The very irony of the term "inhumanity" itself, or of the hackneyed phrase "man's inhumanity to man," is linguistic testimony to the ambiguity of our situation.

Why do we call "inhuman" what so manifestly describes what humans have in fact done, do, and go on doing? A much more concrete and ominous testimony to the precariousness of humanity, of our self-definition, is afforded by the nuclear arsenals which we take so much for granted. Humanity has the capacity for self-annihilation in the blizzard of a nuclear winter. Even if we do not seek such an event, it is not at all clear that we have the will, or the imagination, or the creativity to do what is necessary to avoid it. What is the human thing to do? What is it to be human? Where do we come from? Where are we headed? How do we get there?

Our anthropologies, in the broad sense I intend here, are the answers that our concrete lives give to such questions. Our anthropologies are defined by the stands we take, by the causes with which we identify ourselves, by the slogans that we make our own, by the perspectives we adopt and by the stories we tell.[2] This has as much to do with everyday matters (where we buy our homes or send our children to school, our favorite TV programs and news shows) as it does with our "big decisions" or with the newsworthy matters of national and international scope.

All of us have an anthropology in this sense, even those who never heard the term and who never consciously ask themselves what it is to be human, because all of us just in "getting by" take stands, identify with one cause or another, choose between perspectives and recall favorite stories. Consequently all our artifacts (our histories, novels, dramas, movies, poetry, dance, architecture, social institutions, even our jokes, cartoons and dress) implicitly constitute and reveal something of what it means for us to be human. It is possible, then, to analyze these and discern the lived understanding of humanity which they articulate and embody.

Implicit in each of our anthropologies is a bottom line, a value or constellation of values which gives meaning and direction to our lives. That bottom line, which Paul Tillich (1886-1966) called our "ultimate concern," is the functional equivalent of a god.[3] Our ultimate concern is something or someone that gives our life meaning and promises fulfillment, and it is that to which or to whom, consequently, we give ourselves. Sometimes the concern to which we surrender is best described by a term like "God," as in "Yahweh, the God of Abraham and Jacob," or "God the Father of Jesus," or "Allah." In other instances, for example in the case of those whose ultimate concern is difficult to pin down or not clearly divine, the term "god" may not seem appropriate. In such cases, people will describe their ultimate concern with words like the "good of humanity," the "mystery of life," the "wonder of being," "reality itself" or the "unknown." It is also possible that one's "god" can be quite demonic: perhaps it is best described as self-interest, wealth, power, security, fame or hate. Of course, it is always true that one's ultimate concern may not be what it seems. Self-interest can easily mask itself as piety, and self-denial may veil a genuine affirmation of life rooted in the love of neighbor and God.

In any case, we can call "god" whatever serves in this way as the bottom line by which and towards which we direct our lives. It follows that the beliefs, rituals, stories and practices associated with our ultimate concern is the functional equivalent of a religion, and that our understanding and justification of these is the equivalent of theology. In the broadest sense, then, the subject matter of theology is this ultimate concern. So when I use the terms "religion" and "theology," what I have in mind initially is something broader than what we usually mean by those terms. Religion and theology, so conceived, have to do with our lived relation to our ultimate concern and our concrete understanding of it.

In this sense, all of us, whether we know it or not, are already engaged in theology. We are already, in a minimalistic and broad sense, religious. In defining what it is to be human, we are also defining our "gods." This is true whether we think of this bottom line as a finite concern which we create or discover, as an infinite God who is revealed to us or as a meaningless void. Consequently, our theology, as well as our anthropology, is revealed in the stands we take, in the causes with which we identify ourselves, in the slogans that we make our own, in the perspectives we adopt and in the stories we tell. What's more, there is a correlation between our anthropologies and our theologies. Every lived understanding of humanity entails a "god," at least implicitly. Likewise, every ultimate concern entails at least an implicit anthropology. Thus it is possible to analyze one's stands, causes, slogans and stories to discern not only their vision of humanity but also their ultimate concern.

This correlation between anthropology and theology means that it is possible to focus the thrust and bottom line of one by inquiring about the other. We can break into the meaning and truth of a people's lived anthropology (their stories, perspectives, behavior, etc.) by inquiring about its implied theology (ultimate concern). Likewise, it is possible to uncover the meaning and cash value of a people's theology (their religious rituals, beliefs, practices, etc.) by inquiring about its implied anthropology. The effort to analyze and elaborate this correlation in a methodic and precise way, to get at the religious meaning and truth of people's circle of understanding, is what I mean by theological anthropology.

This is the first sense in which theological anthropology is the secret for breaking into the Christian faith's charmed circle. More fundamental and specifically Christian senses will be elaborated in later chapters.[4] It will also be necessary to explain how such an approach can incorporate liberation theology's emphasis on the hermeneutics of suspicion and engagement, but the immediate need, which we will address in the next chapter, is to illustrate exactly how theological anthropology provides a key for unlocking the meaning and truth of an alien circle of understanding.

Notes

1. For further development of this notion of humanity's questionableness, cf. John Macquarrie, *In Search of Humanity: A Theological and Philosophical Approach* (New York: Crossroad, 1983), esp. pp. 10-37; Jürgen Moltmann, *Man: Christian Anthropology in the Conflicts of the Present*, trans. John Sturdy (Philadelphia: Fortress Press, 1971), esp. pp. 1-21; Wolfhart Pannenberg, *What Is Man: Contemporary Anthropology in Theological Perspective*, trans. Duane A. Priebe (Philadelphia: Fortress Press, 1970), esp. pp. 1-13, and *Anthropology in Theological Perspective*, trans. Matthew J. O'Connell (Philadelphia: The Westminster Press, 1985), esp. pp. 27-142; Karl Rahner, S.J., *Foundations of Christian Faith: An Introduction to the Idea of Christianity*, trans. William V. Dych (New York: The Seabury Press, 1978), esp. pp. 14-115; and Helmut Thielicke, *Being Human . . . Becoming Human: An Essay in Christian Anthropology*, trans. Geoffrey W. Bromiley (Garden City, NY: Doubleday & Company, Inc., 1983), esp. Chapters 1-3.

2. For illuminating illustrations of the role which story plays in our self-understanding and self-definition, see Michael Novak, *Ascent of the Mountain, Flight of the Dove: An Invitation to Religious Studies* (New York: Harper & Row, 1971); and Stanley Hauerwas, *Vision and Virtue* (Notre Dame, Indiana: Fides Publishers, Inc., 1974) and *Truthfulness and Tragedy* (Notre Dame, Indiana: University of Notre Dame Press, 1977).

3. For his use and explanation of the term see his *Systematic Theology* (Chicago: The University of Chicago Press, 1967), esp. vol. I, pp. 11-15, and *Theology of Culture*, ed. Robert C. Kimball (New York: Oxford University Press, 1959), esp. pp. 40-51.

4. See the conclusions to Chapters 13, 17 and 18.

5. The Ring Shout

The "ring shouts" of plantation slaves in the Antebellum South offer a striking and very concrete illustration of the correlation between theology and anthropology. Enslavement had thrown the Africans into an entirely foreign environment. They were cut off from their families, languages, cultures and religions. They were forced into situations which, even when they were not brutalizing, were inherently dehumanizing. The wisdom of their native cultures could offer little help. They had been cast into an alien world that lived by a very different wisdom.

It is a wonder that so many were able to maintain their identity as persons, when the circles into which they had been thrust were so bent on reducing them to a subhuman level. The historian Albert J. Raboteau has demonstrated that many overcame these dehumanizing assaults on their dignity and personal worth, in part, because of their appropriation of Christianity.[1] "In the midst of slavery, religion was for the slaves a space of meaning, freedom, and transcendence."[2] This space, however, was not won easily. For the African slaves, the white man's religion was certainly something like what we have been describing as a charmed circle. To grasp its meaning and appropriate its truth, the Africans had to break out of their former circles of understanding and break into a quite new, and indeed often hostile, circle. The key for doing so, was their concrete experience of the human condition, that is to say, their experience of enslavement and of mutual support and comfort in the singing, dancing and ecstasy of the "ring shouts."

The ring shouts were related to the broader and more inclusive category of the Afro American spirituals with which we are more familiar today. Evangelical Protestantism's ecstatic camp-meeting revivals, although they were an alien circle for the Africans, nevertheless possessed many characteristics akin to the heritage of dance and spirit-possession found in West Africa: rhythmic clapping, dancing in a circled group and styles of singing or "shouting" that either led up to, or resulted from, experiences of enthusiastic and ecstatic possession by the spirit. Because of these familiar resonances, the slaves found in the camp revivals a congenial point of contact between their old worlds and this new Christian world. It is not surprising, then, that one of the principal means for their appropriation of this new circle of understanding was ring shouts of their own. These frequently lasted until the early hours of the morning and often had to be held in small groups out of range from the master's hearing, in "hush harbors," hidden under blankets or way back in plantation hollows.

In these ring shouts and in the spirituals, African gods and imagery were replaced by Biblical figures and Christian imagery, so that a new Afro-American and Christian form of song and worship was developed. This new idiom reflected the Christian understanding through the prism of the slaves' experiences of joy and sorrow, fellowship and hardship, ecstasy and oppression.

> Images of the Bible, from Genesis to Revelation filled the hymns and spirituals which the slaves sang in church, in the fields, and in the quarters. Themes and events from the Old Testament were used by the slaves to interpret their own experience by measuring it against a wider system of meaning. Simultaneously, the biblical symbols were translated in the light of the slaves' own day-to-day experiences. For the vast majority of slaves who could not read, hymns and spirituals were their channel to the word of God.[3]

In this way the Christian circle became their own.

Raboteau contends that conversion to this new circle "equipped the slave with a sense of individual value and a personal vocation which contradicted the devaluing and dehumanizing forces of slavery. In the prayer meetings, the sermons, prayers and songs, when the Spirit started moving the congregation to shout, clap and dance, the slaves enjoyed community and fellowship which transformed their individual sorrows."[4] In this fellowship of the shouts, their songs "articulated the slaves' vision of a 'new heaven on earth,' and as the spirit started working and the shouting broke out, vision became real in ecstasy. And for a time, at least, the sorrow and toil of the individual's life were assuaged and given meaning."[5] For a time, a new and free space was created within their circle.

Raboteau's account is rich with the historical testimony of those who believed they were sustained and in that sense "saved" by their conversion to this circle of faith. He relates the words of a contraband in Beaufort, S.C.

> O missus! I could not hab-libbed had not been for de Lord — neber! work so late, and so early; work so hard, when side ache so. Chil'en sold; old man gone. All visitors, and company in big house; all cooking and washing all on me, neber done enough. Misus never satisfied — no hope. Noting, noting, but Jesus, I look up. O Lord! How long? Give me patience! patience! O Lord! Only Jesus know how bad I feel; darsn't tell any body, else get flogged. Darsn't call upon de Lord; darsn't tell when sick. But . . . I said Jesus, if it your will, I will bear it.[6]

The slaves' religion, however, was not simply otherworldly and compensatory in a way which distracted them from the injustice of their fate or pacified them. They heard in the Christian Gospel, and particularly in the Old Testament exodus of Israel out of slavery, a message of hope for a liberation from physical as well as spiritual bondage. Raboteau reports that Francis Henderson concluded from sermons he heard in a Methodist church, "that God had made all men free and equal, and that I ought not to be a slave."[7] Raboteau also tells of Clayborn Grantling who,

> born a slave in Dawson, Georgia, in 1848, recalled the sight of slaves "sold in droves like cows . . . white men wuz drivin' 'em like hogs and cows for sale. Mothers and fathers were sold and parted from their chillun; they wuz sold to white people in diffunt states. I tell you chile, it was pitiful, but God did not let it last always. I have heard slaves morning and night pray for deliverance. Some of 'em would stand up in de fields or bend over cotton and corn and pray out lout for God to help 'em and in time you see He did."[8]

As Raboteau explains it, slave religion had a this-worldly impact, not only because it led some to acts of violent rebellion, but also because it enabled many to assert and maintain a sense of their personal dignity and worth. In fact, "the religious meetings in the quarters, groves, and 'hush harbors' were themselves frequently acts of rebellion against the proscriptions of the master."[9] Even the "humming" of slaves could be so construed. Raboteau notes that

> William Sinclair whose early childhood was spent in slavery in Georgetown, South Carolina, claimed that when slave owners forbade the slaves to sing "One of these days I shall be free/ when Christ the Lord shall set me free," they "hoodwinked the master class by humming the music of this particular song, while the words echoed and re-echoed deep down in their hearts with perhaps greater effect than if they had been spoken."[10]

It is true that from Colonial times, white Christians also saw themselves as a new Israel, and that poor whites knew suffering, hardship and oppression. But, as Roboteau observes, they identified themselves for the most part with the Israelites who had already entered the promised land. Although they often sang the same verses as blacks and certainly identified in their own way with these verses, white Christians did not hear in them the same poignant messages of sorrow and hope, or of God's anger and love, that were so apparent to a people who, like the Israelites in bondage under the Pharaoh, were actually enslaved — actually driven like hogs and cows for sale. "As a result," Raboteau concludes, "the slaves' identification with the children of Israel took on an immediacy and intensity which would be difficult to exaggerate."[11]

Although the slaves were not consciously elaborating either an anthropology or a theology, the ring shouts and the spirituals clearly developed and articulated a vision of God and of humanity distinct from the understanding of their masters. That vision deserves much more extensive and scholarly attention than to date it has been given. We are indebted to the pioneering efforts of scholars like Raboteau to retrieve that spiritual journey for us. But even with what little we have gleaned from his research, the relevance of the ring shouts should be evident for our own efforts to break into the Christian circle of understanding. As we have seen, the shouts were born of necessity. The question at issue for the slaves was their very humanity, their survival. By no means did all slaves turn to the Christian God. There is ample evidence that "some saw Christianity as meaningless, a sham, and a white man's religion."[12] Those who did turn to Christianity, however, found that with it they were able to articulate a vision of life that enabled them to survive in a system that denied their personal worth and identity. Their experience of slavery and of the fellowship and ecstasy of the ring shouts, that is to say, their lived anthropology, was the secret which enabled them to break into the charmed circle of the masters' faith and appropriate its truth, often more originally than the masters themselves. The slaves found a God who was credible and effective for them. They found a saving truth. Their experience of this God and saving truth, that is to say, their lived theology, was, in turn, the secret that enabled them to find hope and dignity in their lives despite the dehumanizing conditions which they endured.

The slaves' struggle to maintain their humanity through the imaginative reappropriation of Christianity in the ring shouts was faithful to the dynamics of the Biblical tradition itself. The stories of creation and fall in Genesis, for example, are themselves creative adaptions of other peoples' theological anthropologies or at least alternatives to them. Attending to the correlation between anthropology and theology in these different traditions enables us to break into a circle of understanding which might otherwise seem no more than outdated and irrelevant mythology.

An insight into the character of these earlier theological anthropologies has been provided by the discovery of other ancient stories of creation, particularly *Enuma elish*.[13] The first fragments of this account were unearthed by archaeologists in the middle of the nineteenth century. Later discoveries eventually provided enough information to reconstruct much of the text and to conclude that it originated in Babylon around 2000 B.C.E. Although scholars agree that Genesis was composed at a significantly later date, few argue for a direct dependence. Rather, most conclude that the Hebrew author, whether directly familiar with *Enuma elish* or not, certainly knew accounts similar to it.

The work of two scholars in particular, John L. McKenzie and Thorkild Jacobsen, is helpful for recovering the theological anthropologies articulated in Genesis and in these other accounts.[14] There are notable differences between McKenzie's and Jacobsen's interpretations, particularly as concerns *Enuma elish*'s meaning and significance, which we cannot pretend to resolve here. There is enough of a consensus in their research, however, and in that of other biblical scholars and Assyriologists, to provide us with the necessary groundwork for breaking into Genesis' circle of understanding.

Enuma elish tells about the origins of the universe and about how order and meaning were created within it. The beginnings of the world are pictured as a watery chaos personifed by the mingling of Tiamat (female — the powers of the salt waters of the sea) and Apsu (male — the powers of the fresh waters). From their union, the gods came to be. The gods, however, were unruly. Their noise disturbed Apsu's sleep. Despite Tiamat's reluctance, he determined to destroy them. Somehow the gods learned of his plan. Ea, god of the rivers, saved the day by putting Apsu to sleep with a spell and then killing him. Jacobsen emphasizes that this first victory was won by a single god acting on his own initiative and saving the day without permanently overcoming the virtual anarchy of the divine community.[15] In any case, there was peace for a time. But then the gods began to disturb Tiamat. The text is vague about how. Tiamat, along with her new consort, Kingu, set out to destroy her progeny. Neither Ea nor his father Anu, god of the heavens, was powerful enough to stand up to her. The gods eventually found in Marduk, son of Ea, a leader and warrior capable of saving them. Having secured their allegiance, Marduk prepared to do battle.

> He made a bow, designed it as his weapon,
> let the arrow ride firmly on the bowstring.
> Grasping (his) mace in his right hand,
>   he lifted it,
> hung bow and quiver at his side,
>   set the lightning before him,
> and made his body burn with searing flame.
> He made a net wherein to encircle Tiamat,
> bade the four winds hold on,
>   that none of her escape.
> The south wind, north wind,
>   east wind, west wind,
> gifts from his (grand-) father Anu,
>   he brought to the edges of the net.[16]

After the expected verbal sparring, they joined in deathly battle. The text is quite vivid in its detail, highlighting Marduk's cunning and fierceness as warrior king.

> Tiamat and the champion of the gods, Marduk,

engaged,
were entangled in single combat,
  joined in battle.
The lord spread his net encompassing her;
the tempest, following after,
  he loosed in her face.
Tiamat opened her mouth as far as she could;
he drove in the tempest
  lest she close her lips.
The fierce winds filled her belly,
her insides congested and (retching)
  she opened wide her mouth:
he let fly an arrow, it split her belly,
cut through her inward parts
  and gashed the heart.
He held her fast, extinguishing her life.[17]

After routing her followers, Marduk returned to Tiamat. He crushed her skull with his mace and split her like a shellfish into two parts. From one half, he created the heavens. He posted guards and ordered them not to let her waters escape. Many scholars see this as a reference to the common Mesopotamian picture of the world. The sky was imagined as a dome or tent-like structure which kept out the waters from above, while the earth, like a disk, kept out the waters from below.

Marduk next determined stations for all of the gods in his new creation. He established constellations for each of the twelve months. He fixed the monthly course of the moon, and created the night and the day. In this way order was now created out of what once was chaos. In gratitude the gods, even those who had sided with Tiamat, pledged their obedience to him. He accepted their praise and expressed his wish to build, at a place he would call Babylon, a city and temple in which to dwell. To lighten the burden of the gods, and perhaps to avoid ill feeling, he then hit upon the idea of creating humanity to do the gods' menial work. Kingu was slain and from the blood of this enemy humankind was fashioned. In the end, Marduk

ruled supreme from the towering temple, or ziggurat, which had
been created for him at the center of creation.

Jacobsen sees several levels of meaning in the text. The
early section appears to be an account of the world's origins
based on observations about how new land came into being from
the silt carried by rivers to the sea basin. The mingling of Apsu
and Tiamat leads to the successive births of Lahmu and
Lahamu (representative of silt formed in the primeval ocean),
Anshar (horizon of the heavens), Kishar (corresponding rim of
the earth), An (god of the heavens) and so forth. Jacobsen de-
tects a more fundamental line of imagery, however, reflecting
the emergence of Babylon as the dominant monarchy of
Mesopotamia. *Enuma elish* charts the origin of the gods
(theogony) as a movement from anarchy at the time of Ea's confrontation with Apsu, to the primitive democracy which elects
Marduk to leadership, and finally to the permanent monarchy
established by Marduk's creation of the world, humanity and
the god's dwelling place at the base of the heavens in Babylon.
Jacobsen sees a clear parallel between this emergence of order
in the heavens and the Babylonian monarchy's supplanting of
the democracies of more ancient Sumerian cities. He suggests
that such a reading would also account for the rather obvious
theme of parricide entailed in Ea's poisoning of Apsu and Marduk's slaying of Tiamat.[18]

From this, it is clear that the myth is more than a fanciful
story about the gods. It is an outline, celebration and justification of Babylon's and Marduk's rise to power over a united
Mesopotamia, but projected poetically back to mythical times
and made universal.[19] As such it tells us something first of all
about Babylonians' ultimate concern, or theology in the sense
defined earlier. Creation, and so order and reality itself, originate out of chaos. This chaos predates even the gods. The gods
themselves are identified with the forces of nature. Their power
is awesome compared to man's, but still limited. Their origins
and affairs are known. Thus these forces of reality are not altogether eternal or transcendent, at least not in the Christian
sense of the terms.

Marduk, the fierce and cunning warrior and born leader, is able to create order out of the primeval chaos. His world, however, is born of struggle. Commentators such as McKenzie argue that there are good reasons for seeing such struggle, from the myth's perspective, as an abiding characteristic of reality itself. Myths, in this view, are not histories of past events, but rather accounts of once-upon-a-time events that speak just as much of the present and the future, as of the past. As struggle must be an abiding feature for any empire that wants to maintain control of its subjects and territories, so struggle is an abiding characteristic of life itself. "In this myth," McKenzie contends, "the struggle between order and chaos is constant in material reality; the cycle gives the victory to one, and then to the other. Neither ever emerges finally supreme, and reality remains this unstable equilibrium of conflicting forces."[20] Jacobsen proposes a more positive view, arguing that the myth sees the universe grounded in divine power and divine will which unifies the cosmos "under the leadership of a single ruler who governs through consultation, persuasion, and conviction."[21] But even Jacobsen would have to admit that the image of persuasion here is, to say the least, a bit coercive.

The myth also reveals something of the Babylonian view of humanity. Marduk's creation of humankind, however ingenious, is an afterthought. The raw material is the blood of his vanquished enemy, Kingu. The meaning of human existence is found in nationalistic identification with the warrior god. To be human is to serve the gods and the empire. Jacobsen stresses the value which such order brings to humankind: "ultimate power is not estranged from mankind, but resides in gods in human form who act understandably. The universe is now moral and meaningful and expression of a creative intelligence with valid purpose: order and peace and prosperity."[22] But we would also have to note that the gods are made understandable by bringing them down to humanity's level, and that the order with which humankind is blessed is not one in which people appear to have much personal worth outside their identification with the empire. Moreover, even if one does not grant McKenzie's emphasis on dualistic struggle, the element of conflict cannot be altogether ignored. In picturing the origin of things as struggle for domination between the female principle of chaos and the male principle of order, the myth suggests more of an estrangement within the cosmos and within humanity than Jacobsen's account seems to acknowledge.

There are numerous indications within Genesis that its author and original audience were familiar with stories like *Enuma elish*. The text appears to have the image of primeval watery chaos in mind when it says in Gen. 1:2 that in the beginning "the earth was formless void," that "there was darkness over the deep," and that "God's spirit hovered over the water." Verses 6 thru 8 seem to allude to a picture similar to Marduk's splitting of Tiamat's body to create the heavens:

> God said, "Let there be a vault in the waters to divide the waters in two." And so it was. God made the vault, and it divided the waters above the vault from the waters under the vault. God called the vault "heaven."

There are other biblical texts which make more direct references to the mythical struggle between God and a primeval sea monster. Isaiah 27:1 reads:

> That day, Yahweh will punish,
> with his hard sword, massive and strong,
> Leviathan the fleeing serpent,
> Leviathan the twisting serpent:
> he will kill the sea dragon.

Isaiah 51:9 is just as explicit.

> Awake, awake! Clothe yourself in strength,
> arm of Yahweh.
> Awake, as in the past,
> in times of generations long ago.
> Did you not split Rahab in two
> and pierce the Dragon through?

In Genesis, as in *Enuma elish*, the creator puts the moon and stars in the heavens to divide night and day, to establish the months and years and to indicate the seasons and festivals. In Genesis these lights are not dieties, but it seems clear that a similiar worldview is in mind.

Although the author of Genesis was surely familiar with descriptions of creation as the result of a god's struggle against chaos, Genesis itself offers a very different picture. There is no mention of struggle. Yahweh is not born of chaos. God's spirit hovers over the water from the beginning. God's word alone is enough to turn this formless void into the heavens and earth. There is no theogony, no biography of God, no gods who can compete with Yahweh. God is there before everything else and in complete power. God is not described, except indirectly. God is not identified with any forces of nature, although it is clear that they must be under God's control. This God is truly transcendent and eternal. There is, of course, an implicit image of God as a craftsman, whose week is filled out, day by day, in the systematic and careful shaping of his intentions into a world that can be seen as good at the conclusion of each step. But note that there is no description of the workman himself, or of his tools. Neither struggle nor domination are at the heart of reality in this account. The wisdom and creativity Yahweh exercises is of a very different sort than the cunning and fierce domination of the warrior god, Marduk.

Even more striking is the image of humanity. Our creation is not an afterthought, but appears to have been God's intent from the beginning. The identification with God could hardly be stronger.

> God created man in the image of himself,
> in the image of God he created him,
> male and female he created them. (Gen. 1:27)

Nor was humankind created for servitude. God blessed the man and woman and made them masters of all the creatures of the earth. There is no hint either, at this point in the text, of estrangement between God and humanity or between man and woman. Genesis 2 goes on to emphasize that sexuality is something good and that it is created by God. At least in the beginning, man and woman were created for companionship, not for the domination of one by the other.[23] They were meant to become one body, and were not meant to feel any shame in front of each other (Gen. 2:24-25).

But here, of course, we run into a difficulty. Genesis 3, in telling the story of the Fall, affirms a fundamental estrangement between God and humanity, and between man and woman. Yahweh curses Adam and Eve, and banishes them from the garden. From that time on, the woman is warned, she will "yearn" for her husband, but "he will lord it over" her (Gen. 3:16). Furthermore, in this chapter it is not at all clear that sexuality itself is something good. After the man and woman eat the fruit, their eyes are opened, they realize they are naked, and then, as opposed to the concluding lines of Genesis 2, they become ashamed of their bodies and sew fig leaves together to cover themselves. Yahweh's curses reinforce the impressions of a negative view of sexuality. Not only will the husband lord it over the woman, but God vows to multiply her pains in childbearing. God even curses the fertility of Adam's crops.

Accursed be the soil because of you.
With suffering shall you get your food from it
every day of your life.
It shall yield you brambles and thistles,
and you shall eat wild plants.
With sweat on your brow
shall you eat your bread,
until you return to the soil,
as you were taken from it. (Gen. 3:17-19)

McKenzie notes that "both ancient and modern interpreters have been quick to see in the 'forbidden fruit' the meaning which it has acquired in popular speech — the pleasures of sex," and that "some have thought that the man and the woman sin-

ned by some form of illicit sexual pleasure."²⁴ But citing the
positive view of sexuality at the end of Genesis 2, McKenzie rejects the common interpretation that the fruit signifies the pro-
hibition of sexual relations. Once again, the secret for breaking
into the text's circle is attention to the correlation between anthropology and theology, and between the Hebrews' theological
anthropology and that of their neighbors. The Canaanites wor-
shipped fertility. They were very conscious that human survival depends on the fruits of the soil, on the fertility of one's cattle, and even on women's fertility, for children are necessary to
share a man's burdens, provide for him in old age and carry on
his name. Thus, not without some justice, fertility was seen as
humanity's ultimate concern, its god, its Ba'al. The fertility
cults sought to understand, worship and control this sacred
power of life. In particular they sought to influence the cycles of
natural fertility (the birth, death and rebirth of the seasons) by
ritual acts of sexual intercourse between the high priest (or the
king) and a priestess. Worshipers shared in this divine power of
Ba'al through union with sacred prostitutes. If fertility is god,
then in the ecstasy of sexuality man comes closest to knowledge
and union with the divine. In this anthropology, woman is
deified for her sexual aspects, but she has no personal dignity.
She gives pleasure and bears children, but is still man's prop-
erty.

Archaeology has established that the serpent was a common sexual symbol among these cults. In this light, the serpent
and the tree of life, whose fruit will make Adam and Eve like
gods, seem clear references to such cults. It would have been obvious to Genesis's original audience. Sexuality itself, then, is
not the evil. The evil is making a god of sexuality. The author
warns that those who make an idol of fertility will lose the very
thing they are trying to attain. We cannot control our world or
find ultimate reality through sexuality. As important as healthy
progeny, cattle and crops are, there is more to life than that. As
fulfilling as sexuality is, it not always "divine" even in the
figurative sense, let alone divine in any real sense. Indeed,
making a god of sexuality and worshiping woman or man as a

sexual object warps sexuality and estranges man from woman.
Nor do we become like a god or know god in sexuality as such.
Indeed, making a god, or god-like activity, of our sexuality estranges humanity from all that is truly divine. It is like Michael
Corleone, the godfather in the modern myth by that name, who
seeks the American dream and legitimacy for his "family," but
who tries to achieve that goal according to the mafia's ethic. In
order to save his family, he finally kills his only living brother
and quite totally estranges himself from his wife. Making a god
of the family, he destroys it.

In speaking of God and humanity this way, the author of
Genesis envisioned a very different humanity and ultimate concern than that envisioned by the author of *Enuma elish* or the
worshipers of the fertility cults. Is reality for us ultimately and
finally a struggle against chaos? Is whatever purpose and order
we find in reality ultimately something that has accidentally
spun out of chaos? Or is reality ultimately good, grounded in a
purposefulness there from the beginning? Is the ultimate order
of our world something that can be identified with the powers of
nature, with fertility or with the political hegemony of the
Babylonian empire, or indeed with the political domination of
any of our contemporary empires, democratic or otherwise? Or
is there an ultimate order which transcends the powers of nature and the reach of any political scheme? Is reality made
meaningful by reducing the gods to our level? Or is the meaning
of reality to be found in recognizing a reality that transcends
us? Should we think of ourselves, and so act, as slaves to the
powers of nature, to the gods or to the national political order?
Or should we think of ourselves, and so act, as beings created in
God's image, partners in God's creation, co-creators of our political realms? In accordance with what ideal should we mold ourselves and our world — the ideal of the cunning and fierce warrior god, the ideal of the fertility god who exists to gratify our
needs or the ideal of the creator who calls us to responsibility as
stewards of the world? Is evil something we can blame on the
serpent, on the woman, on the man? Or is evil something for

which we, particularly through our idolatries, are at least partially responsible?

These are, of course, simplistic and loaded questions. They are meant to indicate, though, that *Enuma elish*, the fertility cults and Genesis posed and sought to answer questions similar to the ones we face ourselves today. If these accounts are still revelatory for us, it is not because they pass on some secret about the physical origin of the universe or of humanity, or some direct account of God's doings at the beginning of time. If they are revelatory, it is because they disclose something true and saving about what it means to be human, and about what finally is God for us. Attending to the differences between these accounts, and attending to the correlation between their anthropologies and theologies, enables us to distinguish, at least to some degree, what was taken for granted and what was really at issue. It helps clarify what was really at stake in *Enuma elish*, the fertility cults and Genesis. That is to say, it helps us break into these charmed circles.

Helpful as that might be, however, none of the illustrations in this chapter actually breaks the spell of the Christian circle of understanding. Although many Afro-American slaves found in the God of Exodus a bottom line that gave meaning and direction to their lives, there is no guarantee that people today will come to a similar discovery. Although the ancient Hebrews found vehicles in the myths of their day for expressing their conception of God, or against which to oppose it, that does not mean that people today will hear a disclosure of God in the Genesis stories. The stories themselves do not justify the Christian vision of God and humanity. For many today, the stories are just that — stories or myths which have no real referent beyond ourselves and our imagination. So, if our examination of the correlation of theological anthropology is to break the Christian circle's spell, it is necessary to confront this modern suspicion that theology in the end is nothing more than a disguised anthropology.

NOTES

1. Albert J. Raboteau, *Slave Religion: "The Invisible Institution" in the Antebellum South* (New York: Oxford University Press, 1978). I am indebted to his moving study for the account of slave religion which follows.

2. Raboteau, p. 318.

3. Raboteau, p. 264.

4. Raboteau, p. 318.

5. Raboteau, p. 265.

6. Raboteau, p. 310.

7. Raboteau, p. 310.

8. Raboteau, pp. 310-11.

9. Raboteau, p. 318.

10. Raboteau, pp. 248-49.

11. Raboteau, p. 250.

12. Raboteau, p. 314.

13. "The Creation Epic," in James B. Pritchard, ed., *Ancient Near Eastern Texts Relating to the Old Testament*, 3rd ed., with supplement (New Jersey: Princeton University Press, 1969); the title *"Enuma elish"* comes from the first words of the text, "When on high."

14. John L. McKenzie, *The Two Edged Sword: An Interpretation of the Old Testament* (Garden City, NY: Image Books, 1966, originally published in 1956), esp. pp 95-131; Thorkild Jacobsen, *The Treasures of Darkness: A History of Mesopotamian Religion* (New Haven: Yale University Press, 1976), esp. pp. 167-91.

15. Jacobsen, p. 172.

16. Jacobsen's translation, p. 177.

17. Jacobsen, p. 178.

18. Jacobsen, pp. 183-190.

19. Jacobsen, p. 191.

20. McKenzie, p. 100.

21. Jacobsen, p. 191.

22. Jacobsen, p. 191.

23. See McKenzie, pp. 111-19.

24. McKenzie, pp. 119-20.

II. SIGHTING THE HORIZON

6. Difficulties of the Head

For many of those who see the Christian circle as charmed, even getting its horizon in sight is problematic. Is there anything out there which really corresponds to what believers call God? How can we be sure that God isn't just an illusion, a projection of the believer's imagination, an invention of hope or desperation? Couldn't the story of Jesus the Messiah be explained just as easily, indeed more easily, as the product of human fantasy? Why should this extraordinary tale be given more credence than myths and legends about other men?

Such difficulties have not been easily dismissed, at least in our culture, since the publication in 1841 of Ludwig Feuerbach's *The Essence of Christianity*.[1] The objections he raised there are echoed in the arguments of most modern atheists, including Marx, Freud, Nietzsche and Sartre. The book has had a profound influence on believers as well. In an "Introduction" to it, Karl Barth, perhaps the most influential Protestant theologian of this century, claimed that "no philosopher of his time penetrated the contemporary theological situation as effectually as he, and few spoke with such pertinence."[2]

No doubt, few of our contemporaries have actually read Feuerbach himself. There is no question, however, that arguments like his are behind today's suspicion that Christianity is a charmed circle. It will have to be admitted that his thesis has much in common, as well, with the suggestion of the last two chapters that theological anthropology is the secret for breaking into the Christian circle. Confrontation of his argument thus provides an opportunity both for articulating more precisely the skeptic's difficulties of the head and also, more positively, for

47

clarifying how the notion of theological anthropology can assist in actually bringing into sight the Christian circle's horizon.

Feuerbach's thesis has basically two prongs. On the one hand, he argues that theology is actually disguised anthropology. Its real subject matter is not a God "out there," as we sometimes say, but humanity itself. God is nothing but the best qualities of our own human nature projected or imagined as a being apart from ourselves. Thus, as Feuerbach puts it in the oft-quoted lines of his "Preface," "the true sense of theology is anthropology."[3] If there is in reality no God out there, then it follows that "the secret of religion is atheism."[4] But even though he denies God's existence, this first prong of his argument also has a positive thrust. Feuerbach denies God to free humanity from the tyranny of an illusion. Insofar as humanity's most noble qualities are attributed to another being, he reasoned, humanity is alienated from its true nature and potential. Feuerbach insists that he seeks only to overcome that dehumanizing alienation. His aim is to change "the friends of God into friends of man, believers into thinkers, worshippers into workers, candidates for the other world into students of this world, Christians who on their own confession are half-animal and half angel, into men — whole men."[5]

The second prong of his argument seeks to demonstrate that the usual theological interpretation of religion is essentially and unavoidably contradictory. Again and again in each chapter, he hammers home the same thesis. Either the essence of Christianity is anthropology or its essence is absurd — a charmed and vicious circle.

The persuasiveness of the argument rests at least partially in its beguiling simplicity. He observes, initially, that the predicates or attributes which believers apply to God are all drawn from our own humanity. He contends that this is so because we can only recognize an attribute which comes within our own sphere of vision. That is to say, we can only recognize something which is accessible to our experience and understanding — something which is within our grasp. But that means that anything we are able to recognize must in some way be included within our own sphere. In other words, if it is within our grasp, it must be an attribute of our own existence. As Feuerbach himself put it, "a being's nature is its sphere of vision. As far as thou seest, so far extends thy nature; and conversely. The eye of the brute reaches no farther than its needs, and its nature no farther than its needs."[6]

It follows that knowledge of predicates or attributes outside our sphere of understanding and existence is impossible. We cannot get beyond our own nature. Our imaginations may conceive of beings of a higher kind, but it always turns out that the qualities we give to these beings are drawn from ourselves. They are always qualities through which, in truth, we only image and project ourselves. It is fascinating that in the 1840s he appealed to an example which seems quite contemporary, and one which can be verified readily by a review of today's most imaginative science fiction or a glance at the best special effects contemporary cinematography has to offer.

> There may certainly be thinking beings besides men on the other planets of our solar system. But by the supposition of such beings we do not change our standing point — we extend our conceptions quantitatively not qualitatively. For as surely as on the other planets there are the same laws of motion, so surely are there the same laws of perception and thought as here. In fact, we people the other planets, not that we may place there different beings from ourselves, but more beings of our own or of a similar nature.[7]

Of course, if this is true, then all the predicates or qualities we attribute to God are actually qualities attributable to our own nature. Given Feuerbach's premises, these predicates could be nothing else. "Such as are man's thoughts, such is his God; so much worth as a man has, so much and no more has his God."[8] The argument presumes the correlation between anthropology and theology we discussed in the last two chapters:

"By his God thou knowest the man, and by the man his God."[9]
But Feuerbach pushes the argument much further and in a different direction, concluding that the two, humanity and God, are identical.

God, for example, is supposed to be infinite, Feuerbach says. But if humanity can conceive of an infinite consciousness, then human consciousness must itself be infinite. If our thought can grasp the idea of infinitude, then our thinking itself is in some sense infinite. How could we *think* the infinite, without at least implicitly perceiving and affirming the infinitude of our own power of thought? Likewise, if we can feel the infinite, then our feeling itself must in some sense be infinite. How could we *experience* the infinite, without perceiving and affirming the infinitude of our own existence? So God, for Feuerbach, is nothing but a projection of our humanity, or rather of "the human nature purified, freed from the limits of the individual man, made objective — i.e., contemplated and revered as another, a distinct being."[10]

An appeal to the analogous or indirect character of language about God does not avoid Feuerbach's critique as easily as it might seem. Saying that God in "himself" is distinct from God as we know "him" or describe "him," trades on a specious distinction. How can we know that God is something else in "himself," than "he" is for us, if we can only grasp God in predicates and pronouns derived from ourselves? It is an illusion, Feuerbach insists, to think that we can make a distinction between an object as it is in itself and an object as it is for us, when in fact the only access we have to the object in the first place is through our own conception of it. If anthropomorphic predicates apply to God in some way or other, then God does not really transcend humanity's grasp. If on the other hand, they do not actually apply to God at all, then God is truly indefinable. Of such a God, we could know nothing at all, not even that "he" existed. Not only is such a distinction untenable and unfounded, it also contradicts the very thrust of religious belief which clearly thinks of God as a real being with qualities which can be described, as it were, humanly.

Feuerbach relentlessly applies this logic to the central doctrines of Christian faith. The acknowledgment of divine law, he contends, is nothing else than the recognition of the divinity (absoluteness and necessity) of the laws of human nature. The doctrine of the Incarnation entails a divine love for humanity so great that God becomes man. It is an "orientalism" which means in plain speech that there is nothing higher or more valuable than love of man. The passion and death of Christ mean in effect "nothing else than this: to suffer for others is divine; he who suffers for others, who lays down his life for them, acts divinely, is a God to men."[11] The doctrine of the Trinity "knits together the qualities or powers which were before regarded separately into unity," so that it will be clear that humanity is truly realized only in the integration of understanding, love and compassion, and in a community of persons.[12] The doctrine of Mary as the Mother of God becomes a complement to this notion: love must be embodied. To Feuerbach this is equivalent to "belief in the feminine principle as divine."[13] The doctrine of the Logos, or divine Word, reduces anthropologically to the recognition that "we know no higher spiritually operative power and expression of power than the power of the word."[14] The doctrine of creation out of nothing is ultimately an affirmation of the unlimited power of human imagination. Miracles boil down to the same thing. They are testimony to imagination's power to project the unreal as real. Faith in Providence, in the final analysis, turns out to be faith in humanity's own worth. Heaven and immortality are nothing else than efforts to free the present life from those things which appear as limitations or evil.

Feuerbach applies this sort of analysis to all the central tenets of Christianity. All have a positive anthropological sense. Taken theologically, however, these doctrines are contradictory. In fact, as Feuerbach sees it, faith alienates humanity from everything that is truly human. It was faith, he argues, "not love, not reason, which invented Hell" and which "condemns and anathematises."[15] Indeed, he persists:

> all the actions, all the dispositions, which contradict
> love, humanity, [and] reason, accord with faith. All

the horrors of Christian religious history, which our
believers aver not to be due to Christianity, have
truly arisen out of Christianity, because they have
arisen out of faith.[16]

Such deception and perversion of the truth of humanity
cannot last. Thus, Feuerbach was convinced that Christianity
was on the wane. It was just a matter of time before its secret
would be revealed. Soon it would be clear that the truth of
Christianity is its anticipation of a humanism without God, that
its essence is anthropology without theology.

This prediction, however, has not come true. After almost
150 years, Christianity is still with us and in many quarters
quite vibrant. But such difficulties of the head are also still with
us. There are still many who protest that Christianity is a
charmed circle and who await its demise. Breaking into its circle in this context thus requires taking these difficulties seriously, even as we attempt to show the inherent limitations of
Feuerbach's argument and conclusion.

Notes

1. Ludwig Feuerbach, *The Essence of Christianity*, trans. George Eliot, (New York: Harper & Row, 1957).

2. "An Introductory Essay," p. x.

3. Feuerbach, p. xxxvi.

4. Feuerbach, p. xxxvi.

5. Quoted by Barth, p. xi, from Feuerbach's 1848 Heidelberg lectures.

6. Feuerbach, p. 8.

7. Feuerbach, pp. 11-12.

8. Feuerbach, p. 12.

9. Feuerbach, p. 12.

10. Feuerbach, p. 14.

11. Feuerbach, p. 60.

12. Feuerbach, pp. 65-67.

13. Feuerbach, p. 72.

14. Feuerbach, p. 79.

15. Feuerbach, p. 257.

16. Feuerbach, pp. 257-58.

7. Wounded Humanity

What is humanity's ultimate concern? What horizon finally gives meaning to life? Feuerbach's critique of Christianity gets right to the heart of the matter. God, he charges, is nothing other than our own humanity. Worship of God as one apart from us is detrimental, indeed even demonic, because it alienates us from our own nature. A theological interpretation of Christianity is ultimately dehumanizing. Anthropology alone provides the secret for clarifying the true essence of the Christian circle.

But is human nature itself as divine as Feuerbach claims? How infinite, in reality and concretely, is humanity's love, humanity's justice, humanity's compassion or humanity's consciousness? Since Feuerbach and the advent of modern atheism, has our world really become any less inhuman? We can point to increases in literacy, the eradication of numerous diseases and technological improvements, undreamed of in Feuerbach's time, which affect the quality of life in almost every respect. But, as we observed in Chapter 4, the modern era also has witnessed atrocities against humanity which would have been unimaginable in Feuerbach's day. Human progress has brought us two world wars, the unleashing of nuclear destruction and the creation of a nuclear arsenal capable of destroying the world many times over. Can one really say that there is less poverty, less hunger, less racism, less sexism, less crime or less violence? Has political, social and economic exploitation been eliminated, or has it only taken on different forms and affected different people? Feuerbach's account does not take seriously enough this woundedness of our humanity. The humanity of which he speaks is an abstraction.

The seductiveness and danger of such an abstraction should not be underestimated. It too is a source of dehumanizing bewitchment. This was especially clear to the great voices of Protestant Neo-Orthodoxy like Karl Barth, Emil Brunner, Anders Nygren, Dietrich Bonhoeffer and Reinhold Neibuhr in the years following World War I. Each in their own way protested against the delusory optimism which, for example, left so many of their contemporaries blind to the inherent evil of Nazism. The attempt of theologians such as these to recover the spirit of the Protestant Reformation, and particularly its poignant sense of human sinfulness, provides a sharp contrast to Feuerbach's understanding of human nature.

The German theologian and ethicist Helmut Thielicke, with others speaking out of that tradition, continues this protest against the idolatry of human nature. His recent essay in Christian anthropology describes positions like Feuerbach's as a kind of anthropological docetism.[1] The term refers to an early heresy which denied the reality of Jesus' human body. The Christ of the docetist was not truly of the same flesh as us. His humanity was only an appearance — in reality a sham, a fraud. Likewise, Thielicke charges, the modern conception of human nature is also frequently a sham. We speak all to easily in generalities about love, justice and compassion. We presume that the question of our identity is essentially a private and individual matter. On closer examination, such generalities turn out empty, and the so-called "individual" proves to be "an unreal and shadowy phenomenon that does not really exist."[2]

To illustrate this point, Thielicke offers the example of a businessman who protests to his pastor that love of neighbor sounds fine in general terms, but does not apply to the real world of competition. The man puts it quite directly:

> as a businessman I am in competition. And this, God knows, is hard. My main competitor is geographically very close. His business and house are in the same street. I know him and his family very well personally. They are good people and deserve every

sympathy. Because he is my rival and I also see him almost every day, I am constantly faced by the question, What should be my attitude to him? How am I to love this competitor? Without wanting to boast, I am better at business than he is and more capable in every respect. I also have more capital and flexibility. I have a nose for development. My superiority is so great that as my business flourishes, his declines . . . .

. . . What am I to do? That is the decisive issue. Does loving mean that I should raise my prices, sell poorer goods, and restrict my volume so as to give my rival a chance and halt his decline? Does it mean that I should no longer fight the battle of competition according to its own laws but philanthropically make it easier in a way that is inconsistent with the process? Do I have to go 'half-throttle' as a Christian? Must I be ready to let my business go on the skids financially — for the sake of love? . . . If as a sacrifice to love I cease to be competitive and perhaps have to close down, what will this mean for my employees, to whom I also have an obligation as a neighbor?[3]

Such dilemmas arise from the fact that the demands of love are quite concrete and that our identity is not something private and individual, but rather is defined by the context in which we find ourselves. This context is structured by our own past, both good and bad, by the history of our particular society and by relationships like competition which govern our lives in the concrete.

Our identities are in large part constituted by such structures, be they vocational, economic, political, cultural, social, erotic or religious. Our personal identity cannot be separated from our participation in these structures. Furthermore, we cannot honestly deny that many of these structures are as a matter of fact evil. The world we inherit and inhabit is a dehumanizing one — a world of war, violence, exploitation, racism, sexism and the like. We deceive ourselves if we fail to recognize that our personal identity is very much determined by our involvement in the nexus of such evils. "I myself am part of the nexus," Thielicke insists. "I am not just an effect but one of the causes. Encountering the structured world, I encounter myself."[4] Devout soldiers defending their country, for example, need to be reminded "that the war in which they obey and seek to do God's will is the expression of a secular structure that God does not will."[5] The same must be said to those of us who pay taxes to support such wars, or build nuclear arsenals to prevent them, or support less than ideal legislation in the hopes of achieving compromises that might eliminate some small portion of the root causes behind these armed conflicts. "This situational nexus in which we meet one another," Thielicke insists, "is, as it were, the body of the nexus in which my personhood resides."[6] We cannot escape identification with these evils of our past or with the present evils of our world without turning what we call our human identity into an abstract sham. We are our past, and we are part of the social nexus of evil in our world today, not just its victims.

Here we face a major difficulty with Feuerbach's thesis. What about our concrete humanity? What about our inhumanity to one another? What about humanity's woundedness? Is this not an essential aspect of humanity's real identity? Is the humanity of which Feuerbach speaks anything more than an unreal abstraction? Is humanity truly divine? Quite to the contrary, isn't Feuerbach's humanity an illusion? Isn't it a projection without real substance, a sham, a fraud? Is it in the interest of humanity to minimize its woundedness and inhumanity? Can this wounded humanity save itself? Isn't such a supposition really at root a most dehumanizing kind of bewitchment and delusion? Doesn't worshiping humanity blind us to our woundedness? Have we not here a subtle, docetic alienation from the truth about ourselves? Doesn't such an anthropology deny our need for something more?

When one honestly faces the woundedness and brokenness of the human world, is it really so dehumanizing to hope, as the prophets and Jesus did, for a God who transcends the limits of our humanity — for a God who is more than a projection of our wounded reality?

It is true that there is much about the God of the prophets and Jesus which fits Feuerbach's conception of the divine as a projection of our own humanity. The language of the prophets and Jesus is often anthropomorphic. God speaks to Moses and through him even makes a covenant, a kind of contract if you will, with the people of Israel. The prophets later describe God as a jealous lover. They warn of God's anger and wonder at God's patience. They even speak of God as one at odds with himself, torn between compassion and the demands of justice:

> Ephraim, how could I part with you?
> Israel, how could I give you up?
> How could I treat you like Admah,
> or deal with you like Zeboiim?
> [two cities destroyed by God with Sodom and Gomorrah]
> My heart recoils from it,
> my whole being trembles at the thought.
> I will not give rein to my fierce anger,
> I will not destroy Ephraim again. . . . (Hosea 11: 8-9)

Jesus himself speaks of God as his "father" using the term *Abba* which many scholars believe was an intimate form of address more akin to our "Dad."

It is also true that the God of the prophets and Jesus personifies human ideals. God is compassionate, just, concerned about the poor and downtrodden. In Christ, God suffers and dies for us. As Feuerbach liked to point out, the evangelist John suggested the appropriateness of describing God as love itself.

> God is love
> and anyone who lives in love lives in God,
> and God lives in him.(1 John 4: 16)

Finally, it must be admitted that there is at least some warrant for Feuerbach's claim that the prophets and Jesus emphasize the distance between God, who can be imagined as a transcendent realization of our ideals, and our own concrete humanity which is pictured as unworthy if not depraved. Moses could not look upon God.

> "You cannot see my face," God said, "for man cannot see me and live." And Yahweh said, "Here is a place beside me. You must stand on the rock, and when my glory passes by, I will put you in a cleft of the rock and shield you with my hand while I pass by. Then I will take my hand away and you shall see the back of me; but my face is not to be seen."(Exodus 33: 20-23)

Moses' followers did not dare to approach the mountain where God appeared. Even God's name, Yahweh, is enigmatic. Like a burning bush, the searing presence of God's reality is perceptible, yet mysteriously intangible. We saw earlier that the stories of Genesis, especially in comparison to the myths of their neighbors, emphasize God's transcendence, and humanity's responsibility for the depravity of the world. Adam and Eve protest that the devil made them do it, but God will have none of that. As Isaiah reminds us later,

> for my thoughts are not your thoughts,
> my ways not your ways — it is Yahweh who speaks.
> Yes, the heavens are as high above earth
> as my ways are above your ways,
> my thoughts above your thoughts.(Isaiah 55: 8-9)

But the God of Jesus and the prophets does not always correspond so neatly to the idealized projection of humanity which Feuerbach describes. Nor are the prophets' and Jesus' warnings about human depravity as dehumanizing and alienating as Feuerbach portrays them. The God of the prophets and Jesus is a God who calls humanity to a radically new state. Theirs is a God who sets humanity free, redeems humanity, transforms humanity, sets a new standard and promises a new future for the human race. But also, at the heart of their vision, is a realistic recognition that in the concrete order of things, humanity is not free, not ideal and not able to save itself. The prophets and Jesus call us to look at the world and ourselves as we really are, not as we might project them to be in docetic abstractions. This prophetic conviction emerges from the insight that our world is not as it should be, and that we, insofar as we are part of this unholy world, are not as we should be.

The prophets were not speaking in generalities or platitudes. They were concerned about every facet of life.[7] They protested against the abuses of the legal system:

> Trouble for those who turn justice into wormwood,
> throwing integrity to the ground;
> who hate the man dispensing justice at the city gate
> and detest those who speak with honesty.(Amos 5: 7-10)

They were angered by the dishonesty and greed of the marketplace:

> Listen to this, you who trample on the needy
> and try to suppress the poor people of the country,
> you who say, "When will New Moon be over
> so that we can sell our corn,
> and the sabbath, so that we can market our wheat?
> Then by lowering the bushel, raising the shekel,
> by swindling and tampering with the scales,
> we can buy up the poor for money,
> and the needy for a pair of sandals,
> and get a price even for the sweepings of the wheat."(Amos 8: 4-6)

The prophets condemned the pretensions of wealth, reserving some of their harshest criticism for those who, like the wealthy women of Samaria, showed no concern for the poor:

> Listen to his word, you cows of Bashan

> living in the mountain of Samaria,
> oppressing the needy, crushing the poor,
> saying to your husbands, "Bring us something to drink!"
> The Lord Yahweh swears this by his holiness:
> The days are coming to you now
> when you will be dragged out with hooks,
> the very last of you with prongs.
> Out you will go, each by the nearest breach in the wall,
> to be driven all the way to Hermon.(Amos 4: 1-3)

Nor were the prophets impressed by worship or piety that did not practice what it preached:

> I hate and despise your feasts,
> I take no pleasure in your solemn festivals.
> When you offer me holocausts,
>
> . . . .
> I reject your oblations,
> and refuse to look at your sacrifices of fattened cattle.
> Let me have no more of the din of your chanting,
> no more of your strumming on harps.
> But let justice flow like water,
> and integrity like an unfailing stream.(Amos 5: 21-24)

The prophets would not let Israel claim it knew God or even knew the truth about humanity's identity, unless that knowledge could be shown as a concrete reality. To know God is a matter of the heart, the hands and the feet, not primarily a matter of the head.

Such convictions did not originate from philosophical reflections or speculative projections. It is not just that such speculative thinking was a foreign idiom to them, although that was the case. Nor was it simply a question of mythical language (Feuerbach's "orientalisms") substituting for philosophical reflection. Rather the Israelites' conception of humanity and God

grew out of their historical experience. Their captivity in Egypt
and their exodus provided them with a transformative insight
and revelatory paradigm for understanding all of life. The
theological anthropology elaborated in the Hebrew Scriptures
was formed out of their concrete experience of that originating
event and out of their application of its paradigmatic implications to the practicalities of everyday living.

In light of this process, several things became crystal clear,
at least to the prophets. First, the Israelites could not have
saved themselves. There was no question of escaping on their
own from Pharaoh's harsh and overwhelmingly superior grip.
Second, whatever we make of the marvels reported in the story
of the plagues, the "passover" and the escape across the Sea of
Reeds, there can be no doubt the Hebrews were convinced that
their deliverance was God's doing. Whether the waters actually
divided as Cecil B. DeMille pictured it in *The Ten Commandments*, or whether Exodus 14-15 is a poetic account of a storm
that swallowed up the Egyptian pursuers, the bottom line is the
same: the liberation of the sons and daughters of Israel was
wrought by a fortunate chain of events which answered their
prayers for salvation.

Third, viewing this fortunate outcome as providential
rather than simply fortuitous provided a uniquely disclosive
paradigm for understanding life. The ten commandments provide an outline of this paradigm. The rest of the Torah is commentary and interpretation. To be the people of a God who is
just and compassionate, is to be a just and compassionate people
— a people free of perjury and envy.

> You shall not bear false witness against your neigh-
> bor.
> You shall not covet your neighbor's house. You
> shall not covet your neighbors wife, or his servant,
> man or woman, or his ox, or his donkey, or anything
> else that is his.(Exodus 20:16-17)

To be the people of a God who frees one from dehumanizing

exploitation and violence is to be a people of integrity and peace — a people free of violence and infidelity.

> You shall not kill.
> You shall not commit adultery.
> You shall not steal.(Exodus 20: 13-15)

To be the people of a God who leads one to the joys of life in the promised land, is to be a people who revere life — life in the concrete as it is passed down from generation to generation, life with all its diversity of peoples and traditions.

> Honor your father and your mother so that you may have a long life in the land that Yahweh your God has given you.(Exodus 20: 12)

To be the people of a God who is above every power in this world, is to be a people who is truly free for the fullness and depth of life — a people whose concern is with what is truly ultimate, a people free of all the gods who enslave humanity in vain and dehumanizing pursuits.

> You shall have no gods except me.
> You shall not make yourself a carved image or any likeness of anything in heaven or on earth or in the waters under the earth; you shall not bow down to them or serve them. . . . (Exodus 20: 3-5)

To be the people of a God who providentially touched their lives and concretely changed their political, economic and social standing from that of slaves to that of a chosen people, is to be a people ever mindful of what has been wrought for them and of Who wrought it, not only in their history but, indeed, in creation itself.

> You shall not utter the name of Yahweh your God to misuse it. . . .
> Remember the sabbath day and keep it holy. For

> six days you shall labor and do all your work, but the
> seventh day is a sabbath for Yahweh your God. You
> shall do no work on that day. . . . For in six days
> Yahweh made the heavens and the earth and the sea
> and all that these hold, but on the seventh day he
> rested; that is why Yahweh has blessed the sabbath
> day and made it sacred.(Exodus 20: 7-11)

Applying this paradigm to their lives did not alienate the
Israelites from authentic humanity. Such a God did not dehumanize them. Faith did not bewitch and pervert their identity. Quite the contrary, this God called them out of the inhumanity of slavery, not to become like the Pharaoh enslaved by
power or by the futile quest for immortality, but to be freed from
humanity's own inhumanity for a life of justice, compassion, integrity and peace, open for the fullness and depth of creation. In
this Law, and in this God who could not simply be identified
with their mortal humanity, they found a true freedom and an
authentic humanity. Thus, in light of Exodus, the Israelites
saw themselves as a people drawn into a covenant with God.
They bound themselves to the stipulations of this argeement because they found it liberating, because they found it saving.

The richness and breadth of this paradigm is evident in the
further commentary and interpretations of the Pentateuch. In
its light, one's obligations to slaves, to strangers and even to
enemies are transformed.

> If your fellow Hebrew, man or woman, is sold to you,
> he can serve you for six years. In the seventh year
> you must set him free, and in setting him free you
> must not let him go empty handed. You must make
> him a generous provision from your flock, your
> threshing floor, your winepress; as Yahweh your God
> has blessed you, so you must give to him. Remember
> that you were a slave in the land of Egypt and that
> Yahweh your God redeemed you; that is why I lay
> this charge on you today. (Deuteronomy 15: 12-15)

> You must not oppress the stranger; you know how a
> stranger feels, for you lived as strangers in the land
> of Egypt. (Exodus 23: 9)

> If you come on your enemy's ox or donkey going
> astray, you must lead it back to him. If you see the
> donkey of a man who hates you fallen under its load,
> instead of keeping out of his way, go to him and help
> him. (Exodus 23: 4-5)

The formative influence of the Exodus cannot be missed in such
formulations. It is behind all of the Law. It is the source of the
various cultic regulations too, for these are intended to keep the
people of Israel mindful in one way or another of the events
which liberated them from bondage. There can be no doubt, furthermore, that the bondage in question is all that enslaves and
dehumanizes us, and that those liberated are all who acknowledge God's Law. Consequently, Jews today celebrate the Passover as their own redemption as much as their ancestors' redemption:

> In every generation one must look upon himself as
> if he personally had come forth from Egypt, in keep-
> ing with the biblical command, "And thou shalt tell
> thy son in that day, saying, it is because of that which
> the Lord did to *me* when I went forth from Egypt." For
> it was not alone our fathers whom the Holy one, bles-
> sed be He, redeemed, but also us whom He redeemed
> with them, as it is said, "And *us* He brought out
> thence that He might lead *us* to, and give *us*, the land
> which He swore to our fathers."[8]

Down through the ages, the prophets demonstrated the
breadth and relevance of this paradigm. It provided them with
a tool for uncovering inhumanity in every period and in every
dimension of Israel's life, just as it also provided the basis in
every situation, no matter how desperate, for the hope of deliverance. Their recitations against Israel's infidelity to the cov-

enant and their calls to repentance are concrete testimony against humanity's inhumanity, and witness to the concrete possibility of liberation called forth by the events of the Exodus. It is precisely to this paradigm that Jesus appealed when he went forth preaching, "Repent, for the kingdom of God is at hand" (Matthew 4: 17). And it is to this paradigm that Christians appeal when they confess Jesus as the fulfillment of the covenant.

So with this we come back to the question posed at the beginning of the chapter. Is this the God about whom Feuerbach speaks? Is the heart of this circle of understanding simply a projection of our own humanity? Is a theological reading of this paradigm necessarily alienating and dehumanizing? The answer is no, if as is suggested here, the conviction about the distance between God and ourselves is born of a recognition from concrete historical experience that we, and our world, are not what we should be — not truly free, not truly human. Here the distance between ourselves and God results not from projecting qualities within us to somewhere outside us, but rather results from discovering the reality and truth of the inhumanity of our world, and from acknowledging that inhumanity within us as well. Seen in this light, God hardly can be a mere projection of human attributes. Rather, the God of the prophets and Jesus is revealed in those concrete events of Israel's history and Jesus's story which, against so much evidence to the contrary, testify to a reality which goes beyond the limits of our humanity as we ordinarily know it and which promises to deliver us from our inhumanity.

This is, indeed, a hope — a projection, but with a different ground than the one suggested by Feuerbach's anthropological reading of the Christian circle. Feuerbach's God is not the prophets' and Jesus' God. Nor is Feuerbach's humanity, humanity as the prophets and Jesus saw it. Feuerbach's anthropological critique of Christianity fails to recognize the Christian critique of humanity. Feuerbach does not really take seriously the irony that so much of human history can be described as "inhuman." He simply assumes that humanity is the measure of all. The experiences to which the prophets and Jesus point call for a different "measure" — a measure beyond our wounded humanity capable of transforming us and freeing us.

Notes

1. Helmut Thielicke, *Being Human ... Becoming Human: An Essay in Christian Anthropology*, trans. Geoffrey W. Bromiley (Garden City, New York: Doubleday & Company Inc., 1984), pp. 111-118.

2. Thielicke, p. 112.

3. Thielicke, pp. 113-114.

4. Thielicke, p. 116.

5. Thielicke, p. 117.

6. Thielicke, p. 115.

7. For a very helpful overview see James Muilenburg, *The Way of Israel: Biblical Faith and Ethics* (New York: Harper & Row, 1961), esp. pp. 77- 106.

8. *The Haggadah of the Passover*, ed. David and Tamar de Sola Pool (New York: Bloch Publishing Company), p. 51, as quoted by Muilenburg, p. 51.

8. Saving Mystery

Despite the reservations we have raised about humanity's woundedness, Feuerbach's difficulties of the head remain. Showing that he has not effectively broken into the Christian circle and laid bare its true essence does not by itself get us into the circle. Nor does this critique of Feuerbach establish that humanity's reach actually extends beyond itself. How do we know that we really have anything in the prophets' and Jesus' talk of a saving God? How do we know there is anything more to this than pious hope? If there were some reality beyond our wounded humanity capable of transforming and freeing us from our inhumanity, how could we get it in sight? What about Feuerbach's argument that if there were such a horizon, by its very nature it would be out of reach — beyond the grasp of our understanding and language?

Such questions must be taken seriously and must be addressed. At the same time, we should beware lest the questions themselves bewitch us. Must we assume that objections like Feuerbach's require us to find absolutely indisputable proofs for God's existence? Should it be granted that providing indisputable proofs is in fact what Christians are about when they argue for God's existence? Indeed, can we even presuppose the possibility of establishing a common and neutral point of departure for such arguments? Must we presume that God is known and experienced in the same way that persons or things alongside us in our world are known and experienced? Furthermore, do we have only one alternative: to define the human and divine either as opposed or as identical? The logic of the skeptic's objections requires a "yes" for each question. This logic and the responses to which it leads, however, are themselves questionable.

First, it is an illusion to suppose that the credibility of any effort to interpret the Christian understanding of God requires somehow stepping out of our various circles of understanding onto some neutral turf. All of us (theists, atheists and agnostics alike) stand on ground which already predisposes us towards one way or another of posing and answering the question of God. In Chapter 3 we saw that it is impossible to escape such presuppositions. They are the foundation and framework which enable us to ask questions, see alternatives or draw conclusions in the first place. Bewitchment and ideological captivity do not result from having presuppositions or being guided by them, but rather result from refusing to acknowledge their hold on us and from failing to take whatever measures are possible to critically evaluate their influence on our behavior and thought. Indeed, if anything should raise our suspicions, it is a line of argument that claims to begin from an absolutely objective and neutral point of departure. I am not proposing that here. Every effort is being made to take the spell of the Christian circle seriously, but I cannot help but speak from within that circle, just as everyone else involved in the discussion must be allowed to speak out of their own circle of understanding.

Second, the intent here is not to provide indisputable proofs for the reality of God. The Catholic Church does indeed hold that in principle it is possible to know God's existence "by the light of natural reason."[1] But the Church does not teach, at least as dogma, that as a matter of fact anyone has ever formulated a proof so convincing and beyond doubt that its logic alone can compel one to believe God exists. Nor is it even clear that such logically compelling proof is what the Church intends when it affirms the possibility of natural reason coming to know God's existence "through created things." The believer's arguments have a different function and logic. Custom to the contrary, it is really a bit misleading to speak of "proofs" at all.

One person who argued this point convincingly was the German Jesuit Karl Rahner (1904-84), no doubt one of the most influential theologians of this century.[2] The so-called proofs, he maintained, are not logical appeals from without intended to convince a person of the existence of an object previously quite unknown.[3] Rather the arguments are appeals to the whole person (intellect, will and love). Furthermore, the aim of such arguments is to demonstrate that we can identify God as a reality already experienced and known, at least implicitly and unconsciously, in our experience and knowledge of the world and of ourselves. This line of reasoning needs further explanation.

The important thing to note at the present is that on this view, every genuinely human activity, whether of the head, heart, hands or feet, already reaches out towards God.[4] Rahner readily admitted that this movement or opening out towards God is not the result of a proof — the product, as it were, of the believers' arguments. Either it is already there as an aspect of our human constitution or it isn't. He insisted, however, that reason can discover and display such a dynamism in human thinking, freedom and love.[5] Reason can show that human experience entails an at least implicit and unconscious grasp or anticipation of God. The purpose of the believer's arguments, Rahner contended, is to make this implicit anticipation and unconscious grasp, explicit and conscious; to make thematic and objective what previously was unthematic and unobjective. Our effort to break into the Christian circle can profit from closer attention to this argument, but we must keep its purpose and limits in mind.

First, Rahner's argument cannot induce an experience of God simply by talking about it, any more than talking about profound intimacy, selfless love, untiring fidelity, intense joy or severe anxiety could give rise to such phenomena or convince one who had no experience of such things that they really exist. On the other hand, Rahner cannot try to concretely touch our spirits and hearts through a more direct and personal appeal without giving the impression, especially in light of Feuerbach's critique, of "expressing something subjective or poetic, a mood" too vague to verify.[6] It will be important to keep in mind that Rahner's analysis, by necessity somewhat abstract and removed from experience, is nevertheless rooted in our most concrete and intimate experiences and seeks to bring into sight a reality at the heart of our everyday life.

Second, if the sort of appeal he proposed is successful, there is a sense in which we will be able to say both that reason has discovered God, and that talking of God, despite Feuerbach's objections, has been proven reasonable. The persuasiveness of this contention, as skeptics would surely point out however, rests, in the final analysis, not on the light of reason but rather on the human dynamism towards God which this argument asserts and seeks to conceptualize, and furthermore rests on the whole way of looking at things which such an assertion and conceptualization presuppose.

So on the accounting recommended here, the arguments for God's existence really serve only as "pointers or appeals." They invite us to see if we can discover an experience which in hindsight discloses a reality which might correspond to what believers call God. Their persuasiveness will depend on whether we can understand this appeal to our experience as actually interpreting it more or less correctly.[7] Even though it is true that this invitation's logic is not absolutely compelling, its arguments are not indisputable and its presuppositions are not self-evident to all, a very strong case can still be made that the believer's position is reasonable and credible. Indeed, while admitting that people can, and no doubt do, in good conscience reject arguments such as these as adequate interpretations of their experience, the next chapter will contend that the believer's position has a good deal more to recommend its reasonableness and credibility, than Feuerbach's. For the moment, however, our dialogue with Rahner seeks only to locate more precisely what Christians mean by God and what they mean by calling God a "saving mystery."[8] In particular, closer examination of Rahner's argument provides an opportunity to show both that God is not known and experienced as other beings in the world are, and that believers are not stuck with the alternative of either simply identifying the divine with humanity or acknowledging God as an alienating projection opposed to humanity.

If we are to see what Christians mean when they speak of knowing God, it is necessary in the first place to clarify what "knowing" is. We commonly and too easily assume that knowing is an activity which bridges a kind of gap between ourselves and the world around us. The mind is imagined as reaching out and grasping something outside itself. Knowing God is imagined as one further, if not somewhat problematic instance, of this sort of activity. The process of knowing, however, is really much more complex. Before our minds reach out to the world, they are already in touch with it through the senses. In sensation we are quite literally caught up and absorbed in the world. Knowing begins in the senses and is always rooted in them. The human person is not a mind or spirit located in a separable and dispensable body. Nor is the human person a body to which a mind or spirit has been added. The human person is a radical unity of spirit and body, intellect and senses, self and openness to other. Our first experience, then, is of the unity in our knowing. Our consciousness of these distinctions between spirit and body only comes later when we scrutinize and sort out the processes and structures involved in our knowing, choosing and loving.

On the other hand, the human person is more than an animate sensor of some sort. The unity of spirit and body does not mean that our knowing is limited to what can be grasped empirically. In knowledge and freedom, we are present to ourselves, as distinct from all that impinges on us through the senses. Unlike animals or computers, we are not only in touch with the world around us, we are also in touch with ourselves as distinct from that world. We are aware of ourselves as conscious, self-present and self-determining. Knowing, then, is not only an activity through which we grasp the world about us, but also is the activity through which we first of all recognize ourselves as subjects distinct from that world and from other selves.

This "presence to self" is not some "thing" that we grasp as an object from the outside. Rather self-presence is implicit from the start and intrinsic to every act of knowing. It is not necessary that I explicitly note my presence to self. It is already a fact before my thought turns in on itself to notice. Self-presence is indicated already in our use of first and second person language, for example, when *I* claim to know this, when *you* consider it, or when *we* both decide to do something because of it. To make such a claim as my own, to raise such a question as my own, to act on my own or in concert with others, to truly address another or be addressed by another, I must already be conscious, present to self and self-determining. It is the strange irony of this self-presence, however, that it is so personal and so intimate it can never be adequately objectivized or thematized. Thinking about my self-presence is not the same as that original self-awareness which our thoughts seek to capture. There is an awareness of myself trying to do this which is never quite the same thing as what is thought or described, and which never can be.

Since the self-presence we grasp in this way is not an "object" or a "thing," there is a sense in which we must say that it cannot be objectivized and that it must not be reified. We really grasp it. We truly know it, but we grasp and know it *un*objectively. Nor can what we grasp this way be fitted into normal categories or organized thematically as we do with other "objects" of knowledge. We cannot grasp our self-presence, at least adequately, in a categorical or thematic manner, because we are not talking about something outside us that is known. We have in mind our knowing itself as it is simultaneously grasped or "co-known" along with the objects of our knowledge. Our knowledge of this unobjective, non-thematic, non-categorical self-presence is indirect and reflexive. We can bring our self-presence to light only in hindsight, by directing our thought inward to focus on its own activity.

It is important to note that this reflexive turning of our thinking in on itself to disclose its "presence" as a necessary but elusive presupposition for knowledge, is of a quite different order than the kind of thinking which discloses the objects of the world to us and categorizes them. Rahner called the kind of knowing which discloses objects, *objective* or *categorical* knowledge. He called the kind of knowing entailed in the reflexive grasp of self which is presupposed in objective knowledge but which *transcends* our objective and categorical grasp, *transcendental* knowledge.

It is inevitable that we speak of God as another being alongside us in the world and so picture our knowing him that way, just as we sometimes speak and think of the self as if it were a thing inside us. Such objectifying and reifying language, however, is as inadequate for speaking of God's presence to us and of our knowledge of God, as it is for speaking of our self-presence and knowledge of self. Taking this clue, Rahner's argument for God invites us to ask in hindsight whether our grasp of the world and our presence to self does not presuppose a co-known, unobjective, non-thematic grasp of something more, a "more" that he identifies ultimately with God. As he described it, this "more," this horizon of our self-presence and presence to the world, is itself limitless and hence quite indefinable. It is beyond our objective grasp, despite its being anticipated in the dynamism of knowing, willing and loving, and despite our ability to call attention to it reflexively by attending to this movement. We grasp it transcendentally rather than categorically.

There are numerous facets of human existence to which we could appeal in order to bring this dynamism to light. There are also quite a few places from which our appeal could take its point of departure. The movement of the intellect and our presence to self offer themselves as the most obvious focus and starting point, however, since we have been considering the question of knowing God, and since this was Rahner's own concern in his early and groundbreaking reflections.

This self-presence intrinsic to human knowing about which we have been speaking is not achieved through some sort of autonomous and purely internal activity. We are not born with a full-fledged consciousness of self or with fully formed egos. Self-consciousness emerges step by step through interaction with the world and other selves. In our thoughts, decisions and actions we distinguish objects over against us. We handle them. We judge them as distinct in this way or that, as having this use or that and as valuable or not. It is precisely in this recognition of the object as something standing opposite us, that we become present to ourself as distinct. The point is somewhat of a pun in German, since the word for object (*Gegenstand*) literally means something standing (*stand*) opposite (*gegen*) us. We could visualize this, only very inadequately, of course, by saying that our consciousness must first reach outside itself to the object known, if it is to become present to self.

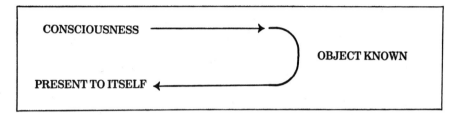

The process through which we grasp something as distinct from ourselves and conceive it as an object of one kind or another is judgment. In judgment, a way of *be*ing is recognized as confined to a particular being, for example a desk, a plant, a person, an emotion or an idea.

"*Be*" in *be*ing is italicized here to indicate that what we are talking about is not some thing, a being (designated by a noun). What we are talking about is the thing's way of existing — its act or process of *be*ing (italicized to emphasize this by calling attention to the noun's verbal connotation).

In judgment, this way of *be*ing (that is to say, the way of *be*ing peculiar to desks, plants, persons, this emotion, this idea or whatever) is recognized as having other instances, or at least the possibility for other instances. That is to say, the particular being (the desk, person or idea) is noticed and affirmed as an instance, a limitation or a confinement of a way of *be*ing that is broader and more inclusive than this particular example or embodiment of it. We could not recognize the limit unless we grasped beyond it towards something more. We could not grasp a tree without also grasping the way of *be*ing peculiar to trees. Recognition of a limit presupposes a grasp of something more. So, when we grasp the particular object of our attention, we are already anticipating and grasping these further possibilities. In other words, if I judge that the thing before me is a desk, I must already have grasped or anticipated the way of *be*ing peculiar to desks. That grasp or anticipation, we could say, is the horizon or backdrop against which I know the object for what it is. We could visualize this, again very inadequately, by saying that our recognition of a particular being presupposes a field of vision which reaches beyond the object, anticipating and grasping the way of *be*ing of which the object is but one instance.

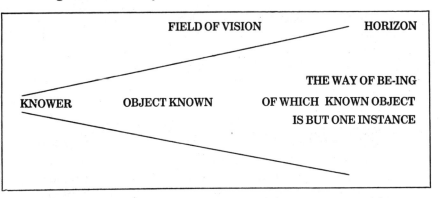

When thought reaches out beyond its immediate object in this way, the term of its grasp is not some thing or some collection of things. When I grasp the tree as a tree, as an instance of that way of *be*ing peculiar to trees, this does not mean that I am simultaneously grasping all trees or that I am grasping some object other than the tree. This may, for example, be that elusive moment when I see my first tree. That is to say, it may be that first moment when the tree in front of me is grasped as a particular way of *be*ing, and when at the same time the way of *be*ing peculiar to trees is grasped in that particular object in front of me. There is no sense stopping here to trouble over which comes first, the grasp of the being or the grasp of its way of *be*ing. These activities are two sides of the same process. Like heads and tails, or the chicken and the egg, one presupposes the other.

Although this particular "way of *be*ing" towards which the intellect reaches is not some thing, it is not nothing or just an abstraction either. When we know the tree as an instance of the way of *be*ing peculiar to trees, we are affirming its reality and grasping it as an instance of a concrete and genuine way of *be*ing. When I say, "That thing there is a tree," I am not just linking ideas or playing with words. I am not simply affirming that the ideas of thing and tree are one. Rather I am affirming that this particular reality is an instance of something real, it is an example of a real and actual way of *being*. In each judgment, a process of this sort comes to such a conclusion.

These conclusions towards which judgment moves are not restricted to any particular way of *being*. All of us, if we are to be self-present, must grasp objects over against ourselves and so also grasp the ways of *being* peculiar to those objects. But we do not all stand before the same objects or even necessarily before the same kinds of objects or the same ways of *being*. Because of our individual circumstances and limitations we are all inevitably oblivious to certain realms of *being*. We can even consciously close ourselves off to entire dimensions of reality, as for example when we decide we don't need or want to know anything about physics, about other people's problems or about our own moral blind spots. Thus, the horizon of our knowing is not limited to any specific being or beings, or even to any particular way of *being*. Our intellect's reach extends beyond itself and beyond every concrete being. This can be visualized by adding to our previous diagram a parenthetical or bottom line to call attention to the "reach" or movement of the intellect towards a "goal" or "term" which cannot be identified with any particular being or way of *being*. This term is pictured by a question mark to indicate its elusiveness.

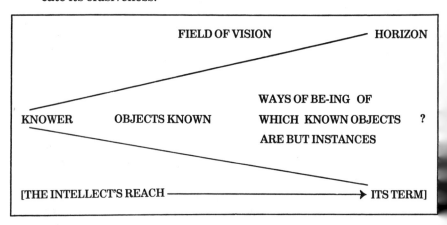

Although the horizon of our knowing is not limited to any specific being or way of *being*, all of us nevertheless anticipate or reach out towards something, towards beings and ways of *being* of some sort. All knowing presupposes this dynamism or movement of the intellect towards its ever broadening horizon. This expanding, ultimate and final horizon cannot itself be an object or even the totality of objects, because to grasp something as an object or as a totality means recognizing it as a limitation or confinement of something "more." Nor can our knowing's horizon be a particular way of *being*, because to grasp something as particular is once again to objectify it, to see its limits and so to see beyond it.

On the other hand, the horizon of our knowing cannot be some sort of empty and limitless void — in effect "nothing" or "nothingness." As we have seen already, our intellect's reach is not empty. Its openness is not a vacant anticipation. Our knowing is an openness for actual beings and for real ways of *being*, or for possible beings and ways of *being* projected by the imagination on the basis of what the intellect has grasped as real. The horizon of this knowing, then, is hardly a void or nothing at all. Indeed, the very ideas "empty openness," "void" and "nothing" could not be conceived in the first place, if we did not already grasp something, and then entertain the possibility of its absence. "Nothing" and "void" are derivative and secondary concepts. They do not refer to anything which can be grasped or experienced, except in light of our previous grasp of a horizon that is real and actual.

Rahner concludes that our knowing must then be an openness for *being* as such. The horizon towards which our intellect reaches is not a being, not the totality of beings, not some particular way of *being* and not a void, but rather is the absolute fullness of *being* itself.

Needless to say, we are dealing here with a very elusive reality and a very slippery concept. *Being* as such, if Rahner's analysis is correct, is the horizon anticipated whenever anything is known. It is presupposed in every affirmation. Our reaching out towards it is the prerequisite or "condition of possibility" for knowing anything at all. But although we are open for *being*, and grasp the difference between *being* and not *being*, still, *being* as such is indefinable. It is not something which can be directly known in itself. Although we grasp it as the horizon of all objective knowledge, we cannot objectify it, describe it or fit it into any of our normal categories. It utterly transcends all such attempts at categorization and thematization. It is, then, in this most radical sense, a mystery: a reality known and named properly only as that which always and finally eludes our grasp.

The situation is analogous to the literal horizon of our field of vision which withdraws itself as we move forward. Broadening or magnifying our vision only intensifies the breadth or depth of its horizon. So too, broadening and deepening our understanding of ourselves and the world about us, only points towards the incalculable fullness and mystery of *being* for which we are open. We can never grasp this horizon itself directly. Our grasp of it is an anticipation, a reaching out, or, as Rahner calls it, a foregrasping (*Vorgriff*). This reaching out towards *being*, or foretaste of it, like our presence to self, is implicit from the start and intrinsic to our knowing. Yet like our presence to self, our reaching out towards *being* as mystery and fullness can be brought to light only reflexively, in hindsight, by directing our thought inward to focus on its own movement beyond every being and particular way of *being* towards *being* as such. We are talking, then, about an unobjective grasp, a transcendental knowing that is intrinsically non-thematic and non-categorical.

We could visualize this by picturing the fullness of *being* as the term of the intellect's reach. This ultimate and mysterious "whither" of the intellect can never be grasped in itself. But we can grasp and describe, however haltingly, the intellect's movement beyond every being or way of *being* towards its elusive horizon. Attending to this dynamism enables us to point to that ineffable goal and to name it, indirectly and reflexively, as the "term" or "whither" of the movement.

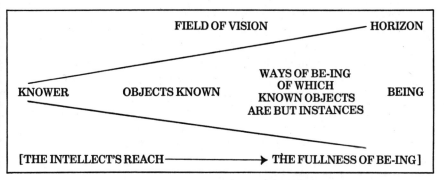

In a very minimal sort of way, this fullness of *being* antici-pated in our knowing is what the believer means by God. God is not some other being alongside us in the world. Nor is God known objectively, the way such beings of the world are known. Rather God is that mystery and fullness of *being*, that elusive but ineffable horizon, presupposed and affirmed in our objective knowledge of the world. Although we have spoken of this hori-zon of our knowing rather formally and abstractly so far, this should not be taken to mean that God must be conceived either as impersonal or as peripheral to our lives.

First, if God is identified with the fullness of *being*, then it is inappropriate to speak of God impersonally as an "it." It is hardly legitimate to equate the fullness of *being* with an inten-sity of *being* less than our own. *Being* as such must include within "itself" pre-eminently that highest way of *being* which we know and that we call personal, even though how God is per-sonal is not something we are able to conceive. Moreover, whenever we speak of God we are pushing language to the limit, since we are speaking about the reality most radically at the limit of our reach. All language about God, therefore, is inher-ently analogical. No pronoun (he, she or it) is truly adequate. At the same time, there are situations in which each can be particu-larly appropriate, as the language of prophets, poets and mys-tics testifies.

Second, anticipation of God as the fullness of *being* is en-tailed in the movement of freedom and love, just as much as in the dynamism of our knowing. Self-determination presupposes that the various factors which affect us or attract us can be seen as possibilities rather than necessities. I do not have to be enslaved by the "craving" for chocolate or real estate, by the "need" for affection or recognition, by the "desire" for success, gratification or power, by the "pressure" of my family, peers or superiors or by the "drives" of my various appetites and ambitions. If I am truly free, then at least some of the time I must be able to recognize the "pull" of these cravings, needs, desires, influences or drives as distinct from myself. I do not have to give in to the pull. I do not have to make it my own. As free or self-determining, I can choose otherwise. Or alternately, I can freely make this exterior determination my own. I can interiorize its "pull" as an expression of my self. An athlete, for example, who accepts the role of playmaker, can recognize the "need" to pass up his own scoring opportunities in order to create better opportunities for his teammates. In freely making this a necessity for himself, he does not give up his freedom. Quite the opposite, he creates a role which gives him more room to play and greater freedom to exercise his gifts, make his mark and define his identity as a competitor. If he succeeds, he will also enhance the freedom of his teammates and coach.

Admittedly, such freedom is not always the mark of human behavior. The athlete's coach and teammates could force a role on him which frustrates his aspirations and gifts, and which restricts his freedom. In the end this would probably constrain the moves open to his teammates and coach as well. This sort of constraint is no doubt the rule much more often than we would care to admit. The point I want to make here, though, is that when and if we do act freely, it is not because we are untouched by reasons and causes outside ourselves. Rather, we act freely when we recognize the reasons and causes which move us as particular possibilities rather than absolute necessities, and when we either make them our own or see them as impositions from without.

To grasp these determinations in this way as possibilities or impositions, and to see both their limits and promise, means

that my freedom, or will, already reaches beyond the factors
which immediately impinge upon me. As with knowing, the
horizon towards which freedom reaches cannot be any particular being or way of *being*, or even the totality of beings. If my will
were determined by some particular thing or way of *being* outside myself, or even the totality of beings, then freedom would
not truly be a *self*-determination. Nor can human freedom be
conceived as an empty openness without cause or reason, for
then freedom would be quite irrational and undetermined. Only
if freedom is rooted in an openness towards the mystery and
fullness of *being* as such, can the will transcend the particular
beings and ways of *being* which impinge upon us. Only if freedom truly reaches out beyond the cravings, needs, desires and
pressures which drive and pull us, can we speak of a genuine
self-determination. So just as in our knowing there is always a
"foregrasp" of more than the object known, so too in freedom
there is dynamism which anticipates more than can be accomplished in any particular decision. In this sense, God for the
Christian is every bit as much the ultimate "term" or "goal" of
our freedom, as God is the "horizon" or "end" of our knowing.

The same dynamism is at work in love, the giving over of
ourself to another. I cannot be grasped by another and give myself over to another, unless I am present to the beloved in all his
or her uniqueness and particularity. As we have already seen,
to know someone as other than myself and to let my freedom be
determined by that other, presupposes the radical openness of
my knowing and freedom for the mystery and fullness of *being*
as such. Thus, inherent in our union with one whom we love is
an opening out and yearning for an intensity of union and a fullness of *being with* others that transcends any specific love of
particular individuals. Our fleeting gestures of love cannot
exhaust love's reach, cannot exhaust our dynamism for loving
and being loved to the utmost. We cannot love truly, without
coming to know that we cannot love or be loved enough.

If this is true, then every act of the intellect, will and love
reaches out towards God as its ultimate horizon. This unobjective presence to God is not something peripheral to our lives. It

is at the heart of our presence to self and presence to the world around us. The more we grasp the world with our heads, hearts and hands, the more we open out towards God as the mystery and fullness of *being*. Conversely, the more open we are to the fullness of *being*, the more we are able to recognize the world of beings about us. The closer our proximity to God, the more our freedom to be self-determined rather than determined and enslaved by forces outside ourselves. The more open we are for the fullness of love and the more we let ourselves be won over by this yearning, the greater our possibilities for being caught up in the love of another. In these ways our dynamism towards God is central to the formation of our identities as persons. God is the ground of our *being* as well as the horizon of our *being*.

The terms "spirit" and "spiritual," for Rahner and for us in the pages which follow, refer to this openness of the human person for God as mystery. Spirit does not refer to some ghostly thing within us, but rather denotes that dynamism of the person as a whole (head, heart, hands and feet) towards God. In light of this we can refine our visual caricature of this relationship to show the bottom line as the dynamism of spirit (head, heart, hands and feet) towards God as mystery.

	FIELD OF VISION		HORIZON
HUMAN SPIRIT	OBJECTS OF KNOWLEDGE FREEDOM & LOVE	WAYS OF BE-ING OF WHICH OBJECTS KNOWN CHOSEN AND LOVED ARE BUT INSTANCES	BE-ING

[THE DYNAMISM OF THE HEAD, HEART AND HANDS ⟶ GOD AS MYSTERY]

Several final but most important precisions are necessary. The orientation of the human spirit towards God as its horizon is not necessarily a positive one. It is possible to close ourselves off from the fullness of *being*. As we noted earlier in our discussion of humanity's woundedness, we can make gods of beings (of one's family, nation, company, political party or church) or gods of particular ways of *be*ing (of power, getting ahead, material gratification or security). Insofar as we give ourselves over to such finite gods we close ourselves off from God as the mystery and fullness of *be*ing. In this situation the dynamism of the human spirit is obstructed. Its field of vision is clouded, narrowed and closed in on itself. Sight is dimmed, if not blinded. The heart is hardened, if not closed. The hands and feet are restricted, if not enslaved. This situation should be evident to anyone who honestly looks at our world and its history. Not all knowing, choosing and doing can be described as the head's, heart's and hand's reaching out towards the fullness of truth, goodness and love which the believer identifies with God. In this sense, God is not necessarily at the heart of our lives.

Nevertheless, we all still stand before God. If it were not for the openness of the human spirit towards God, we could not fashion gods of our own. The ability to focus on one limited being or way of *be*ing as ultimate presupposes, paradoxically, that we could have reached further. Likewise, surrendering ourselves to the enslavement of consumerism, racism or whatever, is a *self-*determination that presupposes that freedom's reach extends beyond its immediate objective. Ironically, in fashioning gods of our own and giving ourselves over to them, we cut ourselves off from the reality of God at the heart of our *be*ing. In other words, like Adam and Eve, we can make gods of our own only because we have a special relationship towards God. But insofar as our idolatry cuts us off from God, we forfeit our human identity by warping the authentic dynamism and openness at freedom's root. Furthermore, since we live in a wounded world, even when we do not explicity and consciously close ourselves off from the fullness of God's *be*ing, we nevertheless live within structures of *be*ing (ignorance, prejudice, militarism, sexism, racism, totalitarianism, consumerism, etc.) which frustrate the authentic dynamism of our *be*ing, obscure our true identity and belie our freedom.

This distortion of the human spirit need not be explicit or obvious. We can consciously and explicitly acknowledge God with our minds and mouths, and yet still make a god of our career or be enslaved by our prejudice. So too, it is at least possible that a person who consciously and explicitly denies God, nevertheless may deal with the world and may love others in a way which implicitly reaches out and affirms that fullness of *being* which the believer calls God. Of course, in either case we are talking about a tension within the heart of the person's self-constitution which is contradictory and which would inevitably tug the person's spirit one way or another. But that it is contradictory does not refute the fact that for many of us such a tension is a possibility, if not a reality. Hence, our diagram of the human spirit as a dynamism towards God must be redrawn one last time to picture this potential for distortion: the dynamism of the head, heart and hands can be closed, hardened and enslaved by gods of our own making and thus cut off from its true horizon and ground.

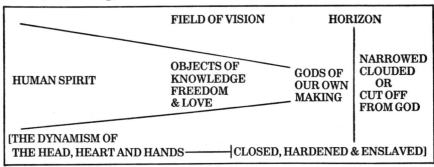

Central to the Christian circle of understanding is the conviction that we all stand before God either affirming or denying this fullness and mystery of *being*. We do so in every act of the head, heart, hands or feet, because in the stances we take towards the beings of our world, we are also already taking a stance which either affirms, chooses and seeks the fullness of *being* or which denies, refuses and turns away from that reality at the heart of our lives. There is no neutral stance.

Equally central to Christian understanding is the conviction that this mystery called "God" is "saving." Much is entailed in that belief, but what we have said so far provides at least a preliminary notion of what is involved. Our presence to self and the world, our freedom and our ability to truly love, hinge on our openness for God. Without that absolute horizon of mystery and fullness presupposed and anticipated in the dynamism of knowing, choosing and loving there could be no true knowledge, freedom or love. At the same time Christian faith warns against underestimating the woundedness of humanity. Although we experience some degree of understanding, freedom and love which provides a basis for pointing to what believers mean by God, both our individual and social identities are fraught with falsehood, enslavement and selfishness. We might just as well have defined God by pointing to "him" as the reality whose absence is manifested in deceit, manipulation and hate. Things are not the way they should be. God, the fullness and mystery of *being*, ultimately eludes our grasp both because the fullness of *being* utterly transcends our limited existence, and because the history of our wounded humanity so utterly constricts our openness for the fullness of truth, goodness and love. Christians are indeed convinced that our reach can extend beyond itself and that we can be saved from ourselves, but only because they believe, as we will see later, that the Spirit of God, revealed in Jesus, is already reaching out towards us in our world and history.

Whether this conception offers a credible framework for answering Feuerbach's objections against the reasonableness of God-talk will have to be addressed in the next chapter. Whether history justifies this faith in a saving mystery, or discloses anything more about God beyond such very formal conceptions as "mystery," "fullness of *being*" and "ground of *being*," will have to be addressed in Part III. For now, I hope only to have offered one path for locating in a very rudimentary way what believers mean when they speak of God.

Notes

1. See Eberhard Simons, "II. Knowability of God," in *Encyclopedia of Theology: The Concise Sacramentum Mundi*, ed. Karl Rahner (New York: The Seabury Press, 1975), pp. 564b-568a; Karl Rahner, S.J. "Proof of the Existence of God," in *Dictionary of Theology*, 2nd ed.(New York: Crossroad, 1981), pp. 416-

418; and Bernard J. F. Lonergan, S.J., "Natural Knowledge of God," in *A Second Collection*, ed. William F. J. Ryan, S.J. and Bernard J. Tyrrell, S.J. (Philadelphia: The Westminster Press, 1974), pp. 117-133.

2. David Tracy, for example, wrote that "there is probably no Catholic theologian writing today anywhere in the world who does not bear Rahner's imprint." ("'All is Grace': A Rooted Radical," *Commonweal*, 20 April 1984, p. 230).

3. See in addition to the essay in the *Dictionary of Theology*, his article "The Experience of God Today," in Theological Investigations, vol. 11, trans. David Bourke (New York: The Seabury Press, 1974), pp. 149-65.

4. Commentators focusing too exclusively on Rahner's early works have sometimes treated this dynamism as if it were a movement of the intellect only. My reasons for holding that this is a misinterpretation and my response to the criticism which such a view generates can be found in "Spirituality for the Head, Heart, Hands and Feet: Rahner's Legacy," *Spirituality Today*, 36 (Winter 1984), 340-54.

5. Rahner, we will see later, holds that this capacity of reason is ultimately grounded in grace. Lonergan comes to a similar conclusion, stating "I do not think in this life people arrive at natural knowledge of God without God's grace, but what I do not doubt is that the knowledge they so attain is natural" (*Second Collection*, p. 133.).

6. "The Experience of God Today," p. 154.

7. "The Experience of God Today," p. 151.

8. The analysis which follows draws freely from the whole of Rahner's writings.

9. Reasonable Risk

The path we have pursued to locate what believers mean by "God" does not conclusively prove that God exists, nor does it break all the way through to the heart of the Christian circle of understanding. It does show, however, that the difficulties encountered in Feuerbach's protest against Christianity are not as insurmountable as they may have seemed. We are not stuck with Feuerbach's alternative: to define God either as opposed to humanity or as identical with humanity. Just as the horizon of our field of vision cannot be identified with the objects which appear against it or with the eyes which behold it, so God conceived as the mystery and fullness of being cannot be identified as another *be*ing alongside us or our world, or as a projection of ourselves.

Of course, the structure of the eye influences what is seen and how it is seen. Fly, eagle and zoologist actually see the world differently. In a sense, we could even say that they see different worlds or that their eyes structure what is seen. But the eye does not create the light which enables it to see nor does the eye really create the objects which it sees. Without the light of a horizon outside it, everything — even the eye itself and its field of vision — would remain hidden in impenetrable darkness. So Feuerbach's thesis that "a being's nature is its sphere of vision" must be turned around to the opposite conclusion: just as the eye's vision presupposes a light distinct from itself, so the openness of the human spirit presupposes a horizon beyond itself and its grasp.

Affirming this utter difference between God and humanity, however, does not at all imply an opposition between the divine and human. Sight presupposes, and really only comes to its own in the presence of, that light from beyond itself. Although light can be blinding, it also is what makes vision possible in the first place. It is at the heart of sight. It saves sight from the darkness. So it is with God who, as the mystery and fullness of *being*, grounds the very possibility of our self-consciousness, knowledge, freedom and love. God so understood is saving rather than alienating, enlightening rather than blinding, freeing rather than enslaving, humanizing rather than dehumanizing.

Thinking of God in this way makes it possible to take the woundedness of humanity seriously. It avoids the "docetism" of anthropologies which, like Feuerbach's, underestimate human evil and make a god of an abstract and sham human nature complete unto itself and capable of saving itself. On the other hand, belief in God need not require equating humanity with depravity, or faith with alienation. It is idolatry, enslavement to gods of our own making, which warps the authentic dynamism and openness of the human spirit at its root, and thus cuts us off from our authentic identity. Faith is not the source of alienation. Rather, it is our own concrete distortion of our consciousness and freedom which warrants the description of so much that we do, and even of us ourselves, as dehumanizing, inhuman or fallen. Because of this fallenness, our concrete reality is only a faint and incomplete distortion of the human spirit's dynamism and openness for God. We are not depraved because we are human, but because we are not what we should be: because we are not truly human, let alone human to the utmost. Faith, properly understood and in so far as it is genuine, does not alienate us from our humanity. Rather, faith calls attention to God as the one and only true horizon of human consciousness, freedom and love. Faith so understood is saving rather than alienating, liberating rather than bewitching, humanizing rather than dehumanizing.

The path we have followed to locate what the believer means by "God" also enables us to meet the objection that we cannot speak of a reality that utterly transcends our grasp, and to meet the converse of this challenge, namely that insofar as

God comes within our grasp the divine must be an aspect of our own identity. As we have seen, the dynamism of knowing, freedom and love reaches beyond itself towards a horizon that can never be directly known. But we can grasp and describe the spirit's movement towards this elusive "whither." Attending to this dynamism enables us to point to God, to name God and to speak about God. What we are able to say in this way, of course, is indirect and limited. Such language is essentially transcendental and analogous because its proper meaning can only be understood in light of (by analogy or comparison with) the movement (transcendence) of the spirit towards its unobjectifiable horizon. In such discourse, language is pushed to the limit, but as long as this is properly understood, the legitimacy and coherence of such talk is defensible. Indeed, from this perspective, there could be no talk at all about the objects which come within our grasp, if our grasp did not also reach beyond ourselves and our world.

Feuerbach's critique of analogy completely misses the mark because he misunderstood this logical difference between our talk about the realities of the world and our talk about God. Certainly believers can and often do make the same sort of mistake, and so end up saying terribly confusing and contradictory things. After all, Feuerbach and his successors are right when they insist that the only vocabulary available for speaking of God is one which draws on our own experience for metaphors, analogies and symbols. But it must not be forgotten that the suitability of this vocabulary is not rooted in some sort of comparison or similarity between God and ourselves. Nor, as Feuerbach legitimately objects, are we able to stand above our nature, as it were taking God's view, in order see how these predicates, properly attributed to us, do and do not apply to God. We are not talking about the same thing as being able to see, for example, how the metaphor "best friend" does and does not apply to a pet. Rather, the "analogy" at issue in our talk about God is rooted in the much more fundamental relation between the dynamism of human knowing, choosing and loving and the ineffable mystery for which it is open. Religious metaphors, analogies and symbols are appropriate for God because they are affirmed in this way as reaching out and pointing radically beyond themselves. At such times they are not predicates which characterize something like our *being* (anthropomorphisms), but rather are predicates which call attention to the concrete ways at the heart of human *being* in which our spirit's grasp of self and world opens out and anticipates the mystery at its limit, and so locates and names that limit as well.

At this point, it could no doubt be objected once again that this sort of response does not actually prove that God exists, or even prove that the mystery of *being* is indeed the same reality believers have in mind when they speak of God. The German philosopher Martin Heidegger (1889-1976) would have objected that as soon as we speak of the mystery of *being* as a fullness or a ground, or as personal, or as existing, we are talking about *being* as if it were a being. Isn't the article "a" a give-away? Doesn't speaking of *being* in this way as existing and personal imply that it is an existent and a person, and so a being rather than the mystery of *being*? Can thought really get beyond its recognition of the difference between beings and *being*? Is recognition of this difference or mystery all that the believer really means by God?[1]

At least in part because of this kind of objection, theologians such as Paul Tillich have maintained that philosophy cannot reach God. Philosophy, Tillich argued, can analyze the polarities of human *being* and show how the disruption which I have called humanity's woundedness leads to a quest for a "ground" or "new being" that would enable us to overcome our estrangement from what we should have been. But philosophy, he insisted, cannot prove the existence of the New Being. Likewise, philosophy can show how we are led to seek after a Power or Ground of being-itself which would enable us to overcome the ever present anxiety of losing our *being* to the forces of physical and spiritual corruption which threaten us with death from the moment of our births. But philosophy cannot get to or prove the reality of such a Ground. For Tillich, the correlation between anthropology and theology discloses philosophy's inability to finally answer the ultimate questions about human existence.[2]

It is not necessary for our purposes to resolve this fundamental and perennial question about whether or not the human
spirit reaches God (Rahner's foregrasp of the Fullness of *Being
Itself*), or only reaches the question of God (Tillich's quest for a
New Being and for the Ground of being-itself), or merely reaches
a mystery which leaves open the question of God (Heidegger's
openness for *being* as not a being but not yet God either). Our
objective here is only to break into the Christian circle of understanding, not to solve all the difficulties which would confront
us once we have gotten in. It is enough, for our purposes, to establish that talking about God and affirming God's existence is
reasonable and no more a risk than any of the other alternatives.

In *Does God Exist?*, Hans Küng develops a line of reasoning
which is quite helpful in this regard.[3] Ultimately, his strategy is
different than the one I have been proposing here. To be quite
honest, I have reservations about some of his central premises.[4]
His notion of belief as a reasonable risk, however, can be appropriated with some freedom and adapted to our effort at articulating a theology for the head, heart, hands and feet.

Küng sympathetically examines the most influential critics
of Christianity, distinguishing between atheists like Feuerbach, Marx and Freud who deny God's existence and nihilists
like Nietzsche who doubt the certainty of reality itself. Küng
concludes that their positions are defensible, and even irrefutable. No definitive and absolutely compelling refutation can be
advanced against their arguments, because these are ultimately based on faiths or doubts which thoroughly insulate
against the logic of contrary positions. There is little use for the
"hypothesis" of God, if one takes as a given, faith in the certainty
of human progress, in the self-sufficiency of science, in the inevitable dialectic of history, in the evident decline of religion or,
with nihilism, in the uncertainty of all that we experience. But
on the other hand, Küng argues, the legitimacy of such faiths
cannot be conclusively proved either.

We have seen this with Feuerbach. He shows that our ideas
of God *can* be simply a projection of our own humanity, or simply

and naively anthropomorphic, but that does not prove that all talk of God *must* be the result of naive projection. Feuerbach shows that Christianity can be dehumanizing, but he does not show that Christianity *must* be dehumanizing. He argues that a more humane world is possible, even inevitable, because the attributes that religion has affirmed as God's are in fact the attributes of humanity itself. But neither Feuerbach's arguments nor the course of human history provide convincing, not to mention conclusive, evidence that this is the case.

The believer's arguments are just as defensible and irrefutable as the skeptic's. But here too, Küng contends, though the arguments are irrefutable, they are not in themselves conclusive. They too presuppose a faith of one sort or another. We have seen as much in our examination of Rahner's case for God.

Does this mean that there is a stalemate? Does this mean that belief and unbelief are equally justified? or equally arbitrary? Is the choice merely a matter of opinion and personal option? Küng says "no." He admits that belief is a risk, but maintains that it is a justifiable risk, indeed, that it is a more reasonable risk than either nihilism or atheism.

For the nihilist, life "in the last resort, is meaningless;" "chance, blind fate, chaos, absurdity and illusion rule the world;" "everything is contradictory, meaningless, worthless, null."[5] Küng admits that it is possible to take such an attitude. Once taken, the persuasiveness of all contrary arguments is undermined. Nihilism puts everything in question. Küng insists that one cannot avoid this challenge. We all must make a fundamental decision to trust or mistrust reality. Furthermore, both fundamental attitudes are a risk. "Reality itself does not extort a Yes or a No, a positive or a negative fundamental attitude. It is not . . . self-evident; the whole is not transparent."[6] But as Küng sees it, the attitude of fundamental trust is the more reasonable choice. Fundamental mistrust means that we in principle close ourselves to reality and to the world. Fundamental mistrust "implies a nihilistic fixation on the nullity of reality and an abysmal uncertainty in regard to all human experience and behavior."[7]

We are not inclined by nature to close ourselves to the reality around us. Something in us "resists a fundamentally negative decision." To consistently maintain an attitude of fundamental mistrust, we have to struggle to overcome this resistance. Our eyes are meant to see, our intellects to know and our wills to strive.[8] Moreover, since reality would of necessity be closed to one who consistently denied it, a "no" to reality cannot be consistently maintained in practice by anyone who continues to traffic in the world.[9]

On the other hand, reality is open to those whose attitude is one of fundamental trust, and their position can be maintained consistently.

> While the No to reality gets entangled in ever greater contradictions, the Yes — as acceptance of uncertain reality — can survive and endure throughout all trials. It is quite possible to combine fundamental trust with mistrust in the individual case. For fundamental trust can also accept the element of truth in fundamental mistrust — the nullity of reality — while, on the other hand, fundamental mistrust cannot recognize any element of truth in fundamental trust, any reality in all the nullity. Hence the attitude of fundamental trust, and this alone, is open to reality in its uncertainty.[10]

Thus Küng concludes that the decision for fundamental trust is more reasonable than the decision for fundamental mistrust. He argues that the same can be said about the decision between atheism and theism. If the skeptic is not a nihilist, then what is the basis of this person's fundamental trust? Küng's survey leads him to conclude that most atheists share the believer's conviction that the existing world with all its injustice is not as it should be, that ultimately and in the end reality must be "different from the apparent, obvious, intrinsically contradictory world" of our experience.[11] But what grounds, he asks, can the atheist give for this faith? Can the atheist answer who we are, where we came from, or where we are going? Can the atheist even ask such questions?

Denial of God implies an ultimately unjustified fundamental trust in reality. Atheism cannot suggest any condition for the possibility of uncertain reality. If someone denies God, he does not know why he ultimately trusts in reality. This means that atheism is nourished, if not by a nihilistic fundamental mistrust, then at any rate by an ultimately unjustified fundamental trust.[12]

Küng argues that the believer, in contrast, can suggest a condition of possibility for fundamental trust despite all the uncertainties of life, because if God exists, then life has an ultimate ground, support and goal.

If God exists,

   • then, despite all the menace of fate and death, I can with good reason confidently affirm the unity and identity of my human existence. Why? Because God is the primal source also of my life;
   • then, despite all the menace of emptiness and meaninglessness, I can with good reason confidently affirm the truth and meaningfulness of my existence. Why? Because God is the ultimate meaning of my life;
   • then, despite all the menace of sin and damnation, I can with good reason confidently affirm the goodness and value of my existence. Why? Because God is then the all-embracing hope of my life;
   • then, against all the menace of nonbeing, I can with good reason confidently affirm the being of my human existence: God is then the being itself in particular also of human life.[13]

Küng asserts that the believer can also account for humanity's woundedness and for the menace of emptiness, meaninglessness, death and nonbeing. How? Because we are not God, and because the world cannot simply be identified with its primal source, meaning and value.[14]

This line of reasoning does not prove that God exists. Belief in God is not based on philosophical arguments. Philosophy can help show that belief is a reasonable decision. Philosophy can help to locate what the believer means by the term "God" and and can help break into the Christian circle of understanding. Philosophy can help the believer explain the grounds for concluding that the risk of faith is more reasonable than the risk of nihilism or atheism. But as Paul Tillich once said, "ultimate concern is ultimate risk and ultimate courage."[15] The risk cannot be avoided. Faith in God is not "provable" in the strict sense. It is not under the spell of logic, philosophy, science or even theology. Such pursuits may clarify the contours of the Christian circle, but they do not constitute its center. It is to that center that we must next turn our attention.

Notes

1. For an extended discussion of the difference between Rahner's and Heidegger's perspectives, see my article "Rahner and Heidegger: Being, Hearing and God," *The Thomist*, 37 (July 1973) 455-88.

2. See Paul Tillich, *Systematic Theology* (Chicago: The University of Chicago Press, 1967), esp. vol. I, pp. 163-210 and vol. II, pp. 19-96; *The Courage To Be* (New Haven & London: Yale University Press, 1952); and *The New Being* (New York: Charles Scribner's Sons, 1955).

3. Hans Küng, *Does God Exist? An Answer for Today*, trans. Edward Quinn (Garden City, New York: Doubleday & Company, Inc., 1980).

4. The difficulties which I have in mind here have more to do with his epistemology than with the doctrinal questions which were at issue when his *missio canonica* (permission to teach theology as a formal representative of the Catholic Church) was withdrawn on Dec. 15, 1979 and when his mandate to teach Catholic theology at Tübingen was withdrawn by the German Bishops on Jan. 2, 1980. (At Tübingen, episcopal approval is necessary to hold a chair in Catholic theology.) Despite these censures, I believe Küng has much to say to us. He now holds a chair in Ecumenical theology at Tübingen and he continues to serve the Catholic Church as a priest.

5. Küng, p. 423.

6. Küng, p. 438.

7. Küng, p. 443.

8. Küng, p. 443.

9. Küng, p. 444.

10. Küng, p. 446.

11. Küng, p. 560.

12. Küng, p. 571.

13. Küng, pp. 567-68.

14. Küng, p. 568.

15. Paul Tillich, *Dynamics of Faith* (New York: Harper & Row, 1957), p. 18.

III. FOCUSING THE CENTER

10. Questions of the Heart

The heart of the Christian faith is not a concept. It is not a particular idea of God. The basis of the Christian faith is not a philosophical demonstration. The Christian circle of understanding finds its center and basis in Jesus Christ. That is to say, it finds its center and basis in an historical person, Jesus of Nazareth, acknowledged as divine — as the Christ, as God's Word become man.

This center of the Christian circle of understanding is no less problematic than its horizon. Even at its heart it is questionable. At issue are not just questions of cogency — questions of the head or of understanding. At issue are more acute and personally involving questions of credibility — questions of the heart or of faith. Are the Christian accounts of Jesus reliable? Does he or his story really touch us today? Is there anything there that really moves us personally? And even if we are moved, is the interpretation of Jesus as the fleshing-out of God's saving Word truly compelling? Indeed, are the claims about Jesus' divinity and his necessity for salvation credible at all? Can Jesus be singled out and acknowledged as God's definitive and saving Word, without presumptuously and cold-heartedly implying that there is no true knowledge of God and no genuine salvation outside of this one man and the particular community which claims him as its founder?

The Reliability of the Christian Account

Such questions of the heart are not new. Objections to the historical reliability of the Christian account of Jesus were already being raised in the eighteenth century. Hermann Samuel

97

Reimarus' *Fragments* provides a striking illustration.[1] Employing the newly emerging science of history, Reimarus (1694-1768) contended that the Christian faith was based on fraud, not divine revelation. The evidence of the New Testament, he alleged, is inconsistent and contradictory. Its "factual" content points to a purely human explanation of Jesus' significance. A nineteenth-century historian recorded the shocking and sometimes devastating impact of this critique.

> The first result was a kind of amazement even on the part of many politicians; displeasure on the part of the more sober and worthy classes; frivolous jesting and deliberate elaboration of the derision, sketched here only in outline. This derision spread immediately among many young educated people from whom these effects extended still wider to the citizens. . . . Many thoughtful and serious young men who had dedicated themselves to the Christian ministry were involved in great perplexity in consequence of their own convictions being thus so fearfully shaken. Many determined to choose another profession for their future labors rather than persevere so long amid increasing uncertainty. . . . [2]

Charles Talbert provides an excellent little introduction to this story in a recent edition of the *Fragments*.[3] In the 1750s, the fervor of the German Reformation had given way to a form of orthodox piety which stressed the notion that faith is an assent to a set of propositions as certain. This orthodoxy was under attack from two directions. Pietism stressed the inner and subjective experience of God's revelation. "The subjective inwardness of the individual was ranked above dogma and external authority. The total content of the faith was regarded as less important than the issue of whether or not one really believed. Subjective experience was made the criterion for the objective validity of the affirmations of faith."[4] The Enlightenment, on the other hand, stressed the role of reason, making it the authority and the criterion of doctrinal truth. In the most extreme cases, reason displaced doctrine altogether.

One of the more influential figures of the time was Christian Wolff (1679-1754). He elaborated a theological synthesis which found a place for both revelation and reason. On the one hand, he held that a truly divine or supernatural revelation, although not contrary to reason, is nevertheless above it. What God reveals cannot be derived from reason. On the other hand, Wolff held that reason establishes the criteria by which revelation must be judged. These criteria are essentially two. First, a genuine divine revelation would have to be consistent. It could not contradict God's nature or the natural order. Second, a genuine revelation would have to disclose something which could not be discovered by reason itself. To be genuine, it must reveal something *super*natural.

In his lectures and essays, Reimarus publicly advocated a position similar to Wolff's. He portrayed revelation and reason as complementary. At the same time, he privately recorded a contrary position in the notes later published posthumously and pseudonymously as the Wolfenbüttel *Fragments*. There he assumed the role of a rationalist, arguing both that the Christian documents consistently contradict themselves and reason, and that the origins of the Christian story could be explained historically without recourse to supernatural occurrences. Although Reimarus' use of the historical-critical method was crude and reductionistic by today's standards, many of his opinions anticipated the conclusions of modern scholarship. Moreover, every generation since his has witnessed its share of popular exposés which do little more than update the kind of objections he had raised in the eighteenth century.[5] It is not possible here to review the whole history of this quest for the "real" historical Jesus behind the gospel portrait of Christ, but sketching a somewhat more detailed picture of Reimarus' position can help to focus the kind of questions, at the heart of doubts, which still cause people to wonder whether Christianity is not a charmed circle.

Reimarus contended that Christian revelation had three essential beliefs. The first, he said, was the belief that Jesus intended to establish through his suffering and death a new religion as the vehicle for humanity's spiritual deliverance. But careful scrutiny of the biblical evidence, Reimarus objected, contradicts this view of Jesus' purpose. Jesus did not actually propose any new mysteries or articles of faith. He preached repentance and the coming of God's kingdom, neither of which were novel beliefs in the Judaism of his day. Nor, Reimarus protested, did Jesus actually reveal any genuine "secrets," "mysteries" or "revelations" to his disciples. Jesus "was born a Jew and intended to remain one."[6] He did not teach any new laws. In fact, he stated quite explicitly that he had not come to abolish the law, but to fulfill it. His further remarks "about the immortality and salvation of the soul, the resurrection of the body to face judgment, the kingdom of heaven and the Christ or Messiah who was promised in Moses and the prophets, were both familiar to the Jews and in accord with the Jewish religion of that day."[7]

Reimarus admitted that Jesus at times "explains his parables, especially to his disciples, and then adds that to them alone it is given to know the secrets of the kingdom of God (Matt. 13:11; Mark 4:11; Luke 8:10). But since these secrets consist merely of an explanation of figurative concepts and the explanation insofar as it is stripped of parable, in turn contains nothing more than the common knowledge of the promised kingdom of God under the Messiah, one must confess that no really new or incomprehensible precepts are to be found among these secrets."[8] Nor did references to Jesus as the "Son of God" convince Reimarus that the doctrine of Jesus' divinity is justified. The phrase did not imply divinity in the Old Testament or in Jesus' day. Reimarus called attention to

> passages from the Old Testament so that it will be seen that the Hebrews understood something quite different by the term, and that it means nothing more than "beloved of God (Jedidiah)" [2 Sam. 12:25]. According to the language of the Scripture God calls those whom he loves his sons, just as today we say to a younger and lesser person, in a spirit of love, "my son." God says to Moses, "And you shall say to

Pharoah, . . . 'Israel is my first-born son . . . Let my
son go that he may serve me'" [Exod. 4:22-23]. Moses
reproaches the Israelites, saying that God has borne
them in the wilderness just as a man bears his son
[Deut. 1:31]. At God's command Nathan must promise Solomon to King David, of whom God says, "I will
be his father, and he shall be my son. . . . "[9]

Similar arguments led him to conclude that all of Scripture's references to God as Father, to Jesus as Messiah and Lord, and to
the Spirit of God could be understood in ways perfectly consistent with Judaism. Read in this way as evidence of the orthodoxy of Jesus' Judaic faith, the Scriptures actually contradict the later Christian doctrines of the Incarnation, Trinity
and Holy Spirit.

Reimarus was just as skeptical that Jesus' baptism could be
seen as evidence of his intention to establish a new religion. In
letting himself be baptized by John, Jesus showed himself a
pious Jew. Reimarus argued that there was no evidence that
Jesus ever understood it otherwise. Jesus himself never baptized his disciples or anyone else. Nor during his life did he ever
commission the apostles to baptize. "Rather, they were told only
to announce the advent of the kingdom of heaven, to heal the
sick, cleanse the lepers, waken the dead, and drive out devils."[10]
One does not hear anything different about baptism until the
risen Jesus in Matt. 28:19 tells the disciples to go out to all the
nations and baptize in the name of the Father, the Son and the
Holy Spirit. But this text was suspect for Reimarus both because
the formula used is open to suspicion (for the reason noted
above), and because the command seems to contradict Jesus'
own practice during his life. To Reimarus Jesus' words are clear
when he

gives the command to his apostles and sends them
out to proclaim the kingdom: "Go nowhere among the
Gentiles, and enter no town of the Samaritans, but go
rather to the lost sheep of the house of Israel" [Matt.
10:5-6]. And he says of himself, "I was sent only to the
lost sheep of the house of Israel" [Matt. 15:24].[11]

Jesus' last supper, too, was in Reimarus' eyes a Jewish ritual "without the least alteration of the prescribed or customary ceremonies."[12] If Jesus saw this Passover meal as an anticipation of his impending death, Reimarus claims, it would have been natural and appropriate for him to indicate this at the customary time for remembrance associated with the blessing of bread and wine. Even if he intended his disciples to continue this as a remembrance of him in future Passover meals, that does not indicate an intention to establish a new religion. Jesus, he reasoned, was a "full-fledged" Jew who had but two intentions. First, "he taught only that the Jews be truly converted and devote themselves to a better righteousness than the external and hypocritical righteousness of the Pharisees."[13] Second, he preached that the kingdom of God, which his fellow Jews were awaiting, had already drawn near and that the Messiah would soon appear. Consequently, for Reimarus "'to preach the gospel' means simply to spread the joyful news that the promised Messiah would appear soon and begin his kingdom. 'Believe the gospel' means no more than to believe that the expected Messiah will come soon for your redemption and to his glorious kingdom."[14]

Even Jesus' words on the cross, Reimarus argued, indicate his intention to awaken the Jews to the hope for a worldly deliverance: *"Eli Eli, lama sabachthani?* My God, my God, why hast thou forsaken me?" (Matt. 27:46) This confession "can hardly be otherwise interpreted than that God had not helped him to carry out his intention and attain his object as he had hoped he would have done."[15] And so, Reimarus concluded, it was clearly not Jesus' intention to suffer and die. His objective was to bring about a "worldly kingdom, and to deliver the Israelites from bondage. It was in this that God had forsaken him, it was in this that his hopes had been frustrated."[16]

How, then, did the notion arise that Jesus intended to establish a new religion? The only explanation which seemed reasonable to Reimarus was fraud. The apostles were men of simple means who gave up their livelihoods to follow Jesus. The Scriptures are quite explicit about their "base" motives. They thought that Jesus would establish the Messianic kingdom and that they would receive back a hundredfold for their sacrifices. When things went otherwise and Jesus was crucified, they deserted him. But once it became clear that the authorities were not going to pursue them as well and that things were going to settle down, Reimarus speculated, the situation must have looked quite different. Having given up their trades to follow Jesus, they now faced poverty and disgrace. But having seen how in living as itinerant preachers with Jesus it had been possible to provide for their needs, and having seen the respect and influence which had come with this vocation, it must have occurred to them that the only viable alternative was to find some pretext for continuing their ministry. Fraud, Reimarus argued, would not have been inconsistent with théir original motivation for following Jesus. Furthermore, such deceit on their part would explain why their accounts are so inconsistent and contradict what can be discerned of Jesus' own intention and teaching.[17]

The crux of this alleged deceit, of course, was the claim that Jesus rose from the dead. Reimarus contended that this second major tenet of the Christian faith is also contradicted by the evidence. He makes a great deal of the claim that Pilate had stationed watchmen who later accepted a bribe from the priests to keep quiet about what they had seen (Matt. 28:11-15). Although Matthew presented this evidence to buttress his account, Reimarus argued, it actually undermines the evangelist's claims. If there had been Roman witnesses and the priests knew about it, why did this not lead to the conversion of at least some of these? Why did none of the other apostles, disciples or evangelists ever appeal to these people as witnesses? Why when Christians were brought before the Roman courts, did they not say "Just ask your countrymen who were there"? How could such an extraordinary and sensational event which the priests and guards knew had actually occurred be kept a secret? "So we can conclude," Reimarus claimed, "only that the event did not take place, otherwise it would have had to be introduced as the sole proof that might have some effect among the heathen, since surely all other evidences were vain and ridiculous in their opinion."[18]

Reimarus goes on to list and examine at length all the inconsistencies in the various gospels' accounts of the resurrection. It is not possible here to recount all of these. Suffice it to say, he is able to make a convincing case that the Scriptures disagree about who first went to the tomb, about the details of what actually happened, about where (Jerusalem or Galilee) Jesus first appeared, about who witnessed the appearances and about what Jesus said. John and Matthew do not even mention the ascension to which they were supposedly witnesses and which was hardly a minor matter.[19] In Reimarus' eyes the allegation that Jesus fulfilled the Old Testament prophecies proves nothing. The crucial question is, do these sayings from the Hebrew Scriptures refer to Jesus? There is in fact no proof that they do actually refer to him other than the premise, which needs to be proved, that they do. The reasoning is quite circular. Because of numerous logical and evidential contradictions of this sort, Reimarus concluded, the claim that Jesus rose from the dead cannot be sustained.

The third teaching which Reimarus regarded as essential to Christian faith was Christ's second coming. This was the easiest for the skeptic to dismiss. The facts of history, he suggested, were quite clear. Jesus did not return and usher in a supernatural kingdom of God.

Reimarus was as skeptical about the external evidence for the Christian account of Jesus as he was of the internal evidence. Miracles, Reimarus observed, require as much investigation as the things they purport to prove. We have already noted his objection that proofs from prophecy argue in a circle and so are logically unsound. He finds other external proofs, such as the deaths of martyrs, equally unconvincing. The sincerity of a person's belief does not prove its truth. People have sacrificed and died for all kinds of crazy ideas. No amount of external evidence, Reimarus insisted, can set straight one single contradiction in the content of the alleged revelation. Rather than being paragons of virtue, Jesus' apostles are just the opposite. Christianity's origins are based on apostolic fraud, not divine revelation.

Today Reimarus' skepticism is neither as shocking nor as revolutionary as it was in 1774. Many of his key assumptions have been invalidated. The difficulties he saw are recognized by modern biblical scholars and the most crucial problems can be adequately resolved. But the fundamental questions he raised still pose difficulties for people today. Is the Jesus of history the same as the Christ of faith? How do we know? What were Jesus' real intentions? Is the New Testament a reliable historical resource at all? Did Jesus claim to be the Messiah? Is the Christian interpretation of Jesus as divine, as God's Word made flesh, contradicted by the evidence of the New Testament, by its logic or by reason? Is apostolic fraud the only reasonable explanation of Jesus' resurrection?

In the next chapter we will consider these issues further, but we should also take notice here and now that justifying the historical reliability of the gospel account of Jesus' ministry and death does not necessarily validate the Christian view of Jesus' significance. From the start, Reimarus was committed to assumptions about the relationship between the human and the divine which precluded such an interpretation. He assumed that belief in Jesus' divinity is credible only if the "*super*natural" character of Jesus' "revelations" and deeds has been demonstrated. Reimarus' conception of the supernatural presupposed that the human (natural) and divine (supernatural) belong to separate and opposed realms. This ruled out, a priori, the possibility of a genuine unity of divine and human in a person or event. It ruled out from the start a revelation of the divine *through* the natural or *through* history. Furthermore, Reimarus' conception of revelation as *propositions* which had a supernatural origin presupposed that Jesus' aim, or God's for that matter, was to provide humankind with information or statements, and so overlooks the possibility that it is not supernatural facts or statements about God, but the reality of God, God's own self or God's love that Jesus revealed.

The Credibility of the Christian Claims

The historical account or facts, therefore, were not all that was at issue for Reimarus. At the heart of his challenge were equally fundamental theological questions about what exactly is meant when Jesus is confessed as the Christ. These are still very much with us. The crucial issue at stake in this "Christological" question is the relationship between the divine and human in Jesus. The question has two sides to it. The first, the Christological question in the narrower sense, concerns the relationship of the divine and human in Jesus himself: In what sense can it be said that Jesus is divine? The second, the soteriological question, concerns the role that Jesus plays as mediator between God and the rest of humanity: In what sense can it be said that Jesus reveals, mediates or communicates God? In what sense does Jesus save humanity? It sometimes seems that Christianity offers a bewildering variety of responses to these questions. This is especially evident in the pluralism of contemporary theology. It must be asked if this "spectrum of views" is not in fact another "specter" which points to the bewitchment of the Christian circle of understanding.

Peter Schineller's description of the diverse models which Christians employ for understanding how Jesus "saves" offers a helpful illustration of this disparity of interpretations.[20] The picture he provides is somewhat incomplete, since it focuses only on the soteriological question. His survey is sufficient, however, for depicting the sort of theological disagreement which for many undermines the credibility of Christian claims.

Schineller proposes four basic views. These are meant to represent the spectrum of logical possibilities. The four positions are mutually exclusive and noncomplementary. As theoretical models they do not directly describe actual theologies. Nor do they provide a sociological overview of the attitudes of contemporary Christians. Of course, if taken too literally, such theoretical or ideal types can easily become obfuscating caricatures. But if this is kept in mind, his models provide a rough framework and overall picture for locating specific theologies and attitudes, and for plotting their relationships.

Each of the four models affirms in its own way that Jesus is the Christ, that Jesus mediates God and, hence, that Jesus provides a way to salvation. They differ in how they understand the relation of Jesus to other possible mediators of salvation. Consequently, they also lead, first, to a different understanding of grace (which for now we can define quite loosely as the mediation of God to humanity), and second, to a different understanding of the Church and its place in this mediation of God. These differences hinge on the question of how dispensable and normative Jesus and the Church are for a person's salvation. Schineller explains that he is using "salvation" here in a very broad sense to mean the activity by which God overcomes what we have called humanity's woundedness. He also is using "Church" in a very broad sense to include "the mainline Churches, that would hold to belief in Jesus as the Christ, as Lord and Savior, and would exercise the sacraments of baptism and the Lord's Supper."[21]

The first model sees Jesus as the exclusive mediator of God to humanity. There are no other mediators. Consequently, other religions are false. Without Jesus and outside his Church there is no salvation. Naturally, life for those who take this view focuses around the Church. So, it could be said that their universe is ecclesiocentric. Since there is no religious truth apart from Christian revelation, orthodoxy is of crucial importance for personal salvation. Schineller describes this model as the conservative extreme of the Christian spectrum, in the sense that it maximalizes Jesus' unique, indispensable and absolutely normative role as mediator of God's grace. Because of this emphasis, the model would ordinarily be associated with a "high" Christology, that is to say, with a view of Jesus which emphasizes his divinity, personal (or hypostatic) union with God and other doctrines, like the Trinity, which are part and parcel of such an emphasis. As scriptural evidence for this position Schineller lists the following.

> "There is no other name in the whole world given to man by which we are saved"(Acts 4:12); "He who believes and is baptized will be saved; but he who does

not believe will be condemned" (Mk 16:15-16); "Without me you can do nothing" (Jn 15:5); "I am the way, the truth, and the life. No one comes to the Father except through me" (Jn 14:6).[22]

"Unless a man is born through water and the Spirit, he cannot enter the kingdom of God" (Jn 3:5) and "If you do not eat the flesh of the Son of Man and drink his blood, you will not have life in you" (Jn 6:53).[23]

Following somewhat freely the chart Schineller provides in his article we can diagram the first model's principal characteristics:

1. EXCLUSIVE MEDIATOR	Ecclesiocentric universe, exclusive Christology	Jesus Christ and Church constitutive and exclusive way of salvation

and we can picture the mediation of the divine as a movement of:

God's saving grace --*through*-- **Jesus Christ** --*through*-- **explicit Church only**

The second model, like the first, insists that Jesus' role in the mediation of God's grace is indispensable and unique. Jesus is constitutive for everyone's salvation. Jesus' necessity, however, is understood in a way which allows for the possibility that God is also mediated to those who do not explicitly belong to the Church or to those who never even heard of Jesus. Here, Jesus' necessity is understood in an inclusive rather than an exclusive way.

This difference can be clarified readily with a very mundane analogy. Suppose a certain university senior's passionate arguments and exemplary behavior persuade the Academic Dean to extend special privileges, like exemption from final exams, to all seniors. This student's efforts would "save" the others from finals, even though many may not have been aware of his mediation with the Dean or may not have even known the student. Indeed, it would be possible that a number of those availing themselves of these prerogatives would assume that their privileges had some other cause or were merited by their own achievements. Nevertheless, the real and indispensable cause of their new freedoms would still be the mediation of that anonymous student.

If Christ's mediation of God is understood to function in an analogous way, then it is possible to imagine his saving grace operating beyond the exclusive confines of explicit Christianity. This allows one to affirm both Christ's necessity for salvation and also God's love for all of humanity. It provides a way to account for scriptural texts like 1 Tim 2:4-6 which emphasize both the Savior's indispensable role and God's universal salvific will: "God our Savior *desires all men* to be saved and to come to the knowledge of the truth; for there is one God and there is one mediator between God and man, the man Jesus Christ, who gave himself as a ransom for all;"[24] or "Acts 17:23, where Paul says that what the Athenians worship as unknown, he proclaims to them in proclaiming Jesus Christ as risen Lord."[25] Theologians working with this model of Jesus as a constitutive mediator of God are thus able to speak of the "anonymous Christianity" and "latent Church" of those who are saved by Jesus without being explicitly aware of this.

Since this model allows for the possibility of genuine knowledge of God and real salvation for those who do not explicitly belong to the Church, this viewpoint is Christocentric rather than ecclesiocentric. It allows for two different ways of estimating the significance and necessity of the Church. On the one hand, it provides a framework for maintaining that the Church, like its founder, is necessary and indispensable in an inclusive way. Referring back to the analogy above, for example, we could imagine the Academic Dean granting senior privileges, but requiring that the student who petitioned him must enlist other students to form an organization that would see to it that the new prerogatives become established as the practice in all senior classes. The privileges of every student would be affected by this organization's work, even though it is likely that not all students would be aware of the group's efforts, and that there might be a good number of students who would never be willing to join the organization or share in its work. Schineller diagrams this first possibility so as to show God's grace coming through Jesus and the Church to all of humanity.

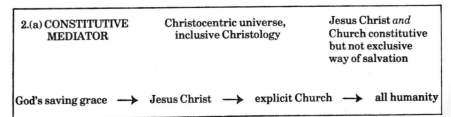

2.(a) CONSTITUTIVE MEDIATOR	Christocentric universe, inclusive Christology	Jesus Christ *and* Church constitutive but not exclusive way of salvation

God's saving grace → Jesus Christ → explicit Church → all humanity

On the other hand, one could also hold that Jesus is constitutive for salvation, but that the Church is dispensable. In our analogy, the Dean could grant senior privileges to all students directly and not require the further mediation of a student organization. This, of course, requires a modification of the previous chart.

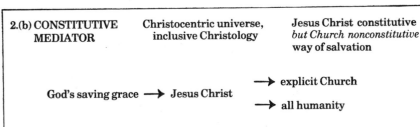

2.(b) CONSTITUTIVE MEDIATOR	Christocentric universe, inclusive Christology	Jesus Christ constitutive *but Church nonconstitutive* way of salvation

God's saving grace → Jesus Christ → explicit Church
→ all humanity

Either of these understandings of Jesus as the constitutive mediator of God would, like the first model, be associated with a relatively high Christology. Although this model also affirms the necessity of Jesus for salvation, it is more open to the possibility of a genuine, if incomplete, truth in other religions. Orthopraxis (living the faith truly) becomes important along with orthodoxy (confessing the true faith), since it is possible for one's life to be affected by Christ's grace without an explicit knowledge of this.

The third model is controversial because it relativizes the necessity of Jesus and the Church much more radically than the second. It sees Jesus as the normative mediation of God "which corrects and fulfills all other mediations,"[26] but it does not regard Jesus as constitutive or necessary for salvation or think of Jesus as necessarily unique or unsurpassable. The key word here is normative. The model does not go all the way to a position of total relativity. Jesus still functions as the measure of all other mediators, and in this sense, at least, he is a superior or ideal type and standard against which the others can be measured. Nevertheless, the position is theocentric rather than Christocentric, since in the end Jesus is not necessary for everyone's salvation. Accordingly, those taking this view appeal to texts which emphasize that although God's love is revealed in Jesus, it is available through other mediations. Schineller cites the first letter of John 4:7-10, which says that God's love is revealed in Jesus, but also that anyone who lives in love, lives in God. Schineller also suggests that a similar thrust could be claimed for Pauline texts where the love of God is *made visible* in Jesus (Romans 8:39).[27]

Picturing Jesus as the normative mediator of God's grace, obviously, relativizes the necessity of the Church. Since one does not have to be a Christian to know and love God, orthopraxis becomes more important than orthodoxy. Typically, the model would be associated with a "low" Christology which stresses the humanity of Jesus.

3. NORMATIVE MEDIATOR	Theocentric universe, normative Christology	Jesus Christ and Church normative but not constitutive way of salvation

God's saving grace	→	Jesus Christ as normative	→ Church
	↘	various religions, all humanity	

The fourth model sees Jesus as just one of many mediators. It embodies an epistemological relativism or skepticism because it refuses to make judgments or comparisons about the various religions. It is still described as Christian, because it acknowledges Jesus as one who mediates God. It is only Christian, however, in the most liberal sense of the term. Many of the mainline Christian Churches would certainly reject the position as heterodox. Schineller nevertheless maintains that the model has a positive dimension "insofar as the adherent stresses even more than the previous position the incomprehensibility of God and the mystery of human subjectivity. It prefers to let God be God; it cautions against making God and His ways into our image, and against trying to judge Him and His ways by our human standards."[28] Thus, this model, like the previous, is theocentric. Its soteriology, however, is nonnormative. Its Christology is low, stressing Jesus' humanity, usually to the detriment of his divinity. It sees orthopraxis as the sole criterion of salvation.

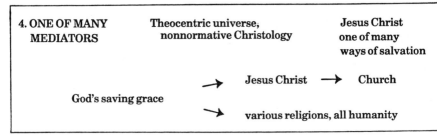

Schineller's overview of this spectrum of views raises an acute question which he does not consider but which certainly must not be avoided. Although the positions he charts are not intended as theological or sociological surveys, one could find numerous representatives of each among believers. Doesn't this disparity of interpretations disclose that the Christian understanding of Jesus' significance is bewitchingly circular? One end of the spectrum preserves Jesus' necessity and indispensability. The cost, however, seems to be the denial that there can be any true mediation of God outside Jesus and the Church. A stance of this sort seems oblivious to the obvious historical and cultural relativity of the Christian faith and of its founder. The other end of the spectrum acknowledges this historicity. It takes most seriously the elements of both the Christian tradition and human experience which might point towards other historical mediations of God's grace. The cost here, however, is a radical relativization of Jesus' and the Church's necessity and indispensability. These are notions which Christians of past generations clearly held as essential to their faith. The positions in between these two ends of the spectrum attempt to do justice to both agendas. Such views, as Schineller argues, are attractive to a great many Christians today. But aren't these positions, in the end, only halfway measures true to neither the Christian faith nor other possible experiences of God's grace? Do we not have here, once again, the specter of a charmed circle? Aren't such Christians trying to have it both ways? They want to find God in Christ without denying that God can be found outside Christianity. They want to identify with Christ as a fellow human without making him just *another* man.

Can the apparent circularity of this logic be justified? Does this diversity of positions demonstrate that at its heart the Christian faith is incredible? How can one make sense of the claim that Jesus is necessary for salvation without either ultimately denying the possibility of any genuine salvation outside of Christ and the community which claims him as its founder or ultimately compromising the claim? Why should such interpretations of Jesus' significance be taken seriously, if they themselves put aside the most crucial beliefs of the tradition they claim to interpret?

Notes

1. From Reimarus, *Fragments*, ed. Charles H. Talbert, trans. Ralph S. Fraser (Philadelphia: Fortress Press, 1970; originally published posthumously and pseudonymously in 1774-78).

2. From Talbert's "Introduction," to Reimarus, *Fragments*, p. 1.

3. Talbert, p. 1.

4. Talbert, pp. 4-5.

5. John H. Hayes, *Son of God to Super Star: Twentieth-Century Interpretations of Jesus* (Nashville, Tennessee: Abingdon Press, 1976), provides a very accessible overview of this phenomenon; the classic overview of eighteenth and nineteenth century lives of Jesus is Albert Schweitzer's *The Quest for the Historical Jesus: A Critical Study of its Progress from Reimarus to Wrede*, trans. W. Montgomery (New York: the Macmillan Company, 1968).

6. Reimarus, p. 71.

7. Reimarus, pp. 71-72.

8. Reimarus, pp. 75.

9. Reimarus, pp. 76-77.

10. Reimarus, p. 104.

11. Reimarus, p. 102.

12. Reimarus, p. 121.

13. Reimarus, p. 123.

14. Reimarus, p. 125.

15. Reimarus, p. 150.

16. Reimarus, p. 150.

17. Reimarus pp. 240-69.

18. Reimarus, p. 159.

19. Reimarus, p   177-200.

20. Peter Schineller, S.J. "Christ and Church: A Spectrum of Views," *Theological Studies* 37 (December 1976) pp. 545-66.

21. Schineller, p. 549.

22. Schineller, p. 551.

23. Schineller, pp. 551-52.

24. Emphasis added.

25. Schineller, p. 553.

26. Schineller, p. 556.

27. Schineller, p. 557.

28. Schineller, p. 560.

11. Jesus of Nazareth

The heart of the Christian understanding is the person Jesus of Nazareth. The placement of this chapter at the center of the book is intended to accentuate his centrality. The irony, of course, is that one chapter, even a prominent one, can hardly do justice to the point. Indeed, Juan Segundo observes in the course of his five-volume reflection on Jesus that it would take readers a good deal more than a few books like his to acquire the background and tools needed to verify the story of Jesus for themselves. It would entail the kind of preparation necessary for a Ph.D.[1] Needless to say, there is no question of trying to do that in a few pages here. A chapter-length survey of even the recent studies of Jesus, such as Segundo's, could provide only a very limited overview.[2] What we can do, is sketch the general lines of the processes which scholars follow in studying the historical record about Jesus and then depict in very broad strokes the resultant portrait.[3]

The Historical Accessibility of Jesus

Certainly that picture is not as complete or detailed as one would like. There is considerable disagreement about many of the specifics. It is clear, today, that Reimarus barely scratched the surface of the problematic. The question about the relationship between the historical events and the Christian account is far more complex than he realized. Questions about the authenticity of particular texts are more difficult to resolve than he imagined. At the same time, however, it is also clear that the Christian account is not a distortion of the record as Reimarus alleged and as many of those outside the Christian circle still suspect.

115

History does not and cannot prove the truth of the Christian understanding of Jesus, but neither does history prove the Christian circle bewitched. Enough of the account can be confirmed to warrant it a credible interpretation and to justify the intellectual honesty of those who rely on it despite their inability to verify every detail themselves.

The line of questioning which Reimarus inaugurated came to be known as the quest for the historical Jesus. In the end it failed. The last truly significant effort along these lines was Albert Schweitzer's study published in 1906.[4] His survey of prior attempts to retrieve the "real" Jesus illustrated the obvious difficulty. Each interpreter found a different Jesus. Moreover, each found his own ideals embodied in Jesus. Rationalists discovered an enlightened teacher and exemplary humanist, but not a miracle worker or Messiah. Romantics uncovered a gentle and inspirational Jesus. For Hegelians, a dialectical understanding of history and myth provided the key for understanding Jesus. Nineteenth century liberals appealed to psychological interpretations. Even Schweitzer's own picture of Jesus as an eschatological prophet forced the evidence. Despite legitimate and suggestive discoveries along the way, it became clear that the gospels do not provide the kind of information or criteria needed to reconstruct a biography of Jesus or a chronological history of even his public ministry. Since then, scholars reacting against the excesses of the quest but also enlarging on its insights have gradually developed reliable processes for historically reconstructing a more modest portrait.

Although this emergence of contemporary biblical scholarship is itself a fascinating history with its own nuances and twists, the discipline's key insights and procedures are not all that controversial or difficult to characterize.[5] By and large its methodology is accepted by the mainline churches and the consensus of university-trained scholars.[6] Among its most important insights is the recognition that the gospels are a unique genre. Their primary intent was not to provide a historical record of Jesus, but to proclaim him as the Risen Lord. The events of his life and death were seen in light of this proclamation. Consequently, the gospels cannot be read as though they were simply historical chronicles of exactly what happened and what was said.

We know from personal experience that events seen in hindsight can look very different than they did at the time. That does not necessarily mean hindsight has distorted the facts. Indeed, what really was happening often becomes clear only in retrospect. The helpful stranger may have been picking pockets, while the suspicious person in the shadows may turn out to be the apprehending officer. Nor are our recollections always as unambiguous as they seem.

For example, I can pinpoint a specific moment in my youth when it was clear that I was headed toward a profession in theology. I am sure my recollection of that moment is true and factual. You would be quite mistaken, however, if you overheard me telling the story and concluded from my account that at the time I even knew what a theologian was. I didn't. But when I tell what happened that isn't obvious, nor is it directly germane to the anecdote. Furthermore, I would be quite naive to assume that my reconstruction corresponds exactly to what occurred or to what another witness would have reported. My recollection is thoroughly colored by subsequent events. But I am certain it would still be true to say that the particular moment in question is not a fiction and was decisive for the direction of my life. This would be true even if it turned out, as it no doubt would, that my memory on many of the precise details was inaccurate, and even if it turned out that a careful investigator was unable to draw any historically certain "facts" from my recollections. One could not conclude from such difficulties that my story was a fraud. Moreover, it would be fruitless to seek from such an anecdote the sort of facts one could expect to discover if it had been recorded on film or written up at the time in a diary or newspaper. Anecdotes of this sort do not provide those kinds of facts, nor does the truth or falsity of such anecdotes necessarily hinge on whether a historian can verify the certainty of all their details.

We encounter similar problems if we approach the gospels as if they were simply historical chronicles. The quest for the historical Jesus did not fail because the gospels are unreliable sources. The quest failed because interpreters like Reimarus misunderstood what kind of sources the gospels were and so asked the wrong sorts of questions.[7]

A second crucial insight of modern scripture scholarship is the recognition that a discernible process of development lies behind the formation of the gospels as we now have them. Many of the *historical-critical* tools which scholars use today are aimed at uncovering the various layers of tradition which constituted this development.

In its effort to explain the remarkable similarities between the first three gospels (Matthew, Mark and Luke), *source criticism* clarified the relationship between these gospels themselves (the so-called *synoptic problem*) and earlier oral traditions. Analysis reveals that the gospels consist of many individual units or pericopae (stories, parables, teachings, prayers and so forth). Investigation of the parallel pericopae of the first three gospels reveals that where Matthew deviates from Mark, Luke usually doesn't, and that where Luke deviates from Mark, Matthew usually doesn't. The *Markan hypothesis* explains this pattern of divergence by proposing that Mark's gospel must have been a common source for Matthew's and Luke's accounts. They diverge from Mark at different points because they wrote their accounts independently. As one would expect, some of this divergent material in Matthew and Luke is unique to one or the other of them. There are many "sayings" of Jesus, however, which are recorded in both their gospels but at different points, and which are not found at all in Mark. To explain this, the *two source theory* contends that Matthew and Luke had access to another source, a collection of Jesus' teachings (generally referred to as the "Q") which they added to the Markan account.

The ease with which each of the evangelists moves and adjusts these smaller units and the ability of each of these units to stand on its own suggests that they were originally handed down independently. Further scrutiny discloses that the narrative linking of the these units is for the most part rather arbitrary: "As he was walking by the Sea of Galilee . . . " (Matt.

4:18); "The Pharisee came up and started a discussion with him . . . " (Mark 8:11); "A man in the crowd said to him . . . " (Luke 12:13). This reinforces the impression that the evangelists were not recounting someone's memory of the exact sequence of events but rather were pulling together units of earlier oral traditions to compose a narrative picture of the sort of thing Jesus said and did during his short ministry to the people of Israel.

Form criticism determines and analyzes the genre of each of these units. For example, is it a narrative, legend, miracle story, saying, parable, allegory, prayer or allusion to the Hebrew Scriptures? The form critic then attempts to reconstruct the context or life setting of each of these units by looking for evidence from the pericope's vocabulary, concerns, implied audience, view of Christ and so forth. Since the oral transmission of these forms follows predictable rules, it is often possible not only to pin down the context of specific passages but also to determine what sort of adjustments would have been likely during the process of oral transmission. Think, for example, how the story leading up to a punch line will often be embellished and made relevant in each retelling while the punch line itself remains unchanged; changing it would ruin the joke. It is a good bet, therefore, that the punch line we hear after the story has gone the rounds for a while is still pretty close to the original version, while it is quite likely that the story itself has undergone substantial transformation. Likewise the study of oral tradition reveals, for instance, that parables in the narrow sense (which are something like concise narrative metaphors) are often expanded into allegories (more comprehensive narratives in which the key elements have symbolic meanings). The reverse is quite rare. The ultimate aim of the scholar, of course, is to determine whether the passage in its present form most likely reflects the context of Jesus' own ministry or the context of later Christian communities (those in Palestine, those of Greek-speaking Jewish converts to Christianity or those of Gentile converts to Christianity).

The versions of the parable of the Great Supper in the gospels of Matthew (22:1-14) and Luke (14:16-24) offer a typical example. As Jesus told it, the parable most likely proclaimed that God's kingdom was coming — even to outcasts and sinners. It is like a man who gives a great banquet, intent on filling his hall. Luke's version preserves that original character but perhaps emphasizes the evangelist's concern with the Church's mission to the gentiles. The householder does not give up when the first guests reject his invitation. He sends out his servant two more times in order to fill all the places. But in Matthew's gospel the "parable" becomes a very elaborate allegory. The man who gives the banquet is made a king to indicate that he stands for God. The occasion is a wedding feast for this king's son, no doubt to symbolize the New Covenant established in God's Son, Jesus. His servants, who stand for the Christian martyrs, are slain. The king takes revenge, suggesting the destruction of Jerusalem, and so forth. Matthew's version clearly addresses the situation of the early Church rather than Jesus' announcement of God's kingdom to the Jews of Palestine.

Further insights are gained by *redaction criticism*, which focuses on the editorial perspectives of the evangelists themselves. Redaction critics seek to determine what is distinctive about each gospel. What does it add, adapt or locate in a different context? What special vocabulary does it use? What themes and incidents does it emphasize? What does this tell about the evangelist's concerns or point of view? A careful study of Matthew's gospel, for example, reveals his special concern to emphasize that Jesus did not come to do away with the law but to fulfill it. This is evident in the incident which his version adds to the parable of the wedding feast. The king notices that one of the guests is not properly attired in a wedding garment and so has the man bound and thrown "out into the dark, where there will be weeping and grinding of teeth" (Matt. 22:14). Just as the right to sit at the banquet table requires appropriate behavior, dressing for the part, we might say, so the freedom to share in God's kingdom will require Christ-like behavior, that is to say, acting the part: living out the spirit as well as the letter of the law. More recently scholars have also exploited the methods of *literary criticism* and *social theory* to clarify the meaning of each of the gospels and the intent of the editors and communities which produced them.

Using such methods, modern scholarship has been able to develop a number of criteria for establishing whether particular details of the biblical accounts are likely authentic. (1) A pericope is probably authentic if it cannot be attributed to or is contrary to the theology of the evangelists, to the concerns of the particular communities which transmitted the oral tradition about Jesus or to the Judaic customs of Jesus' day. There would be no reason to invent something which made it more difficult for the evangelist or the early Christian communities to defend their interpretation. (2) The more primitive a form is, the more likely it is authentic. (3) The shorter or shortest of two or three accounts is probably closest to the original. (4) A detail recorded in diverse sources (e.g. Mark, Q and John) or in a number of forms (e.g. narratives, sayings and prayers) is probably authentic. (5) Irreducible personal idioms like Jesus' use of "Abba" to refer to God or his use of "Amen" at the beginning of his statements are more likely authentic. (6) Doctrinal or linguistic idioms characteristic of the Palestinian Judaism of Jesus' day but not of latter periods may also be indications of authenticity.

The use of such criteria has not led to unanimity about the details of the biblical accounts of Jesus' ministry and teaching, but they have provided the basis for establishing a broad and general consensus about the sort of things Jesus said and did. Examined with these tools, the gospels do yield an accurate portrait of Jesus, even though it is not one which tells us much about the course of his career in all its details and stages, and even though in many cases there can be no certainty about Jesus' exact words. On the one hand there is evidence, as Günther Bornkamm puts it, of "an incontestable loyalty and adherence to the word of Jesus, and at the same time an astonishing degree of freedom as to the original wording."[8] So, although contemporary investigators often probe and question the historical accuracy of particular details much more radically than Reimarus, when it comes to the bottom line their conclusions are generally much more positive. C. H. Dodd put it this way:

> When all allowance has been made for these limiting factors — the chances of oral transmission, the effect of translation, the interest of teachers in making the saying "contemporary," and simple human fallibility — it remains that the first three gospels offer a body of sayings on the whole so consistent, so coherent, and withal so distinctive in manner, style [and] content that no reasonable critic should doubt, whatever reservations he may have about individual sayings, that we find reflected here the thought of a single, unique teacher.[9]

A Man of His Times

So, then, what can we say about this individual, Jesus, and his teaching? First, it is evident that he was a person very much attuned to the eschatological fervor of his day. His contemporaries, or at least those influenced by the Hasidim or "pious ones," saw their history at a crucial turning point. Indeed, some believed history was approaching its final conclusion (the last days, or "eschaton"). This impression had become quite acute in the period from 200 B.C.E. to 70 C.E. (the age of apocalyptic or intertestamental period.) This period was the nation's most heroic, but at the same time its most tragic. Despite the impression one sometimes gets from Scripture, Israel had never been a great world power. In the sixth century before Christ, it had been crushed by Babylon. The temple had been destroyed. The community's leaders had been carried off into captivity. Even after their return from this exile, Israel except for a few brief periods really never escaped domination by foreign powers: first the Persians, then the Greeks (under Alexander the Great), followed by the Egyptian Ptolemies, after them the Syrian Seleucids and finally, in Jesus' day, the Romans.

One of the most severe of these oppressors was the Seleucid ruler, Antiochus IV Epiphanes (175-163 B.C.E.). He was deter-

mined to civilize the Jews by imposing his adopted Greek culture on them. This policy of Hellenization, as it is called, aimed
at destroying all that was distinctive about Judaism. The issue,
therefore, was not simply political independence. Israel's very
identity was at stake. The abolition of its worship and rituals
would have meant the dissolution of its distinctive character as
a people. The pious ones knew that such an attack against Israel's theological anthropology was a mortal threat.

A successful struggle against Antiochus led by Judas Mac-
cabaeus and his brothers restored Israel's independence. The
courage of these Maccabean soldiers became symbolic of the nation's fidelity to its identity, and so to its theological anthropology. Nevertheless, the Hasmonaean reign established by the
Maccabees was not truly a time of restoration. Their govern-
ment rapidly degenerated. "There was corruption in high
places. Bribes were openly offered for preferment in office. Intrigue and murder were the order of the day."[10] Many of the nation's leaders welcomed the influence of Hellenistic culture and
promoted a policy of secularization which extended even to the
High Priesthood. Those who were faithful to the Law now found
themselves in opposition to the royal and priestly families. Israel's identity was thus threatened from within. Jew was at
odds with Jew.

The Roman general Pompey took advantage of this situation when the occasion was offered by a bitter struggle for the
throne between the last Hasmonaean sons, Hyrcanus II and
Aristobulos. The Romans intervened. Jerusalem was conquered. Eventually Herod the Great was established as puppet
king. His restoration of Jerusalem and the temple owed so much
to his allegiance to Rome that it could not really be regarded as
a genuine rebirth of independence. The Herodian dynasty's corruption, tyranny and Hellenistic secularization continued to
threaten the nation's identity. By Jesus' time, Judea had come
directly under the rule of a Roman administrator, the pro-
curator who resided at Caesarea. The Jews' ruling body in
Jerusalem, the Sanhedrin, had been given significant authority
in religious and civil matters but was by that fact forced into a

policy of accommodation. To the pious ones it appeared that Israel's situation was as desperate as ever. This was not a nation covenanted to Yahweh and defined by its fidelity to Yahweh's liberating Law! This was not the land of justice, integrity, honesty, compassion and reverence promised by the prophets! This was not the expected future, the future at the heart of their identity as a people!

Thus the anxiety about the future in Jesus' day was not simply a matter of looking forward to better times. It had to do with Israel's character as people who understood their present situation in light of their past. Their captivity in Egypt and their exodus had provided the key paradigm. The prophetic tradition had always insured that this paradigm drawn from the past was concretely applied to the present. One could not claim to know God, unless that knowledge could be shown as a concrete reality in every dimension of life. That meant a just legal, political, economic and social order. It meant personal integrity and concern for the weak. It meant a love of God and neighbor like the love that God had shown for Israel. Judgment against the present situation as falling short of what the past promised, was at the same time the call for a new future — one that would truly live up to the promise of the past. So the future was envisioned in terms of the past. Prophets like Isaiah, recalling the glory of David's reign, looked for the coming of a son of David worthy of the title who would restore the fidelity to Yahweh that was absent in the present reign. To Ahaz, who was such a corrupt king, Isaiah proclaims:

> Listen now, House of David:
> are you not satisfied with trying the patience of men
> without trying the patience of God, too?
> The Lord himself, therefore, will give you a sign.
> It is this: the maiden is with child
> and will give birth to a son
> whom she will call Immanuel. (Isaiah 7:13-14)

The name Immanuel, which means "God with us," recalls the prophetic act of Hosea who married the whore Gomer and

named the last of their children "No-People-of-Mine" to
dramatize the nation's infidelity to the covenant (Hosea 1:9).
Lest the judgment against the corruption of the present order
be missed by Ahaz, Isaiah emphasizes the future David's fidelity to Yahweh.

> On curds and honey will he feed
> until he knows how to refuse evil
> and choose good. (Isaiah 7:15)

On this "shoot" which springs from the Davidic line,

> the spirit of Yahweh rests,
> a spirit of wisdom and insight,
> a spirit of counsel and power,
> a spirit of knowledge and of the fear of Yahweh.
> (The fear of Yahweh is his breath.)
> He does not judge by appearances,
> he gives no verdict on hearsay,
> but judges the wretched with integrity,
> and with equity gives a verdict for the poor
>   of the land.
> His word is a rod that strikes the ruthless,
> his sentences bring death to the wicked.
> Integrity is the loincloth around his waist,
> faithfulness the belt about his hips. (Isaiah 11:1-5)

The new David will bring peace to Yahweh's people:

> See now, your king comes to you;
> he is victorious, he is triumphant,
> humble and riding on a donkey,
> on a colt, the foal of a donkey.
> He will banish chariots from Ephraim
> and horses from Jerusalem;
> the bow of war will be banished.
> He will proclaim peace for the nations.
> His empire shall stretch from sea to sea,
> from the river to the ends of the earth.
>   (Zechariah 9:9-10)

The future anticipated under such a true son of David is at times quite thoroughly idealized in the prophets. Their descriptions evoke images of Paradise.

> The wolf lives with the lamb,
> the panther lies down with the kid,
> calf and lion cub feed together
> with a little boy to lead them.
> The cow and the bear make friends,
> their young lie down together.
> The lion eats straw like the ox.
> The infant plays over the cobra's hole;
> into the viper's lair
> the young child puts his hand.
> They do no hurt, no harm,
> on all my holy mountain,
> for the country is filled with the knowledge
>   of Yahweh
> as the waters swell the sea. (Isaiah 11:6-9)

The Hebrew Scriptures never explicitly refer to this new David in a technical way as the Messiah (or "anointed one"). When the term Messiah was used in those texts, the reigning king was meant. Nor did the Old Testament use the expressions "the kingdom of God" or "the kingdom of heaven" so common in the New Testament. These ideas, however, were clearly implicit in the prophetic portraits of the future David's reign. By Jesus' day, the expectation of a Messiah and his kingdom had become another way of articulating the judgment that the present order fell short of the promise of the past, and another way of expressing the hope that fidelity to the covenant in the present promised a new divine order in the future. A similar role was played by the images of a new Jerusalem (Jeremiah 31:38-40) and a new covenant:

> See, the days are coming — it is Yahweh who speaks
> — when I will make a new covenant with the House
> of Israel (and the House of Judah), but not a covenant

like the one I made with their ancestors on the day I
took them by the hand to bring them out of the land of
Egypt. They broke that covenant of mine, so I had to
show them who was master. It is Yahweh who
speaks. No, this is the covenant I will make with the
House of Israel when those days arrive — it is
Yahweh who speaks. Deep within them I will plant
my Law, writing it on their hearts. Then I will be
their God and they shall be my people. There will be
no further need for neighbor to try to teach neighbor,
or brother to say to brother, "Learn to know Yahweh!"
No, they will all know me, the least no less than the
greatest — it is Yahweh who speaks — since I will for-
give their iniquity and never call their sin to mind.
(Jeremiah 31:31-34)

This judgment against the present reality and expression
of hope for the future found a new and more radical expression
in the apocalyptic literature of the inter-testmental period. By
this time there were no longer any influential or credible
prophetic voices. The two key elements of the prophetic tradition, divine command and divine promise, were preserved, on
the one hand, in the rabbinic codification of the legal tradition
in the Torah and, on the other hand, in the emergence of the
apocalypses as denunciations of the present order and as proclamations of the advent of a new day. According to D. S. Russell,
"Not only did these apocalyptic books mirror the historical situation out of which they arose, they at the same time actually
helped to create it."[11] They elaborated a theological anthropology which was responsive to the extreme peril of the times. The
first and greatest of these apocalypses was the Book of Daniel,
occasioned by Antiochus' oppression. It is the only apocalypse
that became part of the canonical (officially approved) Hebrew
Scriptures, but there were many others. They profoundly influenced the way Jews understood things in Jesus' day.

Although apocalyptic was essentially a development of
prophecy, it was also quite different. The prophet usually deliv-

ered his oracles in person. They were put into writing much later. The anonymous apocalyptists were more like authors in the modern sense. They wrote out what they had to say following certain literary conventions. The literary form and thematic content were closely related. The apocalyptists were visionaries who saw that Israel's identity was in mortal danger and they were poets who articulated Israel's fears and hopes. Their language, therefore, was imaginative, esoteric, dramatic and highly symbolic. They believed that Israel was at a turning point in its history, so they pictured things in black and white. Evil was pitted against good, the sons of dark against the sons of light, this aeon against the aeon to come. Fantastic imagery, creatures and visions expressed their conviction about the monstrous evils of the time. To emphasize the cosmic proportions of Israel's predicament and God's response, a new or much more significant place was given to angels, demons, astrology and numerology (the use of numbers to predict the future). Since the apocalyptic writers claimed to bring to light God's hidden plan for the future, it was conventional to attribute (pseudonymously) their visions of this secret future to ancient heroes of the past such as Daniel, Solomon, Moses, Abraham, Enoch and even Adam. The secrets attributed to these ancients were interpreted quite differently in each of the apocalypses. There were significant shifts of emphasis and belief. The authors were not systematic and in fact were often quite inconsistent, but they all shared the conviction that the present order was an abomination and that the ultimate triumph of God's kingdom was imminent.

Like the prophets before them, the apocalyptists called on the Messianic imagery of the past. But they radicalized it. Books like Enoch see the struggle of evil on a cosmic scale. The corruption of this world is traced back to the fall of the Angels from the heavenly world. There is a marked tension between this world and the world to come, between the sons of darkness and the sons of light. At the same time, deliverance is seen more as a divine interruption of history and as an other-worldly intervention, than as a this-worldly development. This emphasis on the transcendent, supernatural and supramundane was expressed

in the mysterious figure called "the man" or "the Son of Man."
His first appearance is in the Book of Daniel. The vision reported in the seventh chapter pictures a succession of beasts
symbolic of the nations which had oppressed the people of Israel.
The last of these, whose mouth "was full of boasts," seems a clear
reference to Antiochus. As Daniel watches, the heavenly court
is convened before God, pictured as "one of great age," and the
Son of Man is given authority over all nations.

> I gazed into the visions of the night.
> And I saw, coming on the clouds of heaven,
> one like a son of man.
> He came to the one of great age
> and was led into his presence.
> On him was conferred sovereignty,
> glory and kingship,
> and men of all peoples, nations and languages
>   became his servants.
> His sovereignty is an eternal sovereignty
> which shall never pass away,
> nor will his empire ever be destroyed.
>   (Daniel 7:13-14)

There is considerable scholarly debate about the identity of
this mysterious heavenly figure. In Daniel, the Son of Man does
not appear to be an individual. Rather, the figure appears to
symbolize a corporate reality (the redeemed nation), "in which
the human and the humane triumph over the beastly and the
bestial by the greatness and the power of God."[12] Daniel does not
mention a role for a Davidic Messiah. The Son of Man is evi-
dently another and different image for expressing the same
hope — that God's kingdom will overcome the evils of the present order. It is quite probable that even in Jesus' day the relationship between the Son of Man and Messiah was still ambiguous. Such diversity makes it clear that Jesus' contemporaries were not so much concerned with questions about *how*
God would triumph (through a new David, or a heavenly Son of
Man, or both together), as they were concerned with expressing

their conviction that God *would* triumph. They drew on a plurality of diverse and even conflicting images to unveil the iniquities of the present order and to reveal the coming of a new, holy and divine order.

To the messianic images, the apocalyptists added the ideas of a final judgment day, of the judgment book in which the names of the good and evil are recorded, of eternal reward and punishment, of the places later called heaven and hell, and of the resurrection of the dead. The last of these is perhaps the most important for our understanding the Christian interpretation of Jesus' fate and significance. Scholars have been unable to trace down the origin of this idea. It first appears during the inter-testmental times. There was no significant or developed belief in afterlife in earlier periods. It certainly did not arise out of philosophical speculation or even directly from the interpretation of the Scriptures, although a case could be made that the notion is anticipated in Isaiah 26:19. In Jesus' day, the idea was still rejected by Sadducees, the priestly party and conservative voice of Israel, who certainly had as much claim to authority as any other group at the time. Nor does it appear that there was even universal agreement about the nature of resurrection. Regarding an afterlife, the apocalyptic writings disclose what Russell characterizes as a "bewildering variation."

> Sometimes the righteous are to be resurrected to a kingdom established on this present earth; sometimes it is to be on a 'purified' or renewed earth; sometimes it is limited in duration and precedes the dawning of the age to come; sometimes it is a purely heavenly and 'spiritual' conception in which the idea of resurrection may or may not play a part.[13]

Since the Hebrew tradition conceived the body as an essential aspect of the person, survival after death ultimately would have to mean the resurrection of the body. This was the case in most apocalypses. The sort of body envisioned, of course, would depend on the sort of resurrection envisaged — "a physical body for an earthly kingdom, a 'spiritual' body for a heavenly kingdom."[14] When spiritual bodies were intended, they were imagined as radically transformed and glorified. In those cases, what is envisioned is not simply the resuscitation of the body for life on a renewed earth, but rather an eternal unity with God which perfects and transforms the person, and so also the body. Thus, hope for the resurrection of the body was in effect another way of confessing the belief that the fellowship which the pious had enjoyed with God in this life, and for which the pious may indeed have suffered and died, could not be broken even by death. Certainly for some apocalyptists, hope in the resurrection of the body expressed the conviction that each person's final and ultimate destiny would only be achieved after death either in a transformative and eternal presence with God or in an everlasting and horribly punishing banishment from God's kingdom.

A Man Apart From the Circles of His Day

Jesus' proclamation of the dawning of God's kingdom was clearly a response to such expectations. On the surface, at least, his teaching had much in common with the beliefs of his contemporaries. The Essenes, for example, also awaited the coming of God's kingdom. Rejecting the piety of other Jews as bankrupt, they had established a separate community out in the desert at Qumran. Their vision was apocalyptic. They conceived themselves as a holy remnant awaiting God's victory over the powers of evil. Every dimension of their communal life was guided by a strict, puritanical and ascetical discipline aimed at reinforcing this conception. The practice and symbolism of chastity, celibacy, ritual cleansings and communal meals anticipating the eschaton played an especially significant part in their quest for purity.

One could argue for parallels here with Jesus. As the gospels tell it, he preached the coming of God's kingdom. He used apocalyptic imagery. In the Sermon on the Mount, he called for a stricter observance of the Law. He prepared for his ministry by fasting and praying in the desert. He began his public career by submitting to the ritual cleansing of John the Baptist and saw eschatological significance in his final meal with his disciples. But the differences between Jesus and the Essenes are much more fundamental. Jesus' ministry was not directed to a pious or holy remnant, but to the sinful masses whom the Essenes sought to avoid in their desert commune. Although Jesus used apocalyptic imagery, neither his message nor his idiom was truly apocalyptic. His characteristic form of expression was the parable. The Essenes would have found his freedom with respect to the Sabbath and his life style scandalous. To them, he certainly would have seemed "a glutton and a drunkard, a friend of tax collectors and sinners" (Matt. 11:19). Most significantly, Jesus did not look to the future for the kingdom of God, but proclaimed it as a reality already beginning: " 'The time has come,' he said, and the kingdom of God is upon you. Repent, and believe the Good News' " (Mark 1:15). The thrust of Jesus' message is perhaps clearer to us today in a freer translation suggested by C. H. Dodd's interpretation of the passage: It is zero hour, the hour of decision. Change your lives! Seize this opportunity and find God's presence![15]

One could also point to parallels between Jesus and the Zealots, the rebels based in Galilee who sought the violent overthrow of the Roman occupation. Jesus, after all, was apparently crucified by the Romans on the pretext that he was what we would today call an outlaw or terrorist. Like Jesus, the Zealots proclaimed the coming of the kingdom to the masses. They were also responding to the Messianic and apocalyptic expectations of the time. So it would be unfair to describe them as simply political revolutionaries. No doubt, they too saw themselves as protectors of Israel's religious identity. But the similarity stops there. There is no evidence that Jesus was a warrior or that the coming of God which he proclaimed could be identified with the establishment of a new political order.

There is even considerable doubt about whether the historical Jesus ever accepted the title of Messiah. Although Matthew's account of Peter's confession at Caesarea Philippi suggests that Jesus accepted the designation (Matt. 16:13-16), the most that could be gathered from the versions in the other

A Man of Freedom and God

It was not that Jesus added anything to the Law or questioned the legitimate role of the authorities of his day. It is clear that Jesus was a pious Jew who followed the customs of his people and took part in their temple worship. At the same time, however, there can be no doubting he was convinced that God's reign was an immediate reality which required repentance. Repentance for him was not simply "feeling sorry." Nor did it call for some additional observance. Repentance meant a qualitative change of one's whole being (head, heart, hands and feet). God's will was not to be found through additions to the Law. Jesus took very seriously the notion that the people of Israel were God's sons and daughters called to imitate the love which God had shown them. "You, therefore, must be perfect, as your heavenly Father is perfect" (Matt. 5:48). Such divine love cannot be quantified. To describe such love it is necessary to break out of our accustomed way of seeing things. It requires a new integrity of vision and action.

Luke tells about an interchange with a lawyer which illustrates Jesus' position — both what he taught and his manner of teaching. The lawyer asks Jesus what is necessary to inherit eternal life (Luke 10:25-37). Jesus doesn't propose some new interpretation of the Torah but rather asks the lawyer what he thinks. The lawyer responds "You shall love the Lord your God with all your heart, and with all your soul, and with all your strength, and with all your mind; and your neighbor as yourself." But the man is not satisfied with Jesus' response that "You have answered right; do this, and you will live." He is looking for something more specific from Jesus and is desirous of justifying himself. "And who is my neighbor?" he asks.

His problem, no doubt, was the familiar one. How far do we have to go? Do we sacrifice the security or comfort of our families to satisfy someone else's needs? To what extent? Must we impoverish ourselves? And who really counts here? Relatives? Neighbors? Strangers? Enemies? Jesus responds by telling the story of a man from Jericho who is robbed, beaten, stripped and left half dead. As he lies in the road looking for help, a priest and

Levite pass by without stopping. A Samaritan, however, has compassion and comes to his aid. It must not be forgotten who the Samaritans were. They lived in the region that had been the northern kingdom of Israel before the Assyrian conquest in 721 B.C.E. Although the Samaritans claimed the same God and holy books as their own, the Jews of Jesus' day viewed their piety and lineage as thoroughly adulterated. The Samaritans were no friends to the Jews. They were seen as heretics who had forsaken and corrupted Israel's identity.

Jesus puts the lawyer, and those who hear his parable, into the position of the man from Jericho by asking who, from that person's perspective, is the true neighbor. The answer seems obvious. When it is I who am in desperate need even a Samaritan can be a neighbor, even a Samaritan can be good — and by an extension of that logic, even a Black, or a Jew, or a Latino, or a Greek, or a redneck, or a yuppie or whoever. When it is our own need it is obvious that the requirements of love cannot be quantified. From that vantage point, it seems clear that anyone who passes by should help and that whatever is needed should be provided. Here there is no question about how far to go or about who counts. The obligations of neighborliness cannot be measured out. They extend to as many as necessary and as far as possible.

Jesus' story, thus, reverses our usual way of looking at the question of loving one's neighbor. If we are, as Jesus recommends, to "go and do likewise," then a qualitative, rather than a quantitative, change is necessary. The difficulties behind the lawyer's question are still there. Is it right to compromise my family's security? How can I help if I impoverish myself? His parable does not directly answer these questions but through metaphor challenges the hearer to opt for a different logic. How can I or my family rest secure, while another suffers? How can I or my people possibly enjoy our blessings, while another people is impoverished? The question is especially probing, if like the priest and Levite, I could have helped. Jesus' Sermon on the Mount (Matt. 5-7) lays out the same qualitative calculus for us. His words are harsh:

You have heard that it was said to the men of old,
"You shall not kill; and whoever kills shall be liable to
judgment." But I say to you that everyone who is
angry with his brother shall be liable to judgment;
whoever insults his brother shall be liable to the
council, and whoever says, "You fool!" shall be liable
to the hell of fire. (Matt. 5:21-22)

You have heard that it was said, "You shall not commit adultery." But I say to you that every one who
looks at a woman lustfully has already committed
adultery with her in his heart. If your right eye
causes you to sin, pluck it out and throw it away; it is
better that you lose one of your members than that
your whole body be thrown into hell. And if your right
hand causes you to sin, cut it off and throw it away; it
is better that you lose one of your members than that
your whole body go into hell. (Matt. 5:27-30)

You have heard that it was said, "An eye for an eye
and a tooth for tooth." But I say to you, Do not resist
one who is evil. But if any one strikes you on the right
cheek, turn to him the other also; and if any one
would sue you and take your coat, let him take your
coat and let him have your cloak as well. (Matt. 5: 38-
40)

Dodd argues that such teachings are very much like parables. They give us concrete pictures of the extent to which we
must go, if we are to love each other as God has loved us. These
unexpected pictures, like parables or metaphors, suggest a very
different way of seeing things. The extravagance of the images
stresses the importance of "breaking out of the narrow circle
within which it is natural to confine the love of neighbor."[21] This
implies, of course, that love cannot be adequately defined. It
cannot be hedged in. Where the Law has that effect, it must give
way.

Jesus did not hesitate to live out the implications of his radical vision of God's nearness. He was not hedged in by the Law. His call for repentance was not restricted to those who were scrupulously observant. In fact his ministry seemed especially directed to those who were not observant or who in the eyes of the influential and pious did not count: the heretic, the ritually impure, the sinner, the tax collector, the widow, the orphan, the poor, the foreigner and even the enemy. Although Jesus respected the Sabbath observance, that did not deter him from healing on that day.[22] Nor did he show any reluctance about allowing his disciples to pluck ears of grain on the Sabbath. His freedom with respect to such things was clear in his response to those who questioned him. "The Sabbath was made for man, not man for the Sabbath" (Mark 2:27). Jesus also took exception to the regulations for cleanliness which had become customary among the pious, justifying this with strong words as well. "What comes out of a man is what defiles a man. For from within, out of the heart of man, come evil thoughts, fornication, theft, murder, adultery, coveting, wickedness, deceit, licentiousness, envy, slander, pride, foolishness. All these evil things come from within, and they defile a man" (Mark 7: 20-23). Hence, there can be no doubt that Jesus' response to his people's hopes would have been perceived by the authorities of the day as a threat to Israel's identity. Dodd speaks for most scholars when he concludes that "this was the secret of the fatal breach" between Jesus and these authorities.[23] The difficulty was pinpointed by the Jewish scholar Joseph Klausner.

> The Judaism of that time, however, had no other aim than to save the tiny nation, the guardian of great ideals, from sinking into the broad sea of heathen culture and enable it, slowly and gradually, to realize the moral teaching of the Prophets in civil life and in the present world of the Jewish state and nation. Hence the nation as a whole could only see in such public ideals as those of Jesus an abnormal and dangerous phantasy; the majority, who followed the Scribes and Pharisees (*The Tannaim*), the leaders of the popular party, could on no account accept Jesus'

teaching. This teaching Jesus had absorbed from the breast of Prophetic, and, to a certain extent, Pharisaic Judaism; yet it became, on the one hand, the negation of everything that had vitalized Judaism; and, on the other hand, it brought Judaism to such an extreme that it became, in a sense, non-Judaism.[24]

A Man of Integrity, and Crucified

So Jesus did not fit into the circles of his day. He does not fit into any of our categories: ancient or modern, prophetic or apocalyptic, religious or secular. He is unique. He remains, as Walter Kasper emphasizes, a mystery, and "he himself does little to illuminate this mystery. He is not interested in himself at all. He is interested in only one thing, but interested in it totally: God's coming rule in love."[25] But the reign which he brings comes as a surprise — indeed as a shock. We are not prepared to see the divine reality where Jesus mediates it. Jesus' cause puts him at odds with the authorities of his day, because our wounded humanity is at odds with God's love. It is one thing to speak of imitating God's love, it is quite another to embody it. It is one thing to think of love in general and in the abstract — as an ideal; it is quite another to really see what love demands of us in the concrete — to see what love is as a reality. It is one thing to acknowledge the prophets and saints of the past, quite another to live with one in the present — quite another even to recognize one in the present. "Jesus' violent end," in Kasper's eloquent phrase, "was written into the logic of his life."[26] "Jesus died," Jon Sobrino says in a similar vein, "because he chose to bear faithful witness to God right to the end in a situation where people really wanted a very different type of God. Their condemnation of Jesus indicates that they clearly saw the option he was posing to them. They would have to choose between the God of their religion and the God of Jesus, between the temple and human beings, between the security provided by their own good works and the insecurity of God's gratuitous coming in grace."[27]

That situation was by no means unique to Jesus' contem-

poraries. Christians make it too easy for themselves if they
simplistically blame Jesus' death on the Jews. It is the human
condition to want a God who will satisfy our hungers: a magnifi-
cent and compelling God; a powerful God who will solve our
problems and give us security; a superstar with whom we can
identify and vicariously fulfill our fantasies; a miraculous God,
the *Deus ex machina* of literature and theater who magically
saves us and our world. Jesus could have proclaimed such a God.
Matthew and Luke in their accounts of Jesus' struggle with the
devil in the desert suggest that this temptation was there at the
beginning of his career (Matt. 4:1-11; Luke 4:1-13). What if he
had turned stones into bread? Couldn't he have won the people
of Israel to his Father by proving that this God would satisfy
their needs? How could they have resisted a God who gave them,
as the slang goes, all the "bread" they needed? What if Jesus had
gone along with the zealots' strategy? Wouldn't seizing the
power of the kingdom have been a surer way to bring the people
of Israel under his Father's rule? How could they have resisted
a God who gave them peace, justice and security? How could
they have rejected a God who was in control? What if Jesus had
done something like jumping from the top of the temple tower?
What if he had won converts with such miraculous and mysterious feats, instead of fleeing from those who sought signs and
wonders?[28] Wouldn't his ministry have been more compelling?
Wouldn't Christianity today be much more credible if the power
of miracle were readily at hand to justify the Church's authority
and teaching?

Indeed, as Dostoevski suggests in his story of the Grand Inquisitor, Jesus could be harshly rebuked for resisting these possibilities.[29] To Dostoevski's imaginary representative of religious fanaticism, the devil's three questions to Christ were not
temptations but rather brilliant revelations of the the three
powers which alone could have truly conquered the human
spirit for God and forever held it captive, namely, the powers of
miracle, authority and mystery. This defender of Christianity
condemns its founder for rejecting the very tools required to ac-
complish his mission. Dostoevski's tale is not really that far off

the issue actually addressed in the temptation story of the gospels. The point is not a moral one — that Jesus resisted temptation — but rather has to do with the nature of God's kingdom
and with Jesus' relation to it. Jesus does not take the easy routes
which tempt one to think that our wounded humanity can be
healed simply by the force of some external miracle, authority
or wonder. The comportment of his whole life points in a different direction. Over against a God of power, Jesus proclaims a
God of love. Jesus' Father is a God who calls us in our freedom to
love — to become lovers as God is a lover. Such love does not
seduce, control, coerce or trick. And such love is costly. It calls
for a radical transformation of our wounded humanity. It calls
for a qualitative reversal in the way we look at things and go
about doing things. It calls for an integrity of the head, heart,
hands and feet like that preached and lived by Jesus. Inevitably
such love puts one at odds with our wounded humanity — at
odds with its powers, authorities and magic, at odds with ourselves and our world. Jesus' fidelity to his Father's rule of love
meant resisting such temptations from the beginning of his
ministry to its end. Luke even comments, Sobrino thinks to emphasize this point, that "when the devil had finished all the
tempting he left him to await another opportunity" (Luke
4:13).[30]

So despite Jesus' integrity as a man of freedom and as a
man of God, he is not "the man," the Son of Man, the Messiah or
the Son of God his contemporaries wanted to see. Today most
scholars would agree that Reimarus may have been correct in
holding that Jesus did not claim any of those titles as Christians
later understood them. But at the same time, Jesus very clearly
provoked questions about his identity through what he said and
did. A much more apt designation, it turned out, was the image
in Isaiah of a "suffering servant" who is pictured as one called to
bear witness to God through a life of humiliation, suffering and
death.

> Yet ours were the sufferings he bore,
> ours the sorrows he carried.
> But we, we thought of him as someone punished,

struck by God, and brought low.
Yet he was pierced through for our faults,
crushed for our sins.
On him lies a punishment that brings us peace,
and through his wounds we are healed.

. . . .

By force and by law he was taken;
would anyone plead his cause?
Yes, he was torn away from the land of the living;
for our faults struck down in death.
They gave him a grave with the wicked,
a tomb with the rich,
though he had done no wrong
and there had been no perjury in his mouth.
    (Isaiah 53:4-9)

At one point, Matthew (12:17-21) explictly quotes one of Isaiah's (42:1-4) references to this figure as a description of Jesus. Dodd speculates that this interpretation may indeed go back to Jesus himself. It is quite possible that he saw himself as a representative of the people of Israel called through his trials to establish a new and definitve solidarity between God and themselves.[31] In any case, whether it can be proved historically that Jesus saw this explicitly at the time is not absolutely crucial. In the end, his fidelity to his conception of God's rule did bring him to his death on the cross. Even his death was an expression of his fidelity to this divine call and of his radical, personal integrity — symbolized so appropriately by the head (crowned with thorns), the heart (pierced by a lance), and the hands and feet (nailed to the cross).

    It is not possible here to sort out all the exegetical and historical questions about Jesus' trial, the events which led up to it or how exactly he met his death. Did he forsee what was coming as clearly as the gospels suggest? What were the precise charges against him and by whom were they raised? How did he respond? Can we be historically certain of his final words or are these the fruit of later interpretation? Such questions are certainly of great importance for defining the Christian circle of understanding. For the purpose of breaking into that circle, however, it must suffice to recognize and emphasize the crucial and central role that Jesus' death on the cross has in that understanding. Jesus' death was an expression of his life. It was a consequence of the rule of love which he proclaimed and which Christians believe he inaugurated. It is, therefore, part and parcel of his statement to humanity. "He wanted," Leonardo Boff contends, "to realize the absolute meaning of this world before God, in spite of hate, incomprehension, betrayal, and condemnation to death. For Jesus, evil does not exist in order to be comprehended, but to be taken over and conquered by love."[32] In the end, then, God's reality for Jesus, and for those who follow him, is mediated through the cross. God's love is a call to love — a call to integrity in the face of human woundedness. How and to what extent such integrity is possible for us, is a question that must be left for later. The point to be made now is the Christian conviction that Jesus' comportment and death reveal a new possibility for human existence. Jesus mediates God where we would least expect to find the divine.

The Man Whom God Raised from the Dead

The significance which Christians see in Jesus' death cannot be understood apart from the event which believers call the resurrection. After all, many good and innocent people have died courageously at the hands of human betrayal and malice. In fact, if the atrocities of even our own century are given the weight they deserve, such horrible inhumanity would appear to be the rule rather than the exception. Christians are convinced, however, that Jesus' death was of a radically different and unique nature. It was a death into new life, into resurrected life.

The meaning and import of this notion is not self-evident today, or at least not as self-evident as those of us within the circle of faith sometimes assume. Belief in the resurrection is not the same as belief in the notion we inherit from Greek culture about the survival of an immortal soul after death. Nor is the kind of resurrection about which the New Testament speaks simply a revitalization or resuscitation of the body. It is important to appreciate how different the mental framework of our world is from the conceptual world of Jesus and his contemporaries. Many of us are in a situation analogous to the Athenians who listened respectfully to Paul's identification of his God with their "unknown god" but who could not take seriously the idea of Jesus' resurrection (Acts 17:32) or to the Roman governor Festus who found such talk incomprehensible and quite mad (Acts 26:24). There can be no question of our reconstructing that ancient Jewish world view to which Paul appealed or of actually making it our own. Sloyan cautions that "we can save ourselves a lot of headaches, though, if we realize how much preparedness there was in those times for the notion of being raised from the dead."[33] Among the Jews it was, we have seen, a time of eschatological fervor. By Jesus' day, resurrection was above all a way of articulating the hope for a final conclusion to history which would establish a definitive and eternal solidarity between God and God's people.

Describing or picturing such an eschatological outcome is not as easy as hoping for it or proclaiming it. God is not a reality who can be seen or objectified. Rather, the images and events upon which believers call, to speak of the divine, are derived from the dynamism of our minds, wills and loves towards God's unobjectifiable fullness and depth of be-ing. The divine reality can only be grasped or described indirectly and analogously by appealing to this movement of our spirits, just as our freedom and what we call the "self" (which cannot be seen or adequately objectified) are also only known reflexively and indirectly through our own introspection. It follows that resurrection (the fulfillment of our dynamism towards God) is an event quite beyond description. We can point to our anticipation and yearning for something more complete and more definitive than we are able to achieve by ourselves and on this side of our deaths. We can call attention to the inability of any particular decision in itself to exhaust or even adequately express ourselves and our freedom, or to capture the divine mystery at the root of these. We can observe that our fleeting gestures of love by themselves cannot exhaust love's reach — cannot reach one who loves us absolutely or whom we can love absolutely. We can thus speak indirectly about the fulfillment of these, about a new and uncorrupted humanity, about a healed humanity. But speaking of resurrection in such ways does not directly describe or picture it. Our talk always remains a kind of pointing or anticipation.

It is no wonder, then, that the testimony to Jesus' resurrection is less detailed and precise than the historian in us would like. Resurrection, although an event of Jesus' history, is not historical in the usual sense. One who has been raised by God is no longer caught up in our wounded and finite history. There are ways to speak of such an event and to proclaim it, but not for visualizing it. As a matter of fact, the earliest strata of the Christian tradition (e.g., 1 Cor. 15:3-5) provide very little detail. They announce that Jesus had been crucified, that God had raised him from the dead, that Jesus had appeared to many, and that he had sent his disciples to preach the message of salvation to the world. The historical evidence is very strong that this was the unanimous core of the Christian faith from the very beginning. This center or core, however, was a floating one which can never be precisely tied down, as Kasper put it. "The various statements are, as it were, always on the move to try to put this central point into words,"[34] but the actual center, the resurrection, was not directly reported or described, and as we have seen could not have been — at least not adequately.

Subsequent layers of the tradition do get more specific, but that is where the resurrection accounts become most fluid. Their many discrepancies in detail make things more difficult for the believer, as Reimarus' critique showed. These difficulties cannot be harmonized or explained away. The gospel stories so completely blend theological interpretation, historical detail and legend that it is no longer possible to sort them out. It would seem, for example, that divergences about the places where Jesus appeared are, in large measure, expressions of the particular evangelist's theological perspective. Matthew's text, for instance, about Jesus' appearance to the disciples on the mountain in Galilee (Matt. 28:16-20) is a theological and literary counterpoint to the gospel's Sermon on the Mount (Matt. 5-7). Luke's account of Jesus' appearance in Jerusalem completes his gospel's focus on the Holy City as the destination of Jesus' journey and as the origin of the Church's mission.

Observations such as these have led to a scholarly consensus that the Easter stories are not verbatim records of eyewitness reports. The Christian faith was and is not based on these accounts as such. Rather these stories are recollections, proclamations and interpretations of testimonies and events which are no longer directly available to us. This is the situation even though the stories of the empty tomb and of Jesus' appearances in all likelihood are based on very ancient traditions. In themselves, these accounts simply do not provide the sort of information which someone like Reimarus would need to prove historically that the story of the resurrection is a fabrication, or which the believer would need to prove historically that the resurrection is a fact. Providing details for that sort of historical proof was not the evangelists' purpose. And that, of course, is the difficulty with critiques like Reimarus' which assume that the Eastter stories are historical in the ordinary sense of the term.

But this does not mean that Jesus' resurrection or its recollection and proclamation is just a story or just a matter of personal and subjective faith. Although the resurrection is not an event directly accessible to the historian, there can be no doubt that the evangelists intended to tell of events which they took to be real, objective and historical. On the one hand, they emphasize that something happened to the disciples. They do not speak of visions or dreams, although there certainly was considerable precedent for doing so in apocalypticism. In fact, the Gospel of St. Peter (written around 150 C.E.) which did try to describe Jesus' resurrection was rejected by the Christian community. It is also evident that the evangelists were saying that something happened to Jesus. His tomb was empty. It was he himself whom the disciples recognized. His presence was real and bodily. He talks with the disciples, he eats and in John's version is touched. His presence is so real, Boff comments, "that he can be confused with a traveler, a gardener, and a fisherman."[35]

But on the other hand, it is also clear that in proclaiming Jesus' resurrection the evangelists are confessing God's final and eschatological victory, not simply the resuscitation of Jesus' body. The gospels all indicate that Jesus' disciples recognized him as radically different. He appeared and disappeared apparently quite free of the spatial limitations we ordinarily associate with bodiliness (Luke 24:31; John 20:19,26). It was not always clear initially that it was really him (Luke 24:16; John 20:14; 21:4). Indeed, at first, some doubted that it was him (Matt. 28:17; Luke 24:41). Mark's gospel says quite explicitly that Jesus "appeared in another form" (Mark 16:12), and Paul writing sometime earlier speaks of Christ's body as glorified and radically transformed (1 Cor. 15). All see this event as the fulfillment of eschatological promise. In proclaiming that God raised Jesus from the dead on the third day (traditionally the day of deliverance)[36] and that Jesus sits at the right hand of the Father, the Christian Scriptures affirm that Jesus was what he purported to be: a man who in his very humanity confronted his contemporaries with God, and who in so doing inaugurated humanity's definitive and ultimate encounter with God — an encounter which is mediated and comes to completion in our loving response to the needs of our neighbor.

This gets us to the center of the Christian circle of understanding, but it does not in itself legitimate that circle. Jesus' life, death and resurrection are the basis of the believer's faith, but history no more provides an independent and neutral access to this basis than philosophy. History as such cannot demonstrate that God meets us in this man, Jesus of Nazareth. There is no foundation which can eliminate the risk of faith or the need for courage to go beyond what the evidence "proves" in the narrow sense — no more than you can ever prove your love for another or prove another's fidelity to you. What deed, word or observation can prove love? What deed, word or observation is not open to suspicion? Any you might cite can always be interpreted either way. Love requires a risk and courage, a movement of the heart, that goes beyond such headwork. In most cases the reasonableness of our trust in another, or of their trust in us, is so obvious that we take it for granted, but risk it is, nevertheless. Love that is too sure of itself may indeed mask naiveté, while trust in another's fidelity despite evidence to the contrary may prove, rather than naive, profoundly well-founded.

Other readings of the confession that God raised Jesus from the dead are of course possible. Fraud cannot be ruled out absolutely, even though it seems historically quite unlikely. Self-delusion or hallucination are not impossible, although it is clear that the earliest testimony denies this. It could be argued that resurrection is just a myth or religious metaphor to which the early Church appealed to explain and justify its faith that the eschaton had begun in Jesus. But then we have to face the question, from whence did that faith in Jesus come? How do we explain the dramatic changes, the new conviction and the remarkable courage that came over those original disciples who, when Jesus was seized and crucified, did not have enough faith to stand by him? The evidence all seems to point towards Jesus' life, death and resurrection giving rise to their faith and the Church, rather than their faith or the Church giving rise to the confession of his resurrection.

These, at least, are the reasons which argue for the reliability of the Christian account of Jesus of Nazareth as the man in whom God meets humanity. If we are to break into the heart of the Christian circle of understanding, however, it is not enough to establish the reasonableness of such a conclusion. Nor is it enough to establish that history, while admitting the possibility of other and even opposed alternatives, cannot "prove" more conclusively any of those interpretations. At issue is the question, Just how does God meet humanity in Jesus? It is one thing to say that Jesus is a man of freedom and a man of God. It is quite another to say that he is human to the utmost and that he is divine. It is one thing to say that Jesus suffered because of his fidelity to the coming of God's rule of love, it is another thing to say that Jesus saves humanity from its woundedness. Furthermore, the idea that God is mediated at one unique time and place in a particular individual seems, to say the least, presumptuous and arrogant. These are just the sort of claims which make Christianity so problematic for those outside its circle, and if we are to be perfectly honest, perhaps for many inside as well. If the Christian faith finds its center and basis in the acknowledgment of Jesus as God's Word become flesh, then it is crucial to show that this notion makes sense and is credible. It is to this question that we must now turn our attention.

Notes

1. Juan Luis Segundo, *The Historical Jesus of the Synoptics*, trans. John Drury, Vol. II of *Jesus of Nazareth Yesterday and Today* (Maryknoll, New York: Orbis Books, 1985), p. 45.

2. A great number of such studies have been published in recent years. For very suggestive and helpful surveys see Richard P. McBrien, "The Christ of Twentieth-Century Theology," in his *Catholicism*, Study Edition (Minneapolis, MN: Winston Press, Inc., 1981), pp.469-512; Francis Schüssler Fiorenza, "Christology After Vatican II," *The Ecumenist*, 18 (September-October 1980) 81-89; and Gerald O'Collins, *What Are They Saying About Jesus* (New York: Paulist Press, 1977).

3. Of necessity most studies of Jesus include a chapter which summarizes and characterizes these general lines. Readers looking for a general orientation will probably find quite helpful Raymond Brown's "'Who Do Men Say that I Am?' — Modern Scholarship on Gospel Christology," *Horizons* 1 (Fall 1974) 35-50; and McBrien, pp. 391-437.

4. Albert Schweitzer, *The Quest for the Historical Jesus: A Critical Study of Its Progress from Reimarus to Wrede*, trans. W. Montgomery (New York: The Macmillan Company, 1961).

5. An overview of this development is provided by Stephen Neill, *The Interpretation of the New Testament, 1861-1961* (London: Oxford University Press, 1964); Raymond Brown's essay cited in note 3 provides a helpful characterization of various scholarly and non-scholarly attitudes towards this methodology.

6. See Raymond Brown, *Biblical Exegesis and Church Doctrine* (New York: Paulist Press, 1985), for an analysis of Roman Catholicism's acceptance of historical-critical exegesis, and for his critique of both liberal and conservative misunderstandings of contemporary biblical methodology.

7. For an elaboration of this point see in particular James P. Mackey, *Jesus the Man and the Myth: A Contemporary Christology* (New York: Paulist Press, 1979), p. 50.

8. Günther Bornkamm, *Jesus of Nazareth*, trans. Irene and Fraser McLuskey with James M. Robinson (New York: Harper & Row,1960), p. 17.

9. C. H. Dodd, *The Founder of Christianity* (New York: The Macmillan Company, 1970), p. 21.

10. D. S. Russell, *The Method & Message of Jewish Apocalyptic: 200 BC - AD 100* (Philadelphia: Westminster Press, 1964), p. 15.

11. Russell, p. 17.

12. Russell, p. 327.

13. Russell, p. 369.

14. Russell, p. 376.

15. Dodd, pp. 56-59.

16. Bornkamm, p. 174.

17. Gerard S. Sloyan, *Jesus in Focus: A Life in Its Setting* (Mystic, Connecticut: Twenty-Third Publications, 1984), p. 23.

18. Bornkamm, p. 57.

19. Leonardo Boff, *Jesus Christ Liberator: A Critical Christology for Our Time*, trans. Patrick Hughes (Maryknoll, New York: Orbis Books, 1978), p. 96.

20. Bornkamm, p. 19.

21. Dodd, p. 66.

22. See Mark 3:1-6 (Matt. 12:9-14, Luke 6:6-11), Luke 13:10-17, Luke 14:1-7 and John 5:1.

23. Dodd, p. 77.

24. Joseph Klausner, *Jesus of Nazareth* (English translation, 1925), p. 376; quoted in Dodd. pp. 77-78.

25. Walter Kasper, *Jesus the Christ*, trans. V. Green (New York: Paulist Press, 1976), p. 70.

26. Kasper, p. 76.

27. Jon Sobrino, S.J.,, *Christology at the Crossroads: A Latin American Approach*, trans. John Drury (Maryknoll, New York: Orbis Books, 1978), p. 209.

28. See Matt. 12:38-42 and Mark 8:11-13.

29. From Chapter V in Book V of Fyodor Dostoevski's *The Brothers Karamazov*, written in 1880 and reprinted as *The Grand Inquisitor on the Nature of Man*, trans. Constance Garnett (Indianapolis: Bobbs-Merrill Educational Publishing, 1980).

30. Sobrino, p. 98.

31. See Dodd, pp. 105-16.

32. Boff, p. 119.

33. Sloyan, p. 146.

34. Kasper, p. 129.

35. Boff, p. 127.

36. See Bruce Vawter, "The Third Day," in *This Man Jesus: An Essay Toward A New Testament Christology* (Garden City, New York: Doubleday & Company, Inc., 1973), pp. 39-43.

12. The Humanity of God

In confessing Jesus as Risen Lord the early church proclaimed that God really meets humanity in this man from Nazareth — that in his life, death and resurrection God's presence is no longer a distant hope of the future, but in fact has become a definitive reality of the present. This confession implied a unique relationship between Jesus and the one whom he called Father. Jesus was not just another prophet who announced God's approach. The Risen Christ was recognized by believers as the very fleshing-out of God. Here, in Jesus the Christ, was the One who had been active all along in Israel's history. Here was the concrete embodiment of the Wisdom or Logos which had been at work in creation since the beginning — God's own Wisdom, God's own Logos, God's own Incarnation.

But this posed two difficult problems for the early Church. The first arose from its roots in Judaism. For the Jew, there was only one true God, and that God was above all other realities. How could God be transcendent and one, and yet also be so closely identified with the man Jesus? How could Christians legitimately speak, as they had begun to, of God the Father *and* God the Son, or of God the Creator *and* a Logos or Word of God who was with God from the beginning? Doesn't such language deny God's unity and undermine God's transcendence? The second difficulty arose from the Hellenistic culture in which the early Church emerged. For the Greek philosophical mind, God was eternal, immutable and impassible. How could Jesus, a man born of a woman, someone who obviously was finite, underwent change, suffered and died on a cross, be identified with the transcendent divinity? Is it not a contradiction in terms to speak

151

of a man who is divine or, on the other hand, of God becoming human?

Obviously, the resolution of these questions was crucial to the community's identity as the people who confessed God's eschatologically definitive presence in the Risen Jesus. But it was not easy within the circles of understanding inherited from Judaism and Hellenism to work out a formulation of this faith which was universally appealing and which could prevent misunderstandings and perversions. Controversy and false starts were inevitable as the Church emerged in distinct and diverse centers dispersed throughout the ancient world. Official terminology was not finally hammered out until the definitions of the councils at Nicaea (325) and Chalcedon (451). Nicaea taught that Christ is fully God (*homoousios* with the Father; that is to say, of one being with the Father, or of the same nature as the Father) and fully human (*homoousios* with our humanity; that is to say, of one *being* with us, or of the same nature as us). Chalcedon clarified further that Christ's two complete natures, divine and human, are united in one person. In this personal (or *hypostatic*) union, the human and divine natures are unmixed and unchanged, but also undivided and unseparated. With such terminology, the Church aimed to spell out the implications of its faith in Jesus and to rule out the most egregious misunderstandings and perversions of it. The identity between the man Jesus and God, they claimed, is radical and unique. Jesus is God's Word made flesh: one person, one reality, who as such is both human and divine.

These clarifications, however, present their own difficulties. For many of those outside the Christian circle, and even for many within, such talk makes the Christian faith more not less opaque. How, these people ask, can one reality (or person) have two radically different natures? How can one reality at the same time be two "things" so different as God and man? How can a man be identified with God and yet still be truly and genuinely human? How can God be identified with a particular man without idolatry? without turning something finite into a god? How can God's saving presence be identified concretely with this one man and his particular history without denying God's saving presence to those people and faiths that do not acknowledge Jesus as the Christ? Isn't this presumptuous? Doesn't this contradict the claim that God's "saving designs extend to all," which Catholic Christians, at least, acknowledge as an implication of the Scriptures?[1]

The story of the Church's responses to such questions coincides with the entire history of Christian theology. As important as that history is to understanding the contours of the Christian circle today, it is not possible here to retrace theology's long and complex course. For our purposes, a more contemporary point of entry must do. One line of inquiry is suggested by Peter Schineller's observation, discussed in Chapter 10, that within Christianity today there is a spectrum of widely divergent views about the relationship between Jesus, God and humanity. Do such disagreements today within the circle of belief disclose a fundamental lack of coherence, inherent from the beginning, in the claim of radical unity between Jesus and God? What kind of unity or identity is at issue here? What exactly do Christians mean when they affirm that Jesus *is* God's Word made flesh? How *is* he God's Son? In what senses *is* he divine and in what senses *is* he human?

Clearly the verb "is," in such statements, does not imply the same sort of total identity that is asserted when I say that Erin *is* my daughter, or that the previous chapter *is* central, or that we *are* human. God is not a creature or literally a biological father of the man Jesus or of anyone else. Jesus is not literally a linguistic cipher, utterance or word. So "is" does not have the same meaning or force in each of these examples. Its meaning is not univocal. Its use and force vary. Different sorts of identity are being asserted. But on the other hand, if Christians are not simply equivocating, the identity between Jesus and God must be in some way real, genuine and profoundly intimate. Furthermore, if the believers' affirmations are coherent, then it ought to be possible to determine what sort of identity is actually being affirmed when they claim that Jesus *is* God's Word made flesh, or that Jesus *is* divine and human. At the very least, it would seem, there must be some sort of specifiable analogy with other kinds of identity claims.

Variations in the way Christians understand this unity between Jesus and God can thus be described as embodying different models of identity, just as Schineller classifies different models for characterizing how Jesus mediates God. The scope of the models which I will elaborate, however, is much more restricted than his. Schineller attempts to describe the entire spectrum of views with models that are both exhaustive and mutually exclusive. I have in mind a narrower range of positions which correspond, more or less, to his constitutive and normative mediator models. The positions which I will describe can be understood as mutually exclusive, but I will argue that they need not be, and in fact should not be. Moreover, my aim, unlike Schineller's, is constructive rather than descriptive. The objective is to reach a model for understanding the identity between Jesus and God which will advance our effort to break into the Christian circle. Each successive model will be seen as a further step towards a more adequate interpretation. Of course this also means that the initial models, despite valuable insights, are in my view ultimately inadequate for developing a credible Christian theology of the head, heart, hands and feet.

Two additional reservations should be kept in mind. I believe that each of the proposed models is actually held by a fair number of Christians, at least implicitly, but no attempt will be made here to justify this hunch through sociological analysis. Second, I will examine concrete instances of each model in current theological writing, but I am not claiming that these examples provide a complete and adequate basis for evaluating or even for interpreting the Christologies of the authors cited. Although models can be very helpful for identifying the thrust of divergent theological positions (and that is my aim), this kind of typology is not so well suited for representing all the subtleties of theological discussion or all the nuances of particular theologies.

I am taking it for granted that the Christian tradition affirms both Jesus' humanity and his divinity, and that it believes both that Jesus is necessary for salvation and at the same time that salvation is a real possibility for non-Christians. The rationale for this position will be elaborated in the course of the discussion. In any case, the question I am posing is whether it is possible to come up with a model for understanding the identity between Jesus and God which does not deny Jesus' humanity or the availability of God's saving presence for all people of good will, but that on the other hand does not deny Jesus' divinity or necessity for salvation. Four models will be examined. The range of emphasis extends from the first, which posits a weak identity and so is in danger of compromising Jesus' divinity and necessity for salvation, to the fourth, which posits as strong an identity as possible without compromising Jesus' humanity and the availability of God's saving presence to all people.

Human Paradigm

There are, as I have suggested, many kinds of identity — many ways in which it can be said that a reality *is* "this" or "that." Sometimes the identity can best be described as "paradigmatic." If we asks for example, "What *is* H_2O?" it is perfectly correct and not in the least misleading to answer H_2O *is* water. But it is also quite obviously true that H_2O *is not* water. H_2O is a formula. It is a paradigm or model. It is something that stands for or represents water. It *is not* actually the stuff we drink or with which we splash ourselves. Nevertheless, there is a quite genuine identity between water and H_2O. True, the mathematical model and the reality of water are not strictly speaking the same "being" or thing — that is to say, they are not *ontologically* identical; there is no real identity of their *being*. The paradigmatic identity between water and the formula H_2O, however, is every bit as real as the identity between the reality "water" and any other ciphers or words (whether water, *Wasser*, *eau* or *aqua*) we might use to designate the stuff. We really can come to know things through such scientific models. To know that something is H_2O, and really understand this, can enable us not only to recognize the reality but also to learn new things about its chemistry, properties and "*being*" which we could never discover from the word "water" or perhaps even from splashing around with water itself. In fact, theoretical models like H_2O can enable us to discover realities of which we were previously quite unaware. The recognition of such paradigmatic identities can even enable us to create quite new chemicals and organisms. Therefore, to observe that the identity between H_2O and water is paradigmatic rather than ontological is not to deny that there is an identity or to belittle it.

It is possible to think of the identity between Jesus and God along these lines. Jesus' humanity can be conceived as a paradigm of the divine. It can be thought of as model which represents, stands for, exemplifies or symbolizes the reality of God, but which as a model is nevertheless also distinct from God. It can also be argued that there is an affinity between this conception and very traditional notions of Jesus as divine revealer, teacher and prophet. So understood, Jesus can be described as one who reveals God so truly and fully that to know Jesus is to know God. Or Jesus can be imagined as the definitive teacher or prophet whose mind, heart and spirit are so close to God's, that to know Jesus' mind, heart or spirit is to know God's. In these conceptions the identity between Jesus and God is genuine. The unity is most intimate. At the same time, Jesus is not simply equated with God. Consequently, this model compromises neither Jesus' humanity nor the possibility that God's saving presence is also mediated elsewhere.

Imagining the unity between Jesus and God in this way, as paradigmatic, suggests a way to explain how he both *is* and *is not* divine, *is* and *is not* God's Word, or *is* and *is not* God's Son. In essence, the identity between the human and the divine is seen in "functional" rather than "ontological" terms. Jesus' humanity *re-presents* or *discloses* the divine. So we can point to Jesus and say "Here is God," but still we are pointing to someone distinct from God. It cannot be denied, however, that this move relativizes Jesus' identity with God, and so his uniqueness and his necessity for salvation. Although interpreting the divine-human unity in Jesus as essentially exemplary, disclosive and moral enables us to take Jesus' humanity seriously and to affirm God's saving presence to all people of good will, this gain is purchased at considerable expense. It does not necessarily deny the identity of Jesus and God, but it does deny the ontological character of the identity: Jesus' *"being"* and God's are not the same. Moreover, such a paradigmatic Christology undermines the necessity of Jesus and the Church for salvation. It clearly says something different than Scripture and dogma.

James Burtchaell's *Philemon's Problem* illustrates this difficulty.[2] Burtchaell's position is summed up in his statement: "'Jesus saves'. But so do many others, all by the enablement of the same Father."[3] For Burtchaell, Jesus, as model or revealer "can in no exclusive or particular way be our Savior."[4] "The work of salvation," Burtchaell contends, "is universal; the work of revelation is historically limited. Furthermore, it is not necessary. With or without the incarnation the Father's work would inexorably continue. Jesus' coming is not a necessity: it is a luxury, a grace, and abundance of bounty."[5] This also means, of course, that it is time for Christians to "disavow" the teaching that there is no salvation outside the Church.[6]

I would not want to deny that Jesus' coming is a gift or that God is gracious. Nor do I want to disparage Burtchaell's at times most eloquent articulation of those themes. But is it necessary to dispose in this way of the Christian tradition's testimony to Jesus' ontological unity with the Father, Jesus' necessity for salvation or the necessity of the Church for salvation? Doesn't so radical a revision of Christianity compromise its essential identity? Does credibility require that we affirm a paradigmatic unity to the exclusion of an ontological unity? By no means am I denying the need for Christians to go beyond the formulations of the past to reach clearer and more credible insights into their circle of understanding. What I am questioning is whether such moves require the adoption of a paradigmatic Christology over against a Christology which would affirm that the identity between Jesus and the Father also has an ontological character

Parable of God

In the previous chapters I have contended that the ultimate referent of religious discourse is in the most profound sense of the term a "mystery." Our concepts can never grasp God directly. We must resort to more indirect and analogous forms of speech like Rahner's metaphors "horizon," "asymptotic goal" and "*being* itself," or Tillich's "Ground of Being" and "Ultimate Concern." Sallie McFague's *Metaphorical Theology* and Jerry Gill's *On Knowing God* argue that metaphor is in fact the primary clue for understanding the significance of God-talk in general and of Christological language in particular.[7] More specifically, McFague contends that parable, which is in effect a form of extended metaphor, provides the key needed to elaborate an adequate Christological model for interpreting the identity between the human and divine in Jesus.

Metaphor is a figure of speech in which one thing is likened to another, different thing by being spoken of as if it were that other. The meaning of one word or image is thus brought into creative tension with another. If the metaphor "works," this odd juxtaposition results in unexpected and disclosive meaning which neither image or word would have had by itself. Take, for example, the comment of an officer who dismisses the death of one of his soldiers in an insignificant skirmish: "Look men, war is a game!" No doubt his platoon would not miss the point. He is not simply saying that war is *like* a game. The identity he is asserting between war and game is much stronger than that. His bit of advice would be an "eye-opener" for those serving under him. It would no doubt shed an entirely new light on the value their lives play in his strategy. This would be true even though the officer is speaking metaphorically. Were he to respond to some poor private's shocked look of disbelief by saying, "Son, I was just using a metaphor!" we can be sure this would offer little consolation.

This element of surprise, shock or logical oddness in the metaphor's juxtaposition of ideas or images is crucial. The metaphor is, in words of the philosopher Paul Ricoeur, an "impertinent prediction."[8] It works, Gill says, by crossing "established categories in a startling and fruitful manner."[9] McFague recalls Nelson Goodman's colorful and ironically metaphorical definitions. "Metaphor, it seems, is a matter of teaching an old word new tricks — of applying an old label in a new way."[10] In

another place, he says "a metaphor might be regarded . . . as
a happy and revitalizing, even if bigamous, second marriage."[11]
If these definitions are humorous, it is because most humor is
metaphorical. Humor, McFague, observes "is the recognition of
a *very* unlikely similarity among dissimilars and we laugh because we are surprised to discover that such unlikes are indeed
alike in at least one respect. A great many jokes take the form,
'How is a —— like a ——?' "[12]

So, in metaphor an identity *is* and *is not* asserted. Through
this kind of logically odd juxtaposition "good metaphors shock,
they bring unlikes together, they upset conventions, they involve tension, and they are implicitly revolutionary."[13] Both the
identity and the non-identity are crucial. If the lack of identity
— the "is not" — is lost, then the two words or images simply
become synonyms. Our language offers abundant examples of
such words, "dead metaphors" which no longer call to mind, at
least very vividly, the tension of the original juxtaposition.
Think for example of words like "star" for a luminary in one profession or another, or "bottom line" for one's conclusion or presuppositions, or similar examples through which one could
"make this point." On the other hand, insofar as the tension of
the metaphor is kept alive, it has an ability to upset our usual
way of looking at things and has a potential for actually changing perspectives. Think how the private would react and
perhaps even change after hearing his commanding officer
suggest that "war is a game."

Since it is precisely the specific and unique juxtaposition of
images or words which gives the metaphor its sense, at least
profound metaphors cannot be replaced or paraphrased without
a significant loss or change of meaning. Moreover, metaphors, it
seems, often capture notions which could not be expressed in
more direct speech. We resort to phrases like "broke his spirit"
or "made her day" or "feeling blue," for example, when speaking
of the personal dimension of life, because the self, as we saw in
Chapter 8, is not some "thing" that can be directly observed or
grasped in our concepts and words. But this also implies that
metaphors actually have a primacy over other ways of speaking,

at least for realities like the self and God. Gill and McFague argue that metaphor's primacy is even more basic. "It is not the case," Gill puts it, "that we first develop a set of precise notions and then cast about for a creative metaphor in which to express them. Rather, both our everyday and our specialized insights are frequently initially expressed in metaphors and/or models which later may or may not be refined and precised, depending on our needs."[14] McFague sees this illustrated by the "stages" which Colin Turbayne attributes to the normal "life" of a metaphor.

> Initially, when newly coined, it seems inappropriate or unconventional; the response is often rejection. At a second stage, when it is a living metaphor, it has dual meaning — the literal and metaphorical — and is insightful. Finally, the metaphor becomes commonplace, either dead and/or literalized. At this stage, says Turbayne, we are no longer like the Wizard of Oz who knew green glasses made Oz green, but, like all the other inhabitants of Oz, we believe that Oz is green.[15]

McFague contends that Jesus' parables like "all good metaphors shock, they bring unlikes together, they upset conventions, they involve tension, and . . . in so doing have revolutionary potential."[16] Moreover Jesus' relationship to God was so evocative and transformative that he himself can properly be regarded as a parable of God. McFague believes that a parabolic Christology has the distinct advantage of being able to emphasize the centrality of Jesus' life and work as essential for understanding our relation to God without the disadvantage of too easily and misleadingly identifying Jesus and God. She objects that identification of Jesus and God in more direct ways is not credible in our secular world. People no longer experience or view the everyday world as symbolic of God or imbued with God's presence. Furthermore, identifying Jesus and God more directly, too easily leads to idolatry — to a kind of Jesusolatry. Finally, a too literal identification of God and the "man" Jesus too easily slips into patriarchal and hierarchical images of the divine, which at worst alienate and at best are irrelevant to the experience of most women and minorities.

McFague insists that her position is faithful to the Christian tradition.

> First, given our interpretation of parable as extended metaphor and metaphor as unsubstitutable, Jesus' work is *essential* for our understanding of God. A parabolic christology is not a weak or lightweight christology which sees Jesus merely as a heuristic fiction, helpful but dispensable. A metaphor is not an ornament or illustration, but says what cannot be said any other way; likewise, Jesus as parable of God provides us with a grid or screen for understanding God's way with us which cannot be discarded after we have translated it into concepts.[17]

But on the other hand, she continues, "metaphorical statements *are never identity statements*."[18] Thus a parabolic Christology is open to the possibility of revelation outside Christianity. "If Jesus is understood as *a* parable of God, one which Christians claim is a true one, then other religions can make the claim that they also contain metaphorical expressions of divine reality."[19]

McFague admits that "a parabolic christology relativizes Jesus' particularity while universalizing the God of whom Jesus is a metaphor."[20] She is convinced that feminist and Protestant sensibilities demand a self-consciously iconoclastic, transformative and open-ended theology as opposed to the too-easy identification of the divine and human in the sacramental theology of traditional Christianity. She readily grants that a parabolic Christology relativizes the doctrine of the incarnation, the identity of Jesus and God, the authority of Scripture and so by implication much of the substance of Christian faith.

Is it really possible to pull off this move without thoroughly compromising the Christian faith? Why stop there? Why give the Christ parable so much weight in our understanding of life? Although her parabolic Christology properly focuses on the "is not" dimension of talk about God, it does not really explain the "is" dimension. Why is it that Jesus is so appropriately parabolic

of God? Is there no identity between his *being* and God's? Can
the contrary assertion of generations of Christians be so easily
surrendered? Is the Christian circle of interpretation, after all,
like the green glasses of Oz — perhaps not a dispensible heuris-
tic fiction, but not an outright or in any way eschatological identity claim either? Nor do Gill's or McFague's discussions of
metaphor explain, at least to my satisfaction, why and how the
logically odd juxtaposition of an image or word sometimes has
such evocative force. Why in some cases and not in others? Not
all metaphors work and many eventually die.

By no means am I denying the metaphorical character of
theology and Christology. Theology and Christology must be
ever attentive to the "is not" of its referents. Nor am I denying
the implications that theology must be tentative, open-ended,
liberating and even iconoclastic. These implications must be
taken most seriously. What I am questioning is whether such a
move requires the adoption of a parabolic Christology over
against any Christology which would give more weight to the
ontological and religious issues at stake in accounting for the
identity between Jesus and God.

Dialectical Word

The crucified Jesus, it was argued in Chapter 11, reveals
God where we least expect to find God. This suggests a third
model for understanding the identity between Jesus and the
Father. The cross shatters our expectations about how and
where God's power is manifested and contradicts our assumptions about God's nature. The God of Jesus is at odds with our
wounded humanity — at odds with its powers and loves, its authorities and values, its magic and pretensions. From this perspective, it is the non-identity between the human and divine,
disclosed in the powerlessness and suffering of the crucified
Jesus, which reveals God. God's Word in Jesus is thus dialectical: it is known through its contrary. Those who advocate this
Christological model are thus arguing that an entirely different
logic is necessary to understand the unity of the human and divine in Christ. God's Word cannot be comprehended by ordinary

human logic. Indeed, God's Word contradicts the logic of our wounded humanity and calls for conversion to a perspective that only God can give.

This position has been very influential in Protestant circles since the dialectical theology of Karl Barth at the turn of the century and has taken innumerable forms. Helmut Thielicke's theology, briefly discussed in Chapter 7, offers one variant. For our purposes though, the adaption of Jürgen Moltmann's theology of the cross in the liberation theology of the Jesuit Jon Sobrino provides the most useful illustration.[21]

Sobrino contends that the cross of Jesus requires a "complete break" with our customary way of looking at things. From the Greeks we inherited the notion that thought is analogical — that we come to know something new by seeing an identity (or analogy) between it and another thing with which we are already familiar. Given this theory of knowledge, God's reality is "recognized through what is positive in his creatures: their beauty, order, intelligence, power, and so forth."[22] In the case of the cross, however, this obviously won't work. "It is not at all self-evident that there can be life in death, power in impotence, and presence in abandonment. For the Greek that is nonsense; for the Christian it is a necessity."[23] So we cannot understand the significance of the cross by simply casting about our wounded humanity and world for an analogy. The point is that there is none.

Dialectical theologians have sometimes pushed this notion so far that faith knowledge is radically divorced from other ways of knowing.[24] This, of course, is one of the factors which has fueled the skeptics' suspicion that the Christian circle is bewitchingly cut off from everything else that we know or take to be real.[25] Sobrino, however, does not deny the need for some point of contact between what we already know from the world and what God's Word on the cross reveals. But he does insist that the point of identity is not the analogy of wonder at the root of our ordinary knowledge. Rather it is a dialectical identity which he calls the analogy of sorrow.

Sorrow, as he understands it, is the response that "wells up in the presence of the evil embodied in oppression and injustice."[26] It is a kind of sympathy or co-knowing with the one who suffers in which the lack of identity between our humanity and God, between our world and God's kingdom, is recognized. This recognition is a "hope against hope because it wells up from suffering."[27] It does not arise from our victory over evil or from our domination of the things and events which dehumanize us. So, we are not talking about a knowledge that can be justified from our ordinary way of looking at things. If we simply weigh the evidence of human history, it is not at all clear that "justice finally prevails," that "things are getting better and better" or even that life is fundamentally good. We saw in our discussion of Thielicke (Chapter 7) and Küng (Chapter 9) how strong a case can be made for the radical ambiguity of reality as we experience and comprehend it.

The analogy of sorrow discerns a different logic. Its recognition of injustice and evil is rooted in an identification with another who suffers. Such sorrow in the face of another's plight cannot stand still. If genuine, it cannot just stand by. Sorrow is moved to "recreate" itself into an active and compassionate love which seeks to bridge the distance between the self and the other who suffers. It is precisely in this protest against the misery of the other and in the struggle to alleviate his or her suffering that we have an analogy for recognizing the God disclosed by Jesus on the cross.[28]

This dialectical conception of God requires a kind of "transcendence" which Sobrino contends was "never contemplated or imagined by any philosophy."[29] The cross calls for a conversion and transformation in our ways of thinking and acting. In fact, the cross forces us to rethink the whole question of God. It turns out that God is "recognized through what seems to be quite the opposite" of the divine: namely, through suffering.[30] "God on the cross explains nothing; he criticizes every proffered explanation."[31] Thus a dialectical Christology of the cross calls for a reversal of St. Augustine's notion of the restless heart which will not be content until it rests in God. Instead of the restlessness of our heart pushing us towards God, "it is the cross that makes our heart truly upset and restless; and the repose we find there will be very different from that which human beings regard as repose."[32] The knowledge to which God calls us is thus a discomforting knowledge which requires our conversion and recreation. It is a practical knowledge rather than a theoretical one. It is a knowledge like that shown by God's solidarity with our wounded humanity on the cross of Jesus — a "knowledge born of shared communion with the sorrow and suffering of the other person." [33] This knowledge of God, Sobrino thus insists, "cannot be dissociated from the way that leads to God — a way that passes through the cross."[34]

The dialectical model, therefore, does not offer a theoretical explanation or solution to our question about the identity between the divine and human in Jesus. For someone like Sobrino, Chalcedon's statement about Jesus' divine and human natures, though true, is "much too abstract."[35] To know the humanness of Jesus, Sobrino would argue, it is necessary to attend to the concrete events of Jesus' life and to the specific history of sin (that is to say, the concrete political, religious and human forces) which led to his death on the cross. And to know what "being God" means, it is necessary to attend to the event which reveals God, namely the cross. This event does not explain what "being God" means. No such explanation is really possible. Rather the cross challenges us to follow the path of Jesus — to identify with the poor and oppressed in solidarity with Christ — and thus through participating in this process to experience the divine presence in the approach of God's kingdom.

The cross, in other words, does not offer us any explanatory model that would make us *understand* what salvation is and how it itself might be salvation. Instead it invites us to participate in a process with which we can actually experience history as salvation. It is the same point that we have already reiterated several times: Our knowledge of God and of Jesus as the Son is ultimately a con-natural knowledge, a knowledge based on sym-pathy within the very process of God himself rather than outside it.

The Son reveals himself to us as the Son insofar as we follow his path. The Father reveals himself to us as Father insofar as we experience the following of Jesus as an open road that moves history forward, opens up a future, and nurtures a hope in spite of sin and historical injustice. It is through that experience that we sense that love is the ultimate meaning of existence and feel an unquenchable hope arise within us — a hope against hope because it wells up from suffering."[36]

Conceiving the unity between Jesus and the Father dialectically in this way thus calls into question the very formulation of the question posed at the outset of the Chapter. First, it challenges the assumption that we really know what "human nature" and "divine nature" are. If it is granted that humanity is still an open question for us, and that our achievement of humanity falls so short of the mark that much of our history is more appropriately described as "inhumanity," then abstract statements about Jesus' "true humanity" are quite empty. If talk about Jesus' human nature is to have content, then it must focus on the historical details of his life. Primary among those would be that his nearness to God, his compassion for the outcast, and his fidelity to the coming of his Father's kingdom mediated God's presence where we would least expect to find it, put Jesus at odds with authorities and powers of his day, and ultimately led to his death on the cross. Second, if talk about Jesus' "true divinity" is to have content, then it too must attend to Jesus' cross. Dialectical Christology emphasizes in this way that we cannot comprehend the transcendent God with any of our abstract concepts. Knowing how Jesus *is* and *is not* God is thus, first, a matter of following Jesus and understanding that the path he shares with us (his humanity, his concrete life of love in solidarity with those in need) discloses that God's *being* is love — and more important, demonstrates what these words mean concretely.

On the other hand, the dialectical model also makes clear the sense in which Jesus *is not* God, because from this perspec-

tive "it is not exactly correct to say that Jesus is the manifestation of the Father. . . . The Father is and remains the ultimate mystery of existence and history. The Father is not known
in himself; he is known only through the Son."[37] Thus the dialectical model, like the paradigmatic and parabolic models, understands the identity between Jesus and God "in more operational
terms."[38]

> The Son does not reveal the mystery of the Father in
> such a way that it can be intuited directly. Instead
> the Son reveals to us how one may respond to this
> Father, how one may respond to God. In short, the
> Son reveals the way to the Father, not the Father
> himself. He thus radicalizes a basic insight of both
> the Old and New Testaments: Knowing God means
> going toward God, and accepting the mystery of God
> means being on a continual search for him. Paradoxi-
> cal as it may seem, it is only when we adopt that at-
> titude that we can come to know the innermost real-
> ity of God.[39]

The dialectical model also forces a shift in the question
posed at the outset to this chapter about Jesus' necessity for salvation by focusing the question on the necessity of making love
a concrete and historical reality in solidarity with Jesus. From
this perspective there is no path to God other than Jesus' love of
neighbor and fidelity to the Father. The issue, then, does not
center on whether a person calls himself or herself a Christian.
The decisive issue is whether the person follows Christ. Of
course, we must also recognize, all the while, that our pilgrim-
age to the Father's kingdom leads to the cross. *Our efforts alone*
cannot bring about the kingdom, or even recognize God's presence except dialectically. That qualification granted, however,
several avenues are left open for understanding Jesus' necessity
for salvation. The hard line will insist that our wounded humanity can have no access to authentic human *being* except through
an explicit acknowledgment of Jesus as Lord through his cross
and resurrection.[40] A more moderate position would contend
that conceivably people can follow Jesus' path without con-

sciously acknowledging him, but in that case they would be saved in spite of their wounded humanity and idolatrous religion.[41] Finally, it is possible to maintain from the perspective of a dialectical model that whenever people shoulder the crosses of injustice and oppression, they and their religion are to that extent in solidarity with Christ and so are saved.[42]

There is much to be said for Sobrino's emphasis on the dialectical and practical character of our knowledge of God. In the previous Chapter I underlined that Jesus did not reveal God's presence where we would expect it. Although I suggested in Chapter 8 that God can be identified as the horizon of our knowledge, freedom and love, I also concluded that God eludes our grasp in the most fundamental way, both because the history of our wounded humanity so utterly constricts our openness for God's *be*ing and because God as mystery radically transcends us. In Chapter 9, I emphasized that though philosophy can help show the reasonableness of belief in God, it cannot itself establish the Christian circle of understanding or even lead one to faith that Jesus is the Christ. Chapter 7 emphasized that the woundedness of the human condition is not something that we can overcome ourselves. Part IV will argue, along with liberation theologians, that knowledge of God is a matter of the hands and feet as well as a matter of the head and heart. I agree then, that it is most important to acknowledge the significance of the cross and the practical and dialectical dimension of the Christian circle of understanding. On the other hand, I have also argued that the questions of the head are legitimate. It is not clear that the dialectical model is adequate for dealing with those questions.

It is one thing to say that the logic of faith contradicts our expectations and that it cannot be proven by pointing to our broken world; it is another thing to so emphasize this discontinuity that faith and reason, as such, are opposed and contradictory. Can the problems of the head be completely avoided by appealing to the practical character of our knowledge of God, or by pointing to the non-identity between God and ourselves? Can this be done without turning faith into a charmed circle which

divorces the head from hands and feet, Jesus' humanity from
ours, or Jesus' humanity from his divinity? Doesn't it take an
awful lot of "headwork" to get to the conclusion that knowledge
of God is dialectical? And could one ever get to that conclusion or
be grasped by the question which Jesus' cross raises, without
some prior conception of what human *being* is or of what it could
possibly mean to recognize humanity as wounded, to yearn for
salvation from this woundedness or to hope in a divine *being*
beyond ourselves and our world who could save us from our own
inhumanity? Couldn't one argue that the logical conclusion to
the dialectical approach is the one proposed by the death of God
theologians and some Marxists: namely, that the move from
Jesus to hope and solidarity with those in need does not require
belief in God?[43] How avoid their conclusion that the belief in God
is really no more than a concrete hope against odds and a practical solidarity with those who suffer, exemplified by Jesus, but
by no means requiring belief in a transcendent divinity?

Moreover, does the dialectical model take the identity between Jesus and his Father seriously enough, or does it give
enough weight to the Resurrection or to the presence of Jesus'
Spirit in the Church and through the Church in the world? If the
Son's path leads to the Father, doesn't that entail a unity between Jesus and God which would involve a more positive relation between humanity and divinity than this model seems to
allow? If Christ has sent his Spirit, then shouldn't the effects of
that divine presence be discernable somehow among Christians, if not also in the world? What basis does the the dialectical
model offer for reconciling the affirmations that Jesus is necessary for salvation and that salvation is at least a possibility for
all? It is important to recognize that the salvation question concerns the way people live and not just what they confess in
words. Acknowledging that to be the case, however, does not resolve the problem about how God's Spirit can be manifested to
those who do not believe in Jesus as the Christ.

If the affirmation of Jesus' divinity is entirely dialectical, if
Christians only mean that Jesus leads to and reveals God but
not that the *being* of Jesus and God are somehow ontologically

one, then aren't Christians equivocating when they affirm that he *is* God's Word? If Christians say that Jesus saves, but the fruits of that salvation have effected no change in our humanity, then aren't Christians equivocating when they affirm that Jesus saves us? By no means am I denying that this ontological unity of the human *being* and divine *being* of Jesus must be understood concretely in terms of the love manifested in the cross. What I am questioning is whether there is not something more at stake here and whether the dialectical model expresses this adequately.

Divine Gesture

Each of the previous Christological models have been faulted both for compromising the identity of the human and divine in Jesus and for compromising his necessity for salvation. The aim is to find a model that will not do this and that at the same time will not compromise Jesus' humanity or the possibility of salvation for non-Christians. I believe that Karl Rahner achieves this in his philosophical and theological understanding of what he calls the "realsymbol."[44] His strategy is to probe more deeply the linguistic or symbol-making character of human existence which is at the root of our ability in the first place to make any sort of identity claims, whether paradigmatic, metaphorical, parabolic or dialectical.

At the outset, it is important to recall the understanding of humanity and God elaborated in Chapter 8. Some of the difficulties in conceiving how there can be an identity of the human and the divine come from the tendency to think of God and human persons as objects and to imagine the unity in question as if it were a coming together of two things. This sort of ontic (objectifying or thing-ifying) perspective will not do. God is not some "thing out there" opposed to our humanity. God is not an object at all, nor even objectifiable except in the most indirect way as the "horizon" of our knowledge, freedom and love, or as the "mystery" at the heart of our *being*. But although God cannot be grasped by our concepts and transcends our reach, God is nevertheless implicitly anticipated in the dynamism of our spirit towards its objects. It is true that a person may never recognize this anticipation of God, or that a person can suppress it and even cut it short.We can make gods of finite realities (one's family, political party, ambition, security, etc.) and thus not move out of ourselves, see any broader horizon or experience any true liberation from the cravings, needs, desires and pressures which drive us and pull at us. Ironically, however, even this experience of human existence as closed presupposes that we stand before God. We could not make gods of our own, deny the reality of any ultimate horizon to our existence or refuse to acknowledge any mystery at the heart of life, if it were not for the radical openness of the human spirit for such a horizon and mystery in the first place.

This also means that human persons cannot be conceived adequately as objects. We are subjects, persons. We are embodied spirits. Our consciousness, freedom and love manifest a radical openness which neither we ourselves nor anyone else can sum up or adequately and fully objectify. Nor is our humanity opposed to God, or God's divinity opposed to us. It is precisely our openness and dynamism towards God which enables us to be what we are. Our anticipation of God is the basis and condition of possibility for whatever consciousness, freedom and love we achieve. Proximity to God does not diminish our humanity but, to the contrary, grounds it: the more radical and complete our openness to the divine, the more our capacity for consciousness, freedom and love. Proximity to God is humanizing. Likewise, the achievement of authentic humanity does not diminish our presence to God but, to the contrary, is the result of God's presence as the mystery at the heart of our *being*: the more we truly achieve some degree of knowledge, freedom and love, the closer we come to God.

The identity between the human and divine in Jesus, then, is not the contradiction it first appears to be, if we conceive the unity ontologically (that is to say, if we focus on the character of the sorts of *being* in question, rather than suppose that the problem is simply how to imagine an identity between two different objects or things). Union with God would not make Jesus less human. It would not lessen his potential for human consciousness, freedom and love. Quite the contrary, as Karl Rahner emphasized, only a person whose humanity was completely one with God could be fully and perfectly human.[45] But of course there's the rub. How could such a union between the human and divine come about if God, like an asymptotic goal, transcends and eludes our grasp? How is such a union possible if the woundedness of our humanity has narrowed our horizons, warped our freedom and crippled our reach? If there is unity between God and humanity, it must somehow be established from God's side. But then how imagine such an event? And how would we recognize it?

To answer this Rahner proposes a theology of the symbol. What he has in mind, however, is something more fundamental than what we ordinarily think of as symbol. He is in fact attempting to get at what it is in our consciousness and in reality itself that gives rise to symbols. What is it that makes one reality, image or word symbolic of another in the first place? It cannot just be that there is an agreement or likeness of some sort between the realities in question. With a little imagination we can find some kind of likeness between any two realities. What is it that makes some symbols so peculiarly appropriate, evocative and rich in meaning? What constitutes the difference between genuine symbols and arbitrary signs which stand for another reality simply by convention? It is not just a question about the degree of likeness. An impressionistic painting can be much more symbolic of a loved one than a photograph — a favorite song, or perhaps something ironic like a broken plate, even more symbolic than the painting. Something more basic is at the root of our ability to discover symbolic meanings in things. Rahner contends that the explanation has to do with the symbolic character of reality itself.

Everything that we confront in our world is constituted by a number of somewhat distinct elements or factors. The objects of our world have parts. They have shape, size, weight, color and so forth. We ourselves are constituted by a multiplicity of factors: physical, biological, chemical, psychological, sociological to mention but a few. Our customs and cultures, even our thoughts and words are complex and multifaceted. This multiplicity is not just an extrinsic mental distinction. It is intrinsic to the very nature of these realities. Nothing in our world is absolutely simple. Rahner asserts, therefore, that all finite beings are in this sense multiple. But despite this multiplicity, each reality is still a unity. It is still a particular thing: this chair, not just the separate components that make up a chair; this idea or image, not just an array of disconnected impressions. If there were no unity, the so-called being would be no being at all. It would be merely a juxtaposition of a number of distinct beings. Since this multiplicity which constitutes each being is grounded in a more basic inner unity, there is a sense in which the multiplicity is an expression of the unity. The being is manifested — or to speak a bit anthropomorphically, "expresses itself" — through its multiplicity of characteristics.

It is important to note that the multiplicity of characteristics which express the being are not simply identical with it. We could repaint my car, rebuild the engine and change many of the other components and it would still be my car. Or we could record one of my class lectures on video tape. On that tape would be my voice, my face, my gestures, my ideas, my idiosyncracies — all those factors that incarnated my presence to the original audience — but it would not be me. If, as writers of science fiction imagine, we could make exact clones or androids of ourselves, those would still not be us even though nearly all that goes into our self-constitution and self-expression was cleverly programmed into them. In fact, it is quite literally true that although I am the same person who was born a number of years ago, every cell in my body is now different. We can say that "I'm not the person I used to be." I am not simply identical with my embodiment at any stage of my physical or even of my personal and spritual development.

On the other hand, there is a very real and essential identity between a being and the multiplicity that constitutes its self-expression. A being really constitutes itself in its multiplicity. It is actually made up of its elements, parts and characteristics. Take away the engine, the other components, the interior and the body and you have no car. Take away my voice, my body, my gestures, my ideas, my idiosyncracies (all those things that incarnate me and are reproduced on the video tape) and I would cease to be, at least as far as this world is concerned. Take away the concrete referents of any image or word, make it totally abstract, and it will lose its meaning. In fact the identity between a reality and the multiplicity which expresses it, is as intimate an identity as we can point to in this world. On the one hand, I am my embodiment; I only exist in this physical/spiritual incarnation. Yet on the other hand, my embodiment is also not simply identical with me; to a certain extent, it is something distinct from my*self*.

Rahner calls this self-expression of a being, its "realsymbol." He coins the new word to indicate that what he has in mind here is a symbol in the most fundamental sense. My embodiment, the concrete "me" with all my inhibitions and idiosyncracies, is my "realsymbol," as opposed to a cartoonist's caricature or some other more derivative and secondary symbol of me. All finite beings are symbolic in this sense. Every being in attaining its nature — just to be what it is, to be itself — forms "something distinct from itself and yet one with itself."[46] Every being has its self-expression or "realsymbol" which it both *is* and *is not*. The non-identity or otherness between a being and its "realsymbol" is intrinsic and essential. At the same time, the being's identity with its "realsymbol" is also intrinsic and essential. My concrete embodiment, my "realsymbol," is prior to any other symbol of me and it is irreplaceable.

If beings are indeed symbolic in this way, then one reality, image or word can be symbolic of another because each being is already symbolic in itself. The reason why symbols are different from arbitrary signs, some likenesses more symbolic than others and some symbols richer in meaning than others, is because a symbol has some sort of specific correlation with a being's "realsymbol." A cartoonist's caricature is symbolic of a political figure, for example, because it captures and exaggerates some expression of the official's own reality. The correlation need not be so obvious and pictorial though. Six months after my father's death, my mother broke into tears at the grocery counter because the sweet potatoes in front of her called to mind his idiosyncratic tastes and habits and thus evoked his peculiar relationship to her and the family. Nothing short of a rather long story could begin to explain this; the grocer would have had to know him. Sweet potatoes had this symbolic meaning because of my father's "realsymbol," because of his endearing and eccentric way of fleshing out his vision and passion for life. Such correlations can even be quite dialectical. The star used by the Nazis to "mark" Jews, has become a symbol to that people of their self-identity. Jesus' death on the cross is symbolic because of its correlation with what Christians believe is his real identity.

Of course the line between "realsymbols" and symbols is not always so easily drawn. An artist's portrait of someone is a symbol rather than a "realsymbol," but what of the artist whose creation is more intimately expressive? What of the dancer or singer? Where does artistic expression begin and self-expression end? How distinguish here the "realsymbol" from the symbol? Likewise, symbols can become so familiar, so identified with the reality they symbolize, that they lose their richness and degenerate into mere signs. Moreover, it is not impossible for an arbitrary sign to assume symbolic meaning. So there is a continuum, we might say, between a being's "realsymbol," symbols which have a correlation of some sort with the being's "realsymbol," and signs which arbitrarily designate the being. On this understanding, the kinds of identities described earlier as paradigmatic, metaphorical, parabolic and dialectical are all rooted in the more fundamental symbolic identity and non-identity of a being and its "realsymbol." They are all species of symbol in the broadest sense of the term. Metaphor, parable and dialectic, we could say, trade on the surprising and transformative possibilities inherent in the non-identity, while paradigms, symbols (in the more restricted sense of images or representations of one sort or another) and similes exploit the continuity and similarities inherent in the identity.[47]

This symbolic character of beings is at the root of human knowledge and language. We can recognize beings only because in some sense they already express themselves in their "real-symbols." Without its "realsymbol" a being could not be known at all. In fact, our "realsymbols" — the various roles, gestures, guises and masks which we assume — are the vehicles through which we come to know even our own identities. Moreover, through its "realsymbol" we really can come to know another being in itself. This is most evident in our knowledge of other persons. Through the concrete realities which constitute a person's "realsymbol," that is through the individual's dynamic self-expression in words, gestures and deeds, we can come to know him or her — not just know something about the person, but really know the self. We can really be in communion with the person. Whenever we talk with someone and not just talk at them or about them, there is such *self*-communication.

A person's active self-expression in words, gestures and deed (that is to say, in his or her "realsymbol") is thus essential for there to be any communication of self to another. In a sense one could even say that the words, gestures or deeds *cause* the self-communication. Without the handshake or some similar gesture extended out towards the other person, there could never be an actual coming together. Without some embodied gestures of love, lovers could never reach out and touch each other. But although it is the actual self of the person which is thus communicated through words, gestures and deeds, the self is not simply identical with them. You can have the gestures without a genuine communication of self.[48] So from this perspective, we would have to say that it is the person who causes the "realsymbol" and gives it whatever meaning it has. Symbolic causality thus works both ways. The identity between a being and its "realsymbol" is mutually conditioning. The being expresses itself in its "realsymbol" and at the same time the "realsymbol" fleshes out the being.

I believe that this notion of the symbolic character of beings and knowing provides a model that can handle the problems raised at the beginning of the chapter. If we conceive Jesus as God's "realsymbol," it is possible to affirm a genuine and intimate ontological unity between Jesus' humanity and divinity, and at the same time to affirm the distinction between them which the paradigmatic, parabolic and dialectical models seek to preserve. We have seen that unity between the divine and human is not in itself contradictory. In fact, humanity can be defined as the dynamism toward such union (so long as we keep in mind that the unity would have to be established from God's side). Thus we can imagine Jesus' humanity (his concrete embodiment with all the particularity that this entails) as God's "realsymbol" or as God's "gesture," provided that the words "symbol" and "gesture" are understood in a full, strong and realistic sense as God's self-expression and self-communication to the world and to us. We could then affirm quite literally that such a divine gesture both *is* and *is not* God, just as our "realsymbols," the complex of distinct gestures of all sorts through which we express ourselves, both *are* and *are not* us.

Such a perspective does not deny the "is not" on which the other models focus. To affirm that Jesus is God's "realsymbol" (God's Word made flesh) is not to say that Jesus and the Father to whom he prayed are simply identical. It does not deny the distinction between the human and the divine which Burtchaell and McFague sought to protect. Likewise, it does not require a piety which, as McFague worried, too easily sees God's presence everywhere. Nor does it necessarily equate the divine and the masculine. Understanding Jesus as God's "realsymbol" does not propose an abstraction, as Sobrino was concerned, which purports to comprehend God or which purports to understand either what it is "to be genuinely human" or what it is for Jesus "to be God" apart from the concrete details of his life, cross and resurrection. If a being is only known in its "realsymbol," then there is no grasping it apart from all the historical particularities in which it is fleshed out. I also don't see any reason why this sort of symbolic model can't and shouldn't insist with theologians like McFague and Sobrino that God's revelation comes to us as a shock, as a contradiction of our wounded humanity and as a call for conversion. Nor do I see the symbolic model giving any reason for not joining in their insistence that the God recognized in Jesus remains a mystery, that the Father is not known in himself but only in his Son and that this knowledge of the Son cannot be had apart from Jesus' solidarity with the poorest and most oppressed of our sisters and brothers.

On the other hand, conceiving Jesus as God's "realsymbol" does not require a denial of the ontological identity between the human and divine in Jesus, and so avoids the ambiguity of the other models in this regard. If Jesus' humanity is God's self-expression, then although this humanity is distinct from the divinity, it is not a different being. The "realsymbol" is a being's own self-expression. Jesus *is not simply God*, but Jesus *is* God's Word made flesh. There is no equivocation. As long as we suppose the symbolic character of all *being*, including God's, there should be no hesitation to say straightforwardly as Christians always have said, Jesus *is* divine. Moreover, since the "realsymbol" is not just a communication but rather a communication of the *self*, more than any of the other models it clarifies how it can be said that Jesus actually mediates God, not just something about God. Finally, this model clearly does not undermine or relativize central doctrines of the faith and so contradict the witness of Scripture or generations of Christians. Nor does it require an essential opposition between authentic humanity and God, reason and faith, the Cross and the Resurrection, doctrine and Scripture or the world and the Church.

The model's usefulness can be tested by asking how it enables us to talk coherently about Jesus' knowledge and self-consciousness. If the man Jesus in his very humanity is God's self-expression or "realsymbol," then it seems quite logical that this personal (or hypostatic) unity would affect Jesus' self-consciousness and knowledge. How could a person be one with God and this not have a profound effect on the person's consciousness? Isn't this confirmed by the Gospel reports of Jesus' miracles, knowledge of peoples' hearts and consciousness of his special relationship to his Father in heaven? But, on the other hand, if unity with God means that the person would know all that God knows, would know himself as God's Son and would know God's will as God knows it, could we still say that this is a humanity like ours in all things except sin? What about the Gospel reports, especially as understood in the light of modern biblical criticism, that Jesus *grew* in knowledge and wisdom (Luke 2:52), that Jesus proclaimed the coming of God's kingdom rather than making an issue of his own identity and that Jesus was either unaware of the time of the kingdom's final arrival (Mark 13:32) or was mistaken about it (Mark 9:1)?

Such difficulties are not insurmountable if viewed in light of the perspective just elaborated. Our humanity is ultimately defined by our spirit's openness for God in our knowing, choosing and loving. But this transcendence towards God is an embodied dynamism. Our "reach" is and must be fleshed out in the concrete, worked out in time. In our case, of course, the human spirit's reach always falls short of the mark. We are not God. We are cut off from the mystery at the heart of our *being* by the woundedness of our humanity and the brokenness of our world. If Jesus' humanity is God's (real)symbolic self-expression, then there could be no alienation and no cutting short of his spirit's dynamism towards God. At this level, his humanity would be what we only yearn to be. He would embody an actual reaching in flesh and history of God's presence. He would be one with the horizon which always eludes us.

There is no reason, however, why we can't imagine — in fact it would seem that we must imagine — that Jesus' reach, like our own, had to be worked out, fleshed out and embodied in the concrete and over time. It would be conceivable, then, that at the conscious and explicit level his knowledge would have been conditioned by the language, society, culture and so forth in which he grew up and lived. Certainly we would expect that one who was truly open and genuinely reached for God as none of us has or could, would have understood himself and the world differently than we do, and that such a person would have acted and loved differently — so much more authentically, freely and fully. But it is not necessary for us to suppose that Jesus' knowledge and freedom were omnipotent. Nor would this require that Jesus knew himself to be divine in the way Christians today understand him to be divine. Rather we can know about Jesus' explicit and conscious knowledge and powers only what can be gleaned from Scripture. Anything beyond that, reverent and important as it might be, is speculation.

Needless to say, these remarks do not prove that Jesus is
divine. Nor have they shown how Christians can claim both that
Jesus is necessary for salvation and that salvation is a possibility for all. I have been clear that the former is not my intention.
The latter question will be addressed in the next chapter. What
these reflections do show, I believe, is that the believer's talk
about Jesus' divinity is not necessarily incoherent. Furthermore, although the widely divergent spectrum of interpretations of Jesus' divinity among Christians today certainly reflects a degree of mystification and confusion and so may sometimes justify the charge that this circle of understanding is
charmed, another reading can also be justified: that there is a
profound and multifaceted truth expressed here that is not easily formulated and that lends itself to a plurality of approaches.

It is my contention, then, that these diverse approaches,
rightly understood, can be helpful in expressing a legitimate
pluriformity, that is to say, a plurality which expresses the
unity of a multifaceted truth, rather than an incoherent
pluralism of intrinsically opposed positions. A number of models are needed to explore Jesus' relationship to God.

Those we have discussed are by no means exhaustive, but
they suggest four significant possibilities. First, Jesus' freedom
for the poor, the oppressed and the sinner, Jesus' fidelity to the
coming of God's kingdom and his surrender to what that required, are indeed a human paradigm of the divine. Jesus is, for
Christians at least, paradigmatic of what the teacher, prophet
and priest should be. But that does not preclude the parabolic
aspect of his identity with God evident in the unexpected hum-
bleness of Jesus' origins and particularity, in his surprising
freedom, in his discomforting criticism of this world's loves and
authorities and in his shocking death and abandonment on the
cross. Likewise, the thrust of the claim that Jesus is God's Son
or Word is clearly metaphorical. Yet it is also dialectical. We
cannot really picture the risen Jesus at all except as the contrary of the crucified Jesus.

At the same time, none of these approaches would have real
force unless there were some ontological identity between Jesus

and God. Jesus could truly mediate the Father only if he were in some sense God's own gesture towards us.

If the human Jesus is such a divine gesture, however, then humanity is not what it appears to be. If the humanity of Jesus can be God's self-communication, that means that humanity is not only open for God, but is capable of being taken up into God and expressing God. As Rahner once put it, if Jesus is God's Word, then humanity is the grammar and vocabulary of this divine self-communication.[49] Moreover, if the human Jesus is such a divine gesture then divinity is not what we expect either. It is a love that can empty itself into humanity. It is a love that can be expressed in the human.

The Dutch theologian Felix Malmberg argued that God could not take on something or be expressed in something which was not somehow already God's own and which did not already share somehow in God's own perfection. If the human Jesus can be God's self-expression, or if Adam and Eve can be spoken of as created in the image of God, then not only are humanity and divinity not opposed but humanity as a perfection, as it exists in the Risen Jesus, "must belong to the inner self of God." Because God's Word was fleshed out in Jesus, Malmberg maintained, Christians must affirm the "humanity of God."[50]

All of this, if we can make sense of it in the chapters which follow, would give a new and much more radical meaning to the correlation between anthropology and theology as the secret for breaking into the Christian circle. Admittedly, it raises, as well, a good number of questions to which we must next turn our attention.

Notes

1. See, for example, the "Declaration on the Relationship of the Church to Non-Christian Religions," *The Documents of Vatican II* (New York: America Press, 1966), p. 661.

2. James Tunstead Burtchaell, C.S.C., *Philemon's Problem: The Daily Dilemma of the Christian* (Chicago: ACTA Foundation, 1973).

3. Burtchaell, p. 43.

4. Burtchaell, p. 36.

5. Burtchaell, p. 39.

6. Burtchaell, p. 43.

7. Sallie McFague, *Metaphorical Theology: Models of God in Religious Language* (Philadelphia: Fortress Press, 1982); Jerry H. Gill, *On Knowing God: New Directions for the Future of Theology* (Philadelphia: Westminster Press, 1981).

8. Gill, p. 135, is drawing here from Paul Ricoeur's *The Rule of Metaphor* (Toronto: University of Toronto Press, 1977).

9. Gill, p. 132.

10. McFague, p. 39, quoting form Nelson Goodman, *Languages of Art: An Approach to a Theory of Symbols* (Indianapolis: The Bobbs-Merrill Company, 1968), p. 69.

11. McFague, p. 39, quoting from Goodman, p. 73.

12. McFague, p. 17.

13. McFague, p. 17.

14. Gill, p. 87.

15. McFague, p. 41.

16. McFague, p. 17.

17. McFague, p. 50.

18. McFague, p. 51; emphasis added.

19. McFague, p. 51.

20. McFague, p. 52.

21. See Jon Sobrino, S.J. *Christology at the Crossroads: A Latin American Approach*, trans. John Drury (Maryknoll, New York: Orbis Books, 1978) and Jürgen Moltmann, *The Crucified God: The Cross of Christ as the Foundation and Criticism of Christian Theology*, trans. R. A. Wilson and John Bowden (New York: Harper & Row, 1974).

22. Sobrino, p. 198.

23. Sobrino, p. 199.

24. Rudolf Bultmann, for example, whose dialectical theology is not ordinarily thought of as that radical in this respect, argued for pushing the doctrine of justification by faith alone to its logical conclusion epistemologically, to destroy every false security which we seek in our desire to comprehend God in terms of any knowledge that we have at our disposal. See "Bultmann Replies to His Critics," in his *Kerygma and Myth*, ed. Hans Werner Bartsch, trans. Reginald H. Fuller (New York: Harper & Row, 1961), p. 211; or his *Jesus Christ and Mythology* (New York: Charles Scribner's Sons, 1958), p. 84.

25. See for example, Ronald W. Hepburn's critique of Bultmann, "Demythologizing and the Problem of Validity," in *New Essays in Philosophical Theology*, ed. Antony Flew and Alasdair MacIntyre (New York: The Macmillan Company, 1966; first published 1955), pp.227-42.

26. Sobrino, p. 200.

27. Sobrino, p. 227.

28. Sobrino, p. 200.

29. Sobrino, p. 222.

30. Sobrino, p. 222.

31. Sobrino, p. 222.

32. Sobrino, p. 222.

33. Sobrino, p. 223.

34. Sobrino, p. 228.

35. Sobrino, p. 202.

36. Sobrino, p. 227.

37. Sobrino, p. 387.

38. Sobrino, p. 387.

39. Sobrino, pp. 387-88.

40. Bultmann, for example, even with his call for demythologizing the Scriptures, nevertheless held that all natural religion and natural theology are manifestations of humanity's idolatry and he asserted "that all answers apart from the Christian answer are illusions" ["The Question of Natural Revelation," in his *Essays Philosophical and Theological*, trans. J. C. Greig (London: SCM Press, 1955), p. 98.]; see also "The Problem of Natural Theology," in his *Faith and Understanding*, ed. Robert Funk, trans. Louise Pettibone Smith (New York: Harper & Row, 1969).

41. This is the position of another liberation theologian, Juan Segundo, S.J., articulated quite explicitly in his *The Community Called Church*, trans. John Drury (Maryknoll, New York: Orbis Books, 1973), p. 64.

42. The justification for that alternative will be elaborated in Part IV.

43. Langdon Gilkey argues persuasively that the death of God theology was rooted in dialectical theology in his *Naming the Whirlwind: Renewal of God-Language* (Indianapolis: The Bobbs-Merrill Company, 1969).

44. The initial essay where he explicitly develops this understanding is "The Theology of the Symbol," in his *Theological Investigations*, trans. Kevin Smyth (Baltimore: Helicon Press, 1966), vol. IV, pp. 221-311; but the notion is implicit in most of his Christological writings and grounded in his early philosophical work.

45. "On the Theology of the Incarnation," *Theological Investigations*, vol. IV, p. 110.

46. "The Theology of the Symbol," p. 229.

47. Where these would fit on the continuum between "realsymbol" and sign is not a question of the ontological identity with the being itself but of the degree to which the exploited correlation (identity or non-identity) discloses, calls to mind or resonates with the being's reality. Needless to say, these remarks about the nature of religious discourse do not pretend to any sort of completeness.

48. There is a negative side to this which we can only note here in passing. If you can have such gestures or apparent self-expressions without a genuine self-communication, then this also means that a being's "realsymbol" may not be what it appears to be. Very intimate-sounding talk can be a mask behind which we actually hide ourselves. A handshake which purports to be an extension of the self to another can in fact incarnate the effort to dominate the other. Having sex may be something very different than giving one's self over to another in lovemaking. The person "expressed" to others might not be the real self at all but rather a guise and deception. Or yet worse, the self can be deceived by its own guises. It can be suppressed, our identities confused and our personalities split.

49. "Thoughts on the Theology of Christmas," *Theological Investigations*, trans. Karl-H. and Boniface Kruger (Baltimore: Helicon Press, 1967), vol. III, p. 32.

50. From his unpublished manuscript *The Humanity of God*, ed. Sharon M Burns, which reworked and furthered ideas developed in his earlier works *Über den Gottmenschen* (Freiburg: Herder, 1960) and *Ein Leib — Ein Geist: Vom Mysterium der Kirche* (Freiburg: Herder, 1960).

13. A Spirited Circle

There is, without doubt, a circularity to the Christian understanding. The question is whether the circle is salvific. Is it truly freeing and humanizing? This is not an idle issue. The credibility and significance of the Christian faith centers on the validity of the believers' conviction that "God sent his Son into the world not to condemn the world, but so that through him the world might be saved" (John 3:17). One cannot claim, as Burtchaell does, that Jesus is in no exclusive or particular way our Savior,[1] without turning that faith on its head. To proclaim Jesus as Christ is to proclaim him Savior and Redeemer. Certainly this is the corollary of St. Paul's argument that faith is useless, and believing it is useless, and his preaching it is useless, if Christ has not been raised from the dead (1 Cor. 15:12-19). If Christ has not saved us, why should he be our "Lord"? If he has not saved us, the struggle to break into the Christian circle is not worth the effort.

But why associate salvation so exclusively with that one person? Why is there salvation only in that white Jewish male who lived in an obscure part of the world almost two thousand years ago? And how does he save us? What real effect could he have on us today? Why do his followers insist, in particular, that it was his death on the cross that saved us? Doesn't this make a wrathful despot of the God who requires the sacrifice? How distinguish the power of that cross and the rituals which mediate its significance today, from magic and superstition? Moreover, if Christ is necessary for redemption, how can believers account for the salvation of non-Christians? What about the Risen Christ's command to the disciples reported in Mark's Gospel

(16:16), "He who believes and is baptized will be saved; but he who does not believe will be condemned"? How reconcile that with St. Paul's comment in his first letter to Timothy (4:10) that God "is the savior of the whole human race" even if "particularly of all believers"? Pope John Paul II emphasized this notion very strongly in his first encyclical letter where he expressed the Church's concern (manifested especially in the Second Vatican Council) for the fate of every person in the world

> because man — every man without any exception whatever — has been redeemed by Christ, and because with man — with each man without any exception whatever — Christ is in a way united, even when man is unaware of it: "Christ, who died and was raised up for all, provides man" — each man and every man — "with the light and the strength to measure up to his supreme calling."[2]

How can Christ, or his Church, provide anything to people without them being aware of it? Certainly, the test of the Christological model advanced in the previous chapter is whether it can provide a tool for making some sense of these questions about humanity's salvation.

That we are in need of a Savior is perhaps too easily forgotten much of the time. It is easier to look the other way, than to face problems about which it seems we can do very little. It is easier to find a comfortable rut than to open our hearts and minds to the pervasive suffering and hopelessness in our midst. This, however, is just a further manifestation of our predicament. To the degree that we avoid confronting the pettiness, injustice and malice of our world, we ourselves become enslaved by a flight from freedom and conscience. Flight of this sort narrows consciousness, hardens the heart and debilitates our good work. It too is sin, and "everyone who sins is a slave of sin" (John 8:34). We need to be saved not only from the evils outside, but from the sin within that on any honest accounting it must be admitted we all have made our own.

There should be no misunderstanding. Pessimism about human nature and about humanity's future is not at the root of Christianity's concern with sin, at least not as the Catholic tradition has understood it. Indeed, if God has taken on our humanity in Jesus, then our woundedness can hardly be taken as the last word. That is the difficulty I have with theologians like Thielicke who seem simply to identify humanity itself with the wound (with what tradition has called original sin). On the other hand, if God has taken on humanity to save us, then that act of God's cannot be understood apart from the condition it is meant to remedy. That is why, with theologians like Thielicke, I have aimed to keep the woundedness of humanity in the foreground of our discussion. The Christian truth professes to be a saving truth. It of course assumes, then, that things are not as they should be, that we are not what we should be. Our consciousness, our wills and our love are not nearly open enough, free enough, or potent enough. Even when we do not consciously deny God, our spirit's authentic movement towards the divine is still frustrated and obscured by the woundedness of the human condition. We cannot step out of the web of our language, culture and society which are so thoroughly entangled in the worship of consumerism, hedonism, racism, power, sexism, militarism, nationalism, and hosts of other false gods. Even when we do our best, we are often at our worst. History is replete with humanity's good intentioned misadventures: holy crusades, religious wars, wars to end wars. The present threatens us too at every turn: whether we take up arms to protect the weak or disarm in fear of our own destructive might, whether we write legislation to safeguard the rights of the individual or institute policies to protect the rights of society, whether we call for détente or confrontation, whether we invest or divest.

If our consciousness is clouded, narrowed and closed in on itself, then it needs to be opened to a broader horizon. I argued in Chapter 8, with Rahner, that no horizon short of the absolute fullness of *being*, short of God, can really satisfy that need. But if the woundedness of our humanity has cut short our spirit's dynamism towards the divine fullness of *being*, then nothing less than God's bridging that gap can overcome our consciousness' alienation from its true orientation and goal. Only God's light can free our intellects from their darkness. Likewise, if our freedom is warped, determined by cravings, needs, desires and pressures which drive us and pull at us from the outside, then nothing less than God's presence can liberate freedom so that it truly reaches out beyond such enslavements, so that it truly is an authentic freedom. Only God's touching the heart can liberate it from its captivity. Nor can the impotence of our love be overcome unless the movement of our spirits is converted and reoriented to the absolute fullness of love. Only insofar as the reality of love is made incarnate for us and available for us, can we move out of our self-alienation into the communion for which our mind and hearts and bodies yearn. We can love fully and absolutely only if there is a beloved (an absolute fullness of love) who is truly open to our advances and who invites us and draws us out of ourselves. Only God's love can can empower us to embody the authentic dynamism of the human spirit towards the fullness of truth, goodness and love.

The Christian affirmation of original sin, at least in the Catholic tradition, does not deny that we can see such possibilities even in our wounded humanity and fragmented world. Life is not without love, freedom and knowledge. But it is still a very ambiguous affair. So often our love is impotent, powerless to really and definitively overcome racism, sexism, consumerism, militarism and all the other assaults of our humanity against itself. Our love is powerless even to sustain the majority of our marriages, the reliability of our personal confidences or the honesty of our business with one another. So often we cannot bring ourselves to do what really needs to be done, even when the means are at hand. Few of us are really and truly free! Even in our own nation where it was the intent to institutionalize freedom, it is not always or readily clear whether our elected bodies and free markets reflect and facilitate the people's self-determination or in reality determine and manipulate the public conscience and will.

Nor is it clear that the advances of modern science have really furthered our humanization. Knowledge is a tool for evil as

well as a tool for good. Our skillful exploitation of each other
(personally, socially and politically) at best testifies to the ambiguity of our wisdom, at worst justifies the cynicism which debilitates contemporary society. A good sober and honest look at
the political, social and personal reality of our age — at its terrorism, exploitation, injustice, dishonesty, infidelity and impotence — offers much too much evidence that our hopes for ourselves and our world may be idle dreams, that the principles and
virtues on which we count are largely abstractions which have
never truly been incarnated, that humanity's potential may
never be realized, that our institutions are dehumanizing, that
our own lives are finally empty and insignificant.

And lest the indomitable human spirit rebound, the reality
of death stands there, inevitable and apparently annihilating.
The twentieth century's sanitization and denial of death
through its institutionalization in nursing homes, emergency
rooms, hospitals and memorial parks has not really taken away
death's pain or its presence to our consciousness. Death can only
be hidden for the moment. Just when it seems that the televi-
sion has desensitized our consciousness to the body counts of
one war, a new terrorism of humanity or nature forces itself on
our imagination. As modern medicine seems about to eliminate
the polios and poxes of the past, cancer or AIDS withers away
someone whom we know personally. Even while we try to convince ourselves that people only disappear in other parts of the
world or are murdered in other neighborhoods, someone is murdered close to home, Neighborhoods, too, are dying. Cities like
Beirut are being literally blown apart. Whole peoples on the African continent are starving to death or being denied the most
basic human rights. Totalitarian regimes of the left and right,
and on nearly every continent, do not hesitate to crush and destroy human life. I should not belabor the point. We cannot insulate ourselves from death for long. Once someone close to us has
died, no other death or even our life is ever the same. Death
stands there in its many guises, threatening to annihilate all
that we have become and all that we have created, whether personally or collectively. It is not at all self-evident that life is good,

that things are getting better and better or that there is any-thing beyond us that would empower our love, make us free or give us wisdom.

Humankind, however, needs signs of wisdom, freedom and love if its potential for discerning and committed love is ever to emerge or sustain itself. "When love moves beyond the initial stage of enthusiasm and instinctive attraction," Juan Segundo observes, "it gradually becomes aware of what self-giving really is. It begins to realize that self-giving is the most serious, de-manding, unpredictable, and irreversible adventure that can happen to a human being."[3] Inevitably, he points out, this gives rise to the question of whether love is worth the effort and the risk.

> This question stays with us whether we are ponder-ing basic love for people or the decision to commit our love forever to a person whom we will never wholly know. To love means to lose our autonomy and to be-come dependent on another. And this dependence may end up one day as disillusionment and heartbreak, leaving us empty inside. All love is a gamble, wherein we risk the best and deepest part of ourself.[4]

As we have seen, there is no guarantee that this risk is worth it, that the gamble will pay off. Every act of love, consequently, is also an act of trust and of faith. "It is an act of faith launched into the air, without any precise name or clear content. It is a belief that love is worthwhile,"[5] and possible. It is a hope that defies so much evidence to the contrary.

The same analysis applies to freedom. To be free is to accept responsibility. In freedom there is no one else to take the initia-tive, no one else to follow through, no one else to blame. Genuine freedom is not easy. It is risky. It is something, in spite of so much of our rhetoric to the contrary, from which we generally flee. Even the pursuit of knowledge takes courage. Little of our thinking really breaks new ground. It's safer — every young academic, professional or engineer knows — to follow the conventional wisdom and paradigms. Much of what goes on in our classrooms, gets published in the scholarly journals or gets produced by our technology does not truly advance human knowledge. To genuinely pursue the truth requires a trust that things ultimately make sense, a faith that our intellects can get us somewhere and a courage to follow where the truth leads us.

At the root of the Christian concern with humanity's woundedness is the conviction that because God has become one with our humanity in Jesus' life, cross and resurrection, love is worth the effort, that our faith in humanity despite its failings is well placed, that there is good reason to hope against the hopelessness of our world. If Jesus is God's "realsymbol," God's self-communication, then the movement of our minds, freedom and love towards the fullness of being and love is genuine, not an illusion. If Jesus is God's self-expression, God-incarnate, that really changes what it means to be human. It changes our way of being. It transforms us by giving us a radically new possibility. Our humanity then becomes a real, actual openness for God (or rejection of God), not just an abstract and potential openness for God.

It is like the poor fellow who has no one to love. Without that other person, he cannot be a lover. His potential for love (assuming that there really was no one else) would be an abstraction, a totally unreal possibility, a potential only in the most theoretical sense. But if someone makes themselves available to him, if someone loves him and so is open for his love, or even if there is just someone there who might be open for his love, he is then given a new possibility, a new way of *being*. Only in that situation can he really and actually become a lover (or someone who has failed at love). This is not a possibility he can create for himself. Nor, Christians believe, is this a possibility that we can create for ourselves, apart from what God has wrought in Jesus. But because there is an identity between the divine and human in Jesus, the gap between our wounded humanity and God is bridged. We are redeemed. As the first letter of John puts it, we are able to love because God "loved us first" (4:19).

Salvation, then, is not the result of a juridical decree on God's part. The grace (or gift) of salvation is not just some "thing" that God gives us. If Jesus is God's "realsymbol," then he is God's *self*-communication. The gift in the concrete and created reality of the human Jesus is the transcendent and uncreated reality of God. What we find there is a who: namely, God.

One of the advantages of the "realsymbol" as a model for understanding the unity between the divine and human in Jesus is this manner it offers for conceptualizing how such an identity mediates God. The identity mediates God because it is God's self-gift to humanity, what believers call grace. The identity communicates God's Spirit because it incarnates God's own love, and so shares with us in the person of Christ, the love between the Son and the Father.

We are not talking here about an abstraction. We are talking about a real slice of history. We are talking about Jesus' concrete life, about his proclamation of the coming of God's kingdom and fidelity to it, about his opposition to the preoccupations and priorities of his world, about his identification with the sinner and outcast and ultimately about his abandonment and death on the cross. That, Christians believe, is where God's love is fleshed out and revealed. It is true that this particularity raises problems. It is perhaps even scandalous. Why then? Why in Palestine? Why a Jew? Why a man rather than a woman? If God's love were not particularized, however, it would be an abstraction. Love in general is no love at all. It is had cheaply. God's love, we learn from Jesus, was not cheap. Jesus' "being human to the utmost" was had at the expense of all the particularity which "being human" entails, including suffering and death. That is why Christians attend so closely to what Scripture has to say about Jesus and see in him a norm for themselves, whether they lived in the sixth century or live in the twentieth, whether they are his sisters or his brothers, whether they are black or white. To be saved, to be in solidarity with God, to anticipate being human to the utmost is to be in solidarity through Jesus with humanity in all our diversity.

The conception of Jesus as God's "realsymbol" can also help

clarify how the cross saves us without thinking of this in a magical and superstitious way and without making a wrathful despot of God.[6] A "realsymbol" is what a being creates to express and communicate itself. We "make conversation," "make" a handshake, "make love" or whatever to give ourselves over to another and to "be with" the other. We mentioned in the last chapter that such symbolic gestures actually cause something to happen. What we do in making conversation or in making love really does bring us together. Such gestures create a new *being*, a communion or "we" that was not there before. It is important to emphasize that this "we" (this "*being* of two or more persons with one another") is a reality in itself and is a new reality. A "we" is not simply the sum of two or more "I's" which are next to each other. Two or more minds who are one can think and dream things which the individuals alone would never have dreamed. In the unity of friendship, we can give to each other a freedom and courage that alone we would not dare to risk. When the bond of love between people is fleshed out in the concrete, it is very different than the love one has towards another who is unapproachable and "distant." On the darker side, there is the phenomenon of the mob which has its own mind and will, and which is capable of doing things that would have been unthinkable for any of its members individually. Jesus' cross also creates something new.

Recall that our historical overview of Jesus' life indicated that the cross was not an isolated event in Jesus' career. With scholars like Kasper, I argued that "Jesus' violent end was written into the logic of his life." The fidelity to God and neighbor which Jesus incarnated was ultimately manifested in this last gesture of his life. The point, of course, is that this was not just a gesture or just symbolic. It was a self-expression that summed up and fleshed out all that he stood for and all that he was. And in Jesus' being raised from the dead, Christians believe, it becomes clear that this radical freedom and love incarnated in Jesus express and communicate the ultimate mystery and meaning at the heart of life. In other words, Jesus' cross fleshes out and sums up God's self-communication. So the cross not only reveals that

God is merciful and saving love, the cross is the divine gesture or "realsymbol" which definitively and irrevocably brings that love about and makes it a reality. The cross, then, is the embodied self-expression through which God finally becomes one with all that is human. The cross (along, of course, with the whole history from birth to resurrection of which it is a part) is the gesture which mediates God to us and so causes a divine solidarity with humanity that bridges the alienation created by sin.

So without the cross, real and actual openness for God would be at most something for which we might hope or yearn. God's presence would still be very much out of reach. In retrospect, we might say that it appears that God intended such solidarity from the beginning. In a sense, this movement of God's redemptive love to us was there before Christ. It is the cross, however, that actualized and incarnated this divine plan, and so it is the cross that actually brings it about. Its causality is analogous to marriage vows or the signing of a contract. The vowing or signing actually creates the bond. Those gestures are necessary for the marriage or legal entity to exist. The persons concerned may indeed have anticipated and planned this for years, but that in itself would not constitute a valid marriage or contract. The persons may even have lived together for awhile or already fulfilled many of the obligations of the legal document, but in itself that also would not ordinarily constitute a marriage or contract. Likewise, the Christian believes, Jesus' redemptive life, death and resurrection is necessary for salvation. In it, God's love for humanity is irrevocably and definitively made real and actual. That event gives meaning to all that came before and to all that comes after.

An important qualification must be kept in mind here. To say that God's love has been made real in Jesus' life, death and resurrection, and that this gives humanity an openness for God which we would not have had otherwise, does not mean that all of humanity has accepted that openness. It does not mean that we know all are saved. Certainly we may hope for this. As we saw in Chapter 11, however, the love manifested on the Cross and in the Resurrection is not coercive. It is a love which addresses our freedom. So the very offer of God's love changes us and transforms us, but it does not save us if we refuse it. Moreover, if the concrete history of the world is the arena in which God's love addresses our freedom, then all specifically human activity is implicitly either an acceptance or rejection of that divine love. This now makes explicit the grounds for saying, as I did in Chapter 8, that our consciousness of self and the world, our freedom and our ability to truly love hinge on our openness for God, that this openness is the result of God's saving presence to us in Christ, and that hence every act of the head, heart, hands and feet anticipates solidarity with God or rejects God.

There is a second assumption which must be made explicit. A self-communicative gesture of God, unlike our own gestures, can really do what it sets out to do. Our gestures are always inadequate, always somewhat false and necessarily imperfect because we are. But God is not. God's self-expression, if truly God's and truly self-communicative, would truly express God. One gesture would do it. Another gesture would not produce anything that wasn't already there. So, what appeared to be another gesture would either be somehow one with the first or else bogus. Even in our own cases, one valid marriage ceremony or one signing of the contract is all that is necessary. Going through the ceremony again or signing the documents again (assuming the same parties and covenants) would not create a new (or second) marriage or contract. Indeed, we would not recognize such repetitions as valid. At best they would be renewals of something already established. Now, if God had definitively and irrevocably established solidarity between the human and divine prior to Jesus, then Jesus could not truly be the Christ, God's own Word or "realsymbol." And if Jesus is such a divine gesture, then no renewal is necessary or could replace him and the solidarity he establishes between the human and the divine.

This is not to deny that God's self-communication has a history. Jesus does not reveal or flesh out a new God for the people of Israel. In him the believer recognizes the Logos or Wisdom or

Spirit who according to Scripture had been revealed to the prophets and Moses, to Abraham and Isaac and to Adam and Eve at the very beginning. What happened on the Cross and in the Resurrection, although gratuitous (uncalled for and unexpected), was the fulfillment of the divine promise and covenant which the believer traces etiologically, and so in retrospect, to the very beginning.

Moreover, Jesus as one of the human race had a history and shared fully in our historical reality. To be human, after all, is to live in a specific time and place and is to be part of a greater unity. Our "*being* human" is essentially and intrinsically a "*being* with others." Our consciousness, decisions, loves, language, imaginations — all those things which shape us and through which we determine our shape — are formed by others or in dialogue with others. Jesus was part of this unity, conditioned by it as well as shaping it and giving it a radically new dimension. Jesus was not an isolated otherworldly figure who miraculously dropped from the heavens. He was born of a woman. He had a particular cultural and linguistic heritage, a social and religious heritage, an ethnic and political heritage, a familial and genetic heritage. If Jesus is God's self-communication, then those different heritages set the stage and provide the context for this divine gesture. As Rahner put it, the world constitutes in a radical sense the environment, the setting and even the physical stuff in which God's self-communication is expressed to the non-divine.[7] Consequently the world and its history can be seen as an essential element in God's self-communication.

From a Christian perspective, such a notion is not really so novel. As Malmberg pointed out, if God creates out of nothing then in a certain sense all the effects of this creating (of what traditionally was called God's efficient causality) are a kind of "imparting of Himself." This imparting of self involved in God's creating the world achieves its highest possibility when God assumes as God's very own self-expression the created (and so historically tangible) humanity of Jesus. Consequently, as Malmberg and Rahner put it in their different ways, Jesus is the point at which creation and humanity reach their highest possibility and at which their goal communicates itself most intimately to them.

This Christological model thus provides a way to make sense of the claims that Jesus saves all of humanity and that Jesus is also necessary for salvation. It explains how Jesus could have had a relationship to all those who came before him and how they, at least implicitly, could have had a relationship toward him. Jesus fulfilled what the prophets had anticipated and he endured the injustice and malice against which they had inveighed. In retrospect, the believer can say that wherever there has been movement toward a more authentic love, freedom and wisdom, it must have been in virtue of the Spirit ultimately bestowed in Christ. Bridging of the gap between God and our wounded humanity is not something which could have been effected apart from God's own self-communication. So, wherever and whenever humanity moved towards its true orientation and goal, there was already a yearning, searching or anticipation of what God finally brought about in Jesus. The first letter of John says

> God is love
> and anyone who lives in love lives in God,
> and God in him. (1 John 4:16)

But the letter also says:

> this is the love I mean:
> not our love for God,
> but God's love for us when he sent his Son
> to be the sacrifice that takes our sins away.
>   (1 John 4:10)

So this love of which John speaks redeems what came before. It vindicates that yearning, seeking and anticipation as genuine, just as a marriage or signed contract establish as genuine the falling in love or negotiating that had preceded. If the marriage never happens or the papers never get signed, then what came before is at best an open question, at worst a lie, a false hope, a deception. In the latter case the living together or prior transactions take on an entirely new and perhaps opposite meaning from what they originally seemed to promise.

Humanity has a future as well as a past. If the purpose of God's self-communication in Jesus was to save humanity, then that gesture on God's part is not finished until all of humanity has been touched by this "spirit," and has either accepted or rejected it. By "spirit," I mean both the concrete human *being* (consciousness, freedom and love) of Jesus and the transcendental *being* of the holy Spirit present to us in the gift of love, freedom and truth. If there is acceptance it must, from the Christian perspective, be in virtue of Christ's "spirit," since all love is grounded in God's prior love. This is not a reason to insist, however, that it is no love at all or no salvation at all unless it is an explicitly Christian love. Likewise, if love, freedom and truth are rejected this is implicitly a rejection of Jesus' Spirit and of the coming of his Father's kingdom. A person does not have to know Jesus to reject what he stands for, calls for and ultimately is bringing forth.

This is often seen as an implication of Jesus' parable of the last judgment (Matthew 25:31-46). All the nations — people it could be presumed of all faiths — are gathered before the King. The sheep and the goats are placed at his right and left hands, the former to be rewarded, the latter to be sent away to eternal punishment. The criterion, however, is not what the judged anticipated. Those who inherit the kingdom are actually surprised when the King explains his verdict: "for I was hungry and you gave me food, and I was thirsty and you gave me drink, I was a stranger and you welcomed me, I was naked and you clothed me, I was sick and you visited me, I was in prison and you came to me." To their disclaimers, "Lord, when did we see you?" he responds, "Truly, I say to you, as you did it to one of the least of these my brethren, you did it to me."

The text is a classic to which the Church and theologians have frequently appealed. It also seems likely, however, that Matthew's objective in relating this parable had nothing to do directly with our question about the salvation of non-Christians. There are strong exegetical grounds for holding that the concerns of Matthew and his community were different from ours today.[8] But this does not mean that the parable has nothing to say to our question. The text may not directly have the universalistic meaning which theologians and popes have attributed to it. Still Matthew's concern for relating discipleship of Jesus to identification with the poor and suffering is the root from which that universalistic conviction grew.

These conclusions for which I have been arguing in this chapter give a new and more radical meaning to the images which have guided our discussion up to this point. First, if Jesus is God's self-communication to humanity and if, consequently, the whole of human history is the history of our accepting or rejecting of that solidarity between the divine and human, then the correlation of theology and anthropology takes on a much more profound meaning than it had in the previous chapters.

In the initial efforts to outline the contours of the Christian circle in the first part of the book, I maintained that our concrete determination of who we are (anthropology in the broadest sense) implies an Ultimate Concern or God of some sort (theology in the broadest sense), and that conversely every theology implies an anthropology. In the next section's effort to bring the horizon of Christian faith into sight, I added that "being human" entails an anticipation or reaching out towards God as ineffable mystery and absolute fullness of *being*. Thus, to be human is to reach out towards God, while at the same time any effort to understand God entails an intrinsic reference to what it is to be human. In that very qualified sense we found it even possible to take over Feuerbach's identification of theology and anthropology.

Now a third meaning for theological anthropology can be asserted. The central focus of Christianity is the conviction that God actually meets us in our humanity, that there is a genuine and most intimate solidarity between the divine and human. Our "being human" (that is to say our solidarity of consciousness, will and love with all our brothers and sisters in Christ) is the fleshing out of our acceptance or rejection of God's love.

Christology, as Rahner put it, "is the beginning and the end of anthropology, and this anthropology in its most radical actualization is for all eternity theology."[9] Conversely, because of Christ our theology (both our lived relationship to God in religion and our ideas about God) has practical meaning only in reference to our concrete anthropology. That is to say, the meaning and reality of God is mediated through Jesus' humanity and through our solidarity with him as sisters and brothers across all ages, races, nations and classes. There is a much more intimate, but by no means reductionistic, identity between theology and anthropology than Feuerbach proposed or probably imagined.

If this is true, the notion that Christianity is a charmed circle takes on a quite different meaning as well. We become who and what we are only through our reaching out towards God, a movement which is grounded, however, in God's prior self-gift to us. God is present to us, therefore, not only as distant mystery, but also as fleshed out concretely in Jesus and as personally present in the Spirit of love, freedom and truth which actually touches our consciousness, frees our wills and empowers our love. Our world and our existence, then, in their innermost depths and authentic dynamism are a world to which God is being given, a graced world, a Spirited world, and in this now positive sense a charmed circle. Our world is being made human and being called to be human to the utmost by God's own humanity.

Ours is indeed also a wounded world still in need of salvation, still on its way. But in view of what has been accomplished in Christ and in his "spirit," the wound is not humanity's destiny or its essence. As Malmberg put it, summarizing the teaching of the Church Fathers of the first centuries, Adam's sin — the wound — was limited from within and from the beginning by God's merciful love. "The inner urge of this 'radical' break with God ('radical' in a double sense: humankind at its 'roots' turns 'radically' away from God) to harden itself into a final irretrievable obduracy, was prevented and vanquished from the inside by the stronger urge of grace to go back to God."[10] Humanity, then, is caught up in a circle of love — a circle of love that is divinely inspired, divinely inSpirited, in a most positive sense charmed.

Or so Christians believe! Once again it must be admitted that an effort like this book's to break into the truth of the Christian circle, does not at all establish its truth. The truth can only be found in solidarity with the Savior whom I have argued is at the heart of things for believers. But if God's love is at the heart of things, why is the world still so unloving? If the Spirit of Christ is available to all, why do believers insist so on the necessity of the Church? Indeed, doesn't the sinfulness of those who call themselves the Church undermine the credibility of the claim that Christianity is a divinely charmed circle? We cannot honestly claim to have achieved our aim without at least entertaining these difficult questions.

Notes

1. James Tunstead Burtchaell, C.S.C., *Philemon's Problem: The Daily Dilemma of the Christian* (Chicago: ACTA Foundation, 1973), p. 36.

2. *The Redeemer of Man (Redemptor Hominis),* Vatican Translation (Boston: Daughters of St. Paul, 1979), p. 27 which in part quotes from "The Church Today" *(Gaudium et Spes)* ¶ 10; see *The Documents of Vatican II* (New York: America Press, 1966), p. 208.

3. Juan Luis Segundo, *The Community Called Church*, trans. John Drury (Maryknoll, New York: Orbis, 1973), pp. 56-57.

4. Segundo, p. 57.

5. Segundo, p. 57.

6. I am especially dependent for much of what follows here on Rahner's essay "The One Christ and the Universality of Salvation," *Theological Investigations* (New York: The Seabury Press, 1979), vol. XVI, pp. 199-224. For an anlaysis of Rahner's position, see Leo O'Donovan, "The Word of the Cross," *Chicago Studies* 25 (April 1986), pp. 95-110.

7. Karl Rahner, "Christology in the Setting of Modern Man's Understanding of Himself and His World," *Theological Investigations*, trans. David Bourke (New York: The Seabury Press, 1974), vol. XI, p. 220.

8. John R. Donahue, S.J. "The 'Parable' of the Sheep and the Goats: A Challenge to Christian Ethics," *Theological Studies*, 47 (March 1986), pp. 3-31, makes a strong case that universalistic and ethical application of this text in the official teaching of the Church (e.g. Vatican II, and the teaching of Pope Paul VI

and Pope John Paul II) and especially in liberation theologians does not correspond to Matthew's own meaning or intent. Donahue, nevertheless, sees here an ethic of discipleship through deeds which challenges Christians to a more authentic proclamation of the Gospel.

9. Karl Rahner, *Foundations of Christian Faith: An Introduction to the Idea of Christianity*, trans. William V. Dych (New York: The Seabury Press, 1978), p. 225.

10. From his unpublished manuscript *The Humanity of God*, ed. Sharon M. Burns, RSM, p. 8.

IV. PROJECTING THE VECTOR

14. The Scandal of
the Hands and Feet

In astronomy, a vector is an invisible line joining the center of an attracting body such as the sun with the center of another body, such as the earth, revolving around it. In mathematics, a vector is a force or velocity having direction and magnitude. The vector can also be a line representing such a movement which is drawn from its point of origin to its final position. We could characterize the implications of the last chapter by saying that the Christian circle of understanding posits such a vector. The horizon, goal or final position of the vector is God. Its center or point of origin is Christ. Its embodiment, the vector or line itself, is human history, that is to say, our history insofar as we individually and collectively are touched and transformed by the "spirit" of Christ. There is an essential provisionality and pluriformity to this vector. Each point along its trajectory is partial, still on its way, not yet there. But there is also a definitiveness and unity to the vector which is eschatological: because of Christ and the Spirit, the end is already anticipated in the beginning; the first is included and completed in the last.

One can legitimately ask, however, whether the existence of such a vector is not contradicted by the massive suffering and evil of human history. Is the reality of this vector not belied by Christians themselves and by their Churches? How credible is talk about being caught up in the saving love of Christ's Spirit when the hands and feet of believers are on any sober accounting no less dirtied, complacent, manipulative, exploitive and bloodied than non-Christians'? Talk is cheap. The scandal of the hands and feet, if we are honest, is not easily explained away. For the vast majority of the world's population, the reality of human degradation and suffering is a brutal and constant fact of life. That their hunger, malnutrition, poverty, economic exploitation, political repression, environmental pollution and oppression because of race or religion seem exceptional in our "own world," intensifies rather than mitigates the scandal. If all humanity is one in Christ, where is our solidarity with the masses of our brothers and sisters who are so unfortunate and so victimized? How credible is our belief that God's love was given hands and feet in Jesus, if we are barely conscious, for the most part, even of the plight of those who are near to home?

It is not enough, here, to talk about the woundedness of human freedom or the role that even sin might play in divine providence. The scandal of the hands and feet which I have in mind is not the theoretical question about how a God who is all loving, all good and all powerful could allow suffering or human evil. There is no doubt that resolving such questions poses serious questions for Christian faith. That is but another manifestation of what I have called the problems of the head. Neither such difficulties nor theology's responses to them, however, get at core of what troubles and scandalizes us when we are genuinely attentive to the victims of our world and let their suffering touch us. The problem at its core is not an intellectual conundrum but rather a concrete existential contradiction, not the theoretical question about God's existence but the more fundamental and personally involving soteriological question about the very meaningfulness of human life and the reality of a genuinely humanizing love. The issue is not whether the truth which Christians proclaim is coherent but, rather, whether it is a saving truth.

That is why most people's minds, I suspect, are not changed by Feuerbach's protest against faith as alienating, by Marx's charge that it is an opiate, by Nietzsche's proclamation of God's death, by Freud's critique of religion as an illusion which must be replaced with modern science, or by any of the believer's responses to such theses.[1] No doubt people are moved by one or another of these positions as expressing and validating what they already believed or suspected, but how often do such arguments (the skeptics' or the believers'!) truly bring about a conversion of a person's thinking, commitments and deeds?

The scandal of the hands and feet runs deeper than this. In the face of human pain and anguish, such reasoning is quite impotent; it seems just so much foolish posturing. There are no easy theoretical solutions.[2] Skeptics, on their side, have little difficulty showing how easily faith degenerates into the sacralism of a comfortable piety, cheap grace, lip service orthodoxy and routine obedience to law. The Church itself and theology are not immune to such critiques. Corruption, intrigue, murder, persecutions, inquisitions, holy wars, racism and sexism taint the history, and so undermine the credibility, of the very institutions which purport to be the body of Christ. As the American theologian Matthew Lamb observes, "one can find theologies ideologically supporting almost every bias that ever raised its ugly head in history." He continues,

> No wonder that Catherine of Siena and Dorothy Day often prayed for "the poor theologians." Theologies have abounded attempting to rationalize imperialism, colonialism, racism, sexism, capitalism, militarism, totalitarianism, communism, sacralism, atheistic secularism, consumerism, multinationalism, fascism, anti-Semitism, Nazism, chauvinism, technocratic elitism, clerical authoritarianism, etc. It is difficult to think that theology was ever considered more than a dumping ground of biases.[3]

For many people today, consequently, it is not the idea of God which is problematic but the reality of God in the world, in the Church and in the talk which believers claim mediates the divine. If they do not find there a truth and freedom and love which saves and humanizes — indeed, if what they discover embodied there is suffering and vicitimization, how could they recognize God?

On their side, however, theologians such as Lamb have little difficulty demonstrating that an easy secularism is no refuge from the scandal of the hands and feet either. The emancipation through reason which Feuerbach, Marx and Freud promised has proven itself illusory. Instead of a saving truth, one can point to the myriad ways in which the so-called rationality of modern society, just as frequently as theology, has served to legitimate all the prejudices which have ever corrupted the human heart. The human hand, rather than nature's, has increasingly become the source of suffering in our world. The modern Enlightenment has thus brought what the German theologian Johann Baptist Metz calls "an anthropocentrism of suffering."[4] It is modern rationality which has given us two world wars, the destruction of Hiroshima and Nagasaki, the murder of millions in Nazi, Soviet and Cambodian "work" camps and the insane but seemingly inescapable logic of the nuclear arms race. Nor can we blame sexism and racism on nature, though some have certainly tried. This human responsibility for suffering extends even to realities which we take for granted and do not recognize as orginating with ourselves. "Poverty," Lamb contends, "is man-made, and its present global intensification results more from human stupidity and a shortsighted bias of unenlightened self-interest than it does from a cunningly intelligent greed."[5] He makes the same point with respect to welfarism and colonialism. There can be little question, as well, that the starvation afflicting Africa for a number of years now is as much rooted in the perversity of politics and economics as it is in the capriciousness of nature. Moreover, no one has a monopoly on the defense mechanisms which serve to rationalize such suffering or insulate humankind from our reponsibility for it.

> Conservatives try to atrophy past victories by immunizing the status quo against its critics through legal, economic, humanitarian, and armed force. Liberals make nature the scapegoat for suffering: human failures are ascribed to an unenlightened past which will be absolved by the advance of science and technology. Marxists have no difficulty in attributing the histories of suffering to those enemies of the proletariat who still wield power in history and so impede the inevitable success of the march toward

a party-planned utopia. Such defense mechanisms find their apotheosis in those advocates of technocracy who deny human freedom and dignity.[6]

The scandal of the hands and feet defies a purely theoretical solution. What it makes problematic is not one circle of understanding or another but the meaningfulness, truth and value of our very humanity. Are any of our ideals more than false abstractions? Are any of our deeds more than materializations which enslave and dehumanize? Are any of our beliefs more than deceptive rationalizations? Are any of our faiths or hopes more than self-delusions?

It turns out, then, that the scandal of the hands and feet is not peculiarly the problem of Christian anthropology. It is a scandal which speaks against all of humanity, against all humanisms, against all religions and so against all anthropologies. Lamb rightly warns that this scandal cannot be evaded by a comfortable optimism or a self-assured pessimism. Such optimism in effect trivializes human suffering "with easy assurances of better and brighter tomorrows." "Are the victims of history," he asks, "condemned to die in the waiting rooms of ever more illusory futures?" Pessimism, on the other hand, ends up romanticizing human "suffering with dark forebodings of some impending doom. Do victims struggle to transcend their sufferings only to enter a cynical world of meaningless catastrophe?"[7] Such easy answers cannot circumvent the scandal of the hands and feet.

We, for our part, cannot really claim to have broken into the Christian circle without confronting the scandal which human suffering and our complicity in it poses. If the world is so meaningless, how can there be any ultimate meaning? If the world is so Godless, how can there be a God? Is belief in God even possible for one who honestly faces the overwhelming evil and absurdity of our world and its history? Does the circle of faith we have been describing chart a path which really goes anywhere? Is belief in Christ but another obstacle to our efforts to achieve a more authentic humanity? Is it but another delusion about humanity's destiny and possibilities?

Notes

1. For an extensive overview of their arguments see Hans Küng, *Does God Exist? An Answer for Today*, trans. Edward Quinn (Garden City, New York: Doubleday & Company, Inc., 1980).

2. For an illuminating and provocative critique of such theoretical solutions see Matthew L. Lamb, *Solidarity with Victims: Toward a Theology of Social Transformation* (New York: Crossroad, 1982).

3. Lamb, p. 14; his harsh criticism is by no means advanced as a rejection of the Christian church or its theological tradition, but rather as part of his argument for a more self-critical appropriation of that heritage through an on-going process of reflection which seeks to discern the tradition's values and differentiate these from its disvalues.

4. Johann Baptist Metz, *Faith in History and Society: Toward a Practical Fundamental Theology*, trans. David Smith (New York: The Seabury Press, 1980), p. 108.

5. Lamb, p. 5.

6. Lamb, p. 19.

7. Lamb, p. ix.

15. Fleshing Out Humanity

Jesus, the man from Nazareth, and faith in him as humanity's savior does not do away with the scandal of the hands and feet. Indeed, this intensifies the scandal. If God is love and calls us through Jesus and the Spirit to love, then the inhumanity of the world is even more obscene than it first appears to be. But faith in Jesus not only intensifies the scandal, it also provokes its reversal in the counter question posed for us by his cross and the human potential for love which it actualizes and reveals: How can such love be explained? What significance do such miracles of love have for the meaning of humanity's problematic history? How can we account for love at all, if the love which beacons us in face of evil is not the ultimate meaning of existence, a gift, God's own Spirit, our salvation?

Both this scandal of the hands and feet and its reversal in Jesus' love bring us to a theoretical impasse. Theory cannot overcome evil. Only love, love that is fleshed out concretely, can answer to human suffering and victimization. Nor is such love the fruit of our thinking. Theories cannot generate love. Love cannot be explained or accounted for; love is a risk. It is a matter of faith and trust. It comes as gift and as a grace. Consequently, a credible response to the scandal of the hands and feet calls for a *move* from *thinking* about love to *doing* love.

This move, however, presents us with a further and more intractable difficulty. Do we really know what it is that we are to do? Do we actually know what love is? How confident can we be that the Spirit of Christ truly empowers us with the love of God? Just because we have an abstract notion of love and know how to use the word grammatically does not mean that we know

209

what love calls for, what it is to love in the concrete, or that love
has truly touched us or our world. In the name of well-inten-
tioned love all kinds of victimization has been justified: a distorted love of master for slave, of man for woman, of parent for
child, and of community for individual has frequently enough
denied the beloved's consciousness, censured the beloved's freedom, blocked the beloved's every move and so smothered the beloved's humanity. We must not forget that Christians in the
name of their faith have justified all manner of prejudice and injustice. If theology is to be more than an ideological rationalization for a current cultural bias, it must not only call for a move
from thinking about love to doing love, but also must be itself a
thinking which from the start is *moved by*, *grounded in* and
tested in the doing of love.

This is the guiding insight of the so-called liberation and
political theologies. Pure theory and ideological neutrality are
not genuine possibilities. Knowing the truth is not just a matter
of taking a good look at what's out there, and doing the truth is
not just a matter of giving a good effort.[1] *What we see* is conditioned by where we stand, by the lenses through which we
view the world and the narrative and actions through which we
define ourselves and give shape to our ideas.[2] *What we do*, therefore, is conditioned by this prior "doing" which constitutes our
understanding of ourselves and our world. Consequently, if the
truth which believers embrace and proclaim is in fact to be an
expression of the saving truth of Christ, there must be a constant effort to ferret out and critically examine the lived presup-
postions which inform Christian thinking. Moreover, there
must be an ongoing effort to change that thinking when it does
not promote the concrete and authentic transformation of our
wounded humanity in Christ's "spirit," and finally there must
be a willingness to adjust one's behavior accordingly.

The truth which Christians embrace must respond in this
way to the scandal of suffering and victimization or it will not be
credible to those for whom the reality of love, and so the reality
of God, has become so problematic. If the truth which the believer professes does not in some way reflect the conversion and

transformation of our wounded humanity in the "spirit" of
Christ, then however technically correct, that "truth" will
nevertheless be dangerously partial. The partiality is problematic first of all, because it leaves out what is most important: that
Jesus saves us, that the solidarity which he establishes between
us and his Father inaugurates the kingdom of God, that he
sends the Spirit through whom God offers to make new persons
of us — sons and daughters of us, *true* sisters and brothers of us
all. Equally serious is that such a technically correct but
soteriologically amnesic truth can justify a partiality — that is
to say, a bias — which is complacent about suffering and victimization or, worse,which serves as a rationalization for injustice.
In that case, a dogmatically correct truth is co-opted and per-
verted. It becomes itself a counter-sign and scandal to the good
news of Christ.

That is one of the reasons theologies of liberation are so critical of an exaggerated emphasis on orthodoxy. It is not because
correct doctrine is unimportant. Nor should their criticism be
read as a repudiation of tradition, of historical research or of
theoretical rigor, although most unfortunately that impression
might be given by some of their rhetoric and by the popular nature of much of liberation theology's use of scripture and tradition.[3] What they decry is an orthodoxy whose omissions tend to
privatize faith, thus neutralizing its call for a qualitative transformation and conversion of the whole person — head, heart,
hands and feet.

So, for example, they criticize the separation of the historical from the supernatural because it makes an unreal and docetic abstraction of conversion and of the salvation anticipated by
that turning to Christ's "spirit" of love, freedom and truth.
Likewise, they criticize the simple and absolute identification of
the kingdom of God with any present order or political program
because it denies the distinction between our wounded humanity and the future which God's love in Jesus and the Spirit promises, and because, at the same time, it belies the obvious recognition that the redemption of the world is still far from complete.
Liberation theologians aim to move beyond doctrinal concep-

tions like the hypostatic unity of Jesus' humanity with the
Father or the transubstantiation of bread and wine in the Eucharist because more needs to be said. More needs to be said
about what in the concrete distinguishes Jesus' divine humanity from our wounded humanity. More needs to be said about
what in the concrete distinguishes Eucharistic communion with
God and with our sisters and brothers in Christ from dehumanizing and sinful forms of interdependence with neighbor
which at the same time are a rejection of God's solidarity with
us.

Such positions are not surprising, given the liberation
theologians' point of departure. They are aware of this influence
of their methodological presuppositions on the logic of their arguments and on their eventual conclusions. In fact, they see
their explicit and prior commitment to the poor and marginalized of society as a key for doing theology in a manner that
will more truly be moved by, grounded in and tested in the doing
of love. They are convinced that a credible response to the scandal of the hands and feet which is also faithful to the reality of
salvation in Jesus and his Spirit, must begin, as Boff puts it,
with

> the brutal reality facing the vast majority of people
> on our Christian continent. They are living and dying
> amid inhuman living conditions: malnutrition; a
> high infant mortality rate; endemic diseases; low in-
> come; unemployment; lack of social security; lack of
> health care, hospitals, schools, and housing facilities.
> In short, they lack all the basic necessities that might
> ensure some minimum of human dignity. Such is
> the real-life situation of vast segments of our
> people. . . . [4]

If one begins with the plight of these poor, not only those in Latin
America but throughout our world, then the fascination of so
much of our theological tradition with what I have called the
problems of the head is thrown into question. Hence, liberation
theology often portrays itself in opposition to the dominant
theologies of North America and Europe.

Sobrino, for example, argues that the crisis of belief brought about by the Enlightenment has two stages.[5] The first he traces to Kant and identifies with the concerns of academic theology in the Northern Hemispheres. The concern here is with the intellectual challenge of modern, scientific and secular culture to belief in God. Does God exist? Is God just a projection? Are there truly valid grounds for belief in God? Is it even meaningful to talk of God? Sobrino sees the second stage embodied in Marx's critique of religion as part of the social and economic structures which oppress the majority of humankind. If one begins at this stage, then a quite different set of questions are raised and a different dialogue partner is engaged. Here it is not the philosophical difficulties of the skeptical intellectual which take center stage, but the scandal of the poor and marginalized, the "nobodies" and "non-persons" who have no standing at all in the world of influence or academia. For such persons the question is whether belief in God can be reconciled with suffering and victimization. Is Christianity in any concrete and historical way a saving truth? Does Christianity really free our consciousness, hearts, hands and feet for an authentic humanity?

There is some truth to this distinction which liberation theologians make between the intellectual questions of skeptics and the soteriological questions raised by suffering and victimization. Obviously, however, my argument from the start has been moving towards the conclusion that both the scandal of the hands and feet and the problems of the head must be addressed. Roger Haight also supports this point in his compelling interpretation of liberation theology's alternate vision. "Oppression and the problem of the non-person," he concludes, "is an intrinsic challenge to any faith in God."[6] On the other hand, there is also an inescapable and most fundamental threat to any faith in God posed by those ways of thinking (philosophical, historical or scientific) which preclude the transcendent, whether in an idealistic or materialistic way. A truthful, credible and livable theology faithful to the tradition of Christ cannot afford to slight either intellectual and academic rigor or concrete and humanizing practice. The Christian circle promises the grace of a *saving* truth and of a *truth* that is saving.

Despite this qualification, if one takes seriously the scandal of suffering and injustice and thus pursues the questions of its implicit interrogator, the non-person, it soon becomes clear that classical philosophy and the historical-critical method are not sufficient as tools for thinking through the correlation between our wounded humanity and Christ's good news. Poverty and oppression in their many varieties are social realities. The most obviously relevant methodologies for understanding such phenomena are found in the social sciences (particularly economics, political science and sociology) and political philosophy. Marxist analysis is especially helpful to the extent it has shown how suffering and victimization originate from the economic and political structures of society.

Using such tools to understand human suffering and injustice leads to a greater appreciation of the social and structural dimension of evil and of sin. The point is not that Christians have never before seen the necessity for love of neighbor and social justice. I have already argued that this is a clear imperative in the Hebrew Scriptures and in the New Testament. It is only more recently, however, with the knowledge afforded by the social sciences, that Christians have been in a position to appreciate the extent of human interdependence, its anthropological consequences and its theological implications. From such a perspective, it becomes evident as it could not have been in earlier times, that if love of neighbor and justice are to be genuine realities in our world and history, this requires a transformation of social structures as well as individual conversion. Moreover, from this perspective it becomes obvious that social systems themselves can embody sin — that is to say, our institutions and collective behavior can embody ways of acting and thinking which close us off from the reality of God. Economic, political and social systems can, and do, narrow human consciousness, warp the human will and vitiate humankind's good intentions and good work. There is no question that poverty, suffering and victimization are to a large extent the manifestation of such systemic sin.

Recognizing this, of course, does not change the situation.

It does, however, give our thinking a new direction. It suggests, as Sobrino puts it, that the quandary of suffering "is not to justify God but rather to turn the justification of human beings into a reality."[7] Hence liberation theology emphasizes that social justice is intrinsic and essential to faith, not merely something which is added to faith or which faith encourages.[8] Moreover, endeavoring to give hands and feet to social justice in a world which is sinful requires a recognition of the conflict between victims and oppressors. It means taking sides. It means a preferential option for those who are victimized. It means opposing those who promote injustice.

This should not be read as reversing Christ's command to love even one's enemy, or the conviction that God wills the salvation of everyone. Loving a person does not mean endorsing all that he or she does. Nor does the command to love mean that we must stand by and let one person hurt another even if the first individual only does so indirectly and unconsciously without explicitly intending any harm. I might add that opposing those who promote injustice should not be the expression of any animosity towards persons, but only towards what they are doing. Lest this become an ameliorating excuse for comfortable consciences, however, it is necessary to be mindful that it is persons whom, for example, society puts in jail for doing evil, and that the opposition to love is embodied in us as persons, not merely in the structures of our societies. The need for social and structural transformation to which liberation theology directs our attention, then, cannot be separated from a recognition of personal responsibility or from the need for personal conversion and transformation.

The term which liberation theologians use for this conversion and transformation of persons and social systems is praxis. Praxis does not mean simply practice. Rather it refers to this process of endeavoring to orient one's thinking and acting (both individually and systemically) so that thought and action are truly moved by, grounded in and tested in the doing of love. Praxis in this sense, then, is not opposed to theory as such or opposed to orthodoxy. Rather praxis is an engaged thinking. It is

committed action. This sort of engagement and commitment requires a constant circulation between theory and practice so
that one is informed by the other, moved by the other and tested
by the other. Liberation theologians insist, however, that correct praxis (orthopraxis) requires that priority always be given
to the doing of love in this circulation. Theology, consequently,
is not grounded in abstract theory. Nor does it start with theory.
Theology, as Segundo puts it, is the "second step." The first step
must be faith, and in particular must be a lived faith committed
to making love and justice a concrete reality, committed to giving witness to God's justification of humanity in the "spirit" of
Christ.

Liberation theology is aware that commitment and engagement are not in themselves guarantees of one's living in the
truth. The priority of praxis does not mean that practice by itself
is sufficient for living in the Spirit of truth, freedom and love.
The mutual correlation or dialectic between interpretation and
practice, suspicion and engagement, the critique of our theologies' biases and the recovery of their truths, is an ongoing
task for the particular Christian communities of every age and
in every part of the world. On the other hand, there is no more
fundamental response to the scandal of the hands and feet than
such ongoing, provisional but eschatologically significant efforts to flesh out the humanity to which God calls us through the
Spirit of love, freedom and truth incarnated in Jesus.

Notes

1. See Matthew Lamb, *Solidarity with Victims: Toward a Theology of Social Transformation* (New York: Crossroad, 1982); Juan Segundo, *Liberation of Theology*, trans. John Drury (Maryknoll, New York: Orbis Books, 1976); Johann Baptist Metz, *Faith in History and Society: Toward a Practical Fundamental Theology*, trans. David Smith (New York: The Seabury Press, 1980). Particularly helpful introductions to liberation theology in Latin America are provided by Roger Haight, S.J., *An Alternate Vision: An Interpretation of Liberation Theology* (New York: Paulist Press, 1985); and Robert McAfee Brown, *Theology in a New Key: Responding to Liberation Themes* (Philadelphia: The Westminster Press, 1978). There are of course significant differences, which are not

necessary for us to sort out here, among liberation theologians in Latin America, between them and other liberation theologies and between liberation theologies and the political theologies of Europe and North America.

2. The crucial role which story and narrative play in defining our concepts are very fruitfully explored by Stanley Hauerwas in *Vision and Virtue: Essays in Christian Ethical Reflection* (Notre Dame, Indiana: Fides Publishers, Inc., 1974) and in *Truthfulness and Tragedy: Further Investigations into Christian Ethics* (Notre Dame, Indiana: University of Notre Dame Press, 1977).

3. See Haight's argument (p. 58) that the appearance is deceptive. In any case political and liberation theologians are well aware that undercutting scripture, tradition or modern critical thought violates their own objectives and methodology.

4. Leonardo Boff, *Jesus Christ Liberator: A Critical Christology for Our Time*, trans. Patrick Hughes (Maryknoll, New York: Orbis Books, 1978), p. 268.

5. Sobrino, pp. 33-35.

6. Haight, p. 32; he makes this case throughout the book but especially in in the first four chapters. See also Lamb's argument, esp. pp. 104-12, 124-43. Cf. Gregory Baum's alternate reading in "The Creed that Liberates," *Horizons* 13 (Spring 1986), pp. 136-49.

7. Sobrino, p. 36.

8. Cf. Haight, pp. 64-82.

16. Saving Gestures

The scandal of the hands and feet which makes Christianity so problematic has had as much to do, especially in recent times, with the Church itself as with the question of evil. What has been said about faith as the ongoing effort to flesh out humanity in the "spirit" of Jesus' love, freedom and truth could be interpreted in a way that would aggravate this difficulty with the Church rather than help break into its circle. Christians certainly are not the only people committed to making truth, freedom and love concrete realities in the world. Those outside the Church, even atheists, not to mention admirable people of other faiths, are frequently better at this and more committed than churchgoers. Moreover, there are many people who believe in Jesus, or at least respect him as a model and prophet, and who seek to live in his spirit, but who still do not see any necessity for the Church. Indeed, there can be no question that many of those who thus accept the ongoing task of fleshing out the human love, freedom and truth of Jesus, nevertheless see the Church, its sacraments, its laws and its clerical bureaucracy as an obstacle to this project.

Is the Church necessary? What does it contribute that could not be found elsewhere? Is it not a bureaucratic stumbling block? Isn't the division of the Church into many opposed Churches one of the main obstacles to human solidarity? Don't the Church's rules and regulations actually stifle the spirit of love, freedom and truth? Doesn't its emphasis on the sacraments encourage the superstitious and magical view that salvation can be had apart from love of neighbor? Wouldn't the time devoted to building up the Church be better spent dealing with the urgent economic, social and political problems of our communities and nations?

That there is some validity to the charges implicit in such questions cannot be denied. The Church can be a scandal. It has been and is. It would be naive to suppose that elements of partiality and sinfulness could ever be eliminated this side of God's Kingdom. The Church is a human reality. Still, everything that has been said in the previous chapters, and indeed Christian tradition itself, argues that, scandal and all, the Church has an essential, irreplaceable and salvational function to play.

Our humanity is a dynamic reality. It is also a wounded reality in conflict with itself and its authentic destiny. So being human is an ongoing task: at times a movement of consciousness, freedom and love towards God and at times a narrowing, enslaving and turning in on self which rejects God. The Christian faith, I have contended, is convinced that our woundedness has been limited from within and from the beginning by grace, God's saving gift of Self. The cause of that grace is Jesus, God's own gesture fleshed out in solidarity with our humanity and culminated in the Cross and Resurrection. As such, Jesus is absolutely necessary for salvation. That salvation is also the basis for our humanization and for our coming together in the truth. So when I have spoken about the "spirit" of Jesus, I have intended to emphasize at once both the human and divine. Jesus establishes a *human spirit* of love, freedom and truth with which we can become one, because in fleshing out God's humanity he shares with us the *divine Spirit* of love, freedom and truth.

This divine gesture, literally embodied in Jesus, not only reveals our possibility for such a human dynamic, it establishes and creates that dynamic. Love, we saw, needs such gestures if it is to emerge and be sustained, especially a love that is wounded and closed in on itself. The same need is inherent in our wounded freedom and consciousness. Moreover, the meaning of love's gestures cannot be separated from their content, a content which the authentic gesture seeks to communicate, make explicit, interpret, support, focus and direct.

A kiss that betrays, for example, is not an expression of love, nor is a kiss which is superficial and empty. Nor are things meant to stop at the kiss. The kiss communicates, makes explicit, reinforces, focuses and directs our bearing towards another person. Not all kisses lead in the same direction, but they all head somewhere. The kisses of lovers, of friends, of parent and child, of participants at a Eucharistic celebration move toward different kinds of intimacy. The point is, however, they head somewhere or else are meaningless. The kiss of one who would use us, hurt us or dominate us, or of one who is indifferent to us, aim toward other sorts of relationships. The kiss of whatever kind thus derives its meaning, value and content from the dynamism of which it is a part and expression.

So also, Christians are convinced that the true meaning of the human dynamic of the head, heart, hands and feet aims somewhere and has meaning and content only in virtue of that destination: namely, solidarity with the Spirit of God as concretely embodied and revealed in the Crucified and Risen Jesus. So although it can be said that all genuine expressions of the human spirit, whether explicitly Christian or not, are truly saving, it also must be said that such gestures are incomplete. They must move forward toward a fuller, more explicit unity with God and neighbor in the "spirit" of Christ or become something different, something quite the opposite. Thus, as moments in the human dynamic towards God, rooted in God's prior Self-gift, such genuine expressions of human love, freedom and truth are but the beginnings of faith.[1] They head towards full-fledged faith and are in need of its gestures so that love's, freedom's and truth's contents can be communicated, their meanings become conscious and explicit, their focus be given direction and the possibilities they promise be supported and nurtured.

Indeed, all of us, like Jesus' first followers, are disciples of "little faith." Our wounded love, freedom and truth are but faith beginning, in need of the faith of others and of their faith's saving gestures, lest the dynamic of what is emerging within us be cut short: narrowed, warped and closed in on itself. Faith — that is to say, authentic humanization, the broadening of consciousness, the liberating of freedom and the empowering of love for their true end in God — needs the saving gestures of *people who take a stand for the Spirit of love, freedom and truth fleshed out in the Crucified and Risen Jesus.* Faith cannot live without such people. Humanity, the Christian believes, cannot be saved without such people. Such people are who the Church is called to be.

Conceiving the Church in this way, as people who take a stand for the "spirit" of Jesus, emphasizes that the Church is not a what, not primarily a place or an institution. The Church is persons, persons who sometimes function together as a community and sometimes as individuals in the larger society. Persons, however, cannot take a stand together without some common identity, joint purpose, structures for cooperation and places to meet. Nor can persons even take a stand individually without some common point of reference, language and pattern of behavior which is capable of communicating their stance to others. Consequently, for people to take a stand, either collectively or individually, some sort of organization or institutionalization is necessary. Although Jesus did not found an institution as such, he did take a stand and gathered people around himself as disciples and called them to stand with him. He defined this stance in terms of symbols like the Kingdom of God and the "twelve" (representative of the tribes of Israel) and in terms of a call for a qualitatively radical conversion. Moreover, his "stance" ultimately revealed itself on the Cross and in the Resurrection as God's definitive, irrevocable and saving gesture and self-communication to the world. Thus the Church and its necessity come from this divine/human stance as its tangible and continued presence in history.[2]

Admittedly, disciplines, laws and doctrines, emphasized onesidedly, can stifle the "spirit" to which God calls humanity. This is a danger of which the Church must be ever mindful and which calls for a hermeneutic of suspicion and continuous efforts at genuine and substantial reform, indeed even calls for breaking with our wounded past and present. On the other hand, people who would take a stand for the "spirit" of Jesus cannot do so without structures and institutions of this sort, and

without substantial continuity with the entire history of those
who have stood for Jesus' "spirit" in the past and of those who
stand for it now in other circumstances and in other parts of the
world.

Segundo's interpretation of Paul's instructions to the community at Corinth explains and illustrates the necessity for establishing such rules among people who would take a stand.[3] In
1 Corinthians, Paul responds to the report that one of their
members has been having a sexual relationship with his step-
mother. Apparently this person understood Paul's teaching of
the freedom won in Jesus as a justification for this arrangement.
Segundo emphasizes that this was not a case of someone caught
up in passion for a moment. In effect, this Corinthian was taking
a stance which he believed, despite Paul's admonitions, to be in
the "spirit" of Jesus' freedom and love, Paul urges the Corinthians to "drive out this evil-doer from among you" (1 Cor. 5:13).
Segundo argues, however, that Paul's reason for doing this is
not precisely because the man is a sinner. Paul does not urge
them to separate from everyone who is sinful. Who would be
left?

> When I wrote in my letter to you not to associate
> with people living immoral lives, I was not meaning
> to include all the people in the world who are sexually
> immoral, anymore than I meant to include all usur-
> ers and swindlers or idolworshippers. To do that, you
> would have to withdraw from the world altogether.
> What I wrote was that you should not associate with
> a brother Christian who is leading an immoral life, or
> is a usurer, or idolatrous, or a slanderer, or a drunk-
> ard, or is dishonest; you should not even eat a meal
> with people like that. (1 Cor. 5:9-12)

Segundo points out that Paul does not expel the man to condemn
him. In fact, quite to the contrary, Paul recommends this action
so that the man's "spirit may be saved on the day of the Lord" (1
Cor. 5:5). The reason for Paul's ruling has to do, rather, with the
Church's function as a people who take a stand for the "spirit" of

Jesus. The content, meaning, focus, direction and power of that stand would be drastically compromised if a stance so opposed to Jesus' spirit was passed off as an expression of it or as compatible with it.

> Paul simply draws logical conclusions from the central idea that the Church is, essentially and primarily, a *sign*. It has been placed here precisely and exclusively to pass on to men a certain signification, i.e., a message, something that is to be grasped, comprehended, and incorporated to a greater or lesser degree into the fashioning of history and the world. If *the very existence* of the Church is meant to be leaven in the dough, salt in the meal, and light for all those who dwell in the human household, then the ecclesial community must accept the obligations that derive from its essential function.[4]

Lines have to be drawn today as well, and teachings defined and made normative for the community of believers. Thinking of the Church as people who take a stand should remind us of this necessity. It should also remind us that this people's discernment, formulation and interpretation of such rules and doctrines for itself is an ongoing process. Its purpose must always be to clarify more effectively Jesus' stance for humankind's transformation in the coming of God's Kingdom.

An eschatological dimension is a second aspect emphasized by the conception of Church as people who take a stand for the Spirit of Jesus. The "spirit" of love, freedom and truth fleshed out in him which defines this people's stance is divine as well as human. Christians know, or should know, that their grasp of that divine "spirit" is always partial, provisional and even seriously wounded. The heart of the Christian faith, however, is the conviction that insofar as love, freedom and truth are genuine, concrete and effective, they truly give God's Spirit. The Church, then, insofar as it is a true Church — insofar as its stance is faithful to Jesus' "spirit" — is a reality of God's own Spirit, a source and cause of grace as well as a sign of it. That is why

Catholic Christians have often spoken so confidently of an effectiveness of the Church's sacraments *ex opere operato*, that is as effective by their very performance, "from the work worked." It is not because these signs (these visible manifestations of a stance towards life) have an automatic and magical power in themselves. Rather it is because these signs are rooted in what Jesus Christ has already done and has actually achieved. They are signs of God's stance toward us and its effect on us, rather than signs of something brought about by the merit of the minister or the recipient of the sacrament.[5]

Needless to say, a onesided emphasis on this aspect of the sacraments has often given the misleading impression in Catholic practice and popular theology that the effectiveness of the sacraments has little to do with the disposition of the believer (that is to say, with what comes "from the work of the worker," *ex opere operantis*). That, however, was not the position of the Council of Trent which defined the matter. The sacraments are not magic. The reality which they signify, with which they touch us and to which they call us is Jesus' "spirit" of love, freedom and truth. What saves is the concrete fleshing out of that "spirit" in him and in us through our ongoing conversion, transformation and solidarity in him. Such "realsymbols" of God's Self-gift are essential for focusing the Christian people on their basis in the Spirit, for fashioning them into a community which takes its stand with Jesus' Spirit and for directing them outwards toward the world in that "spirit." The sacraments do this by calling the community's attention to the possibilities for discerning God's saving presence at key moments within its life, which for Catholics are seven: birth (Baptism), coming to maturity (Confirmation), fellowship (Eucharist), alienation and reconciliation (Penance), sexual love and family (Marriage), service to the community (Orders) and illness or death (Anointing).[6]

The stand which the Church takes must not be so narrowly concerned with these gestures that it falls prey to what Segundo calls a kind of "sacramental intoxication." Rather, as he says, the sacraments must "be historically 'true': that is, efficacious with respect to man's liberation in real-life history. In other

words, the sacraments will be valid and efficacious, as Christ intended, to the extent that they are a consciousness-raising and
motivating celebration of man's liberative action in history."[7] So
the people who are the Church have a (real) symbolic or sacramental function with respect to the world. That is what taking a
stand is all about.

From what was said earlier, it should be clear that this does
not mean that the Church is the only place (the only people)
where humanizing action takes place or where humanizing
stands are taken. At the same time, it should be emphasized
that saying this does not decrease the importance of the
Church's function or its particular and unique stand. Rather
this emphasizes the necessity and importance that people
through their concrete stands in history draw attention to the
inextricable connection between human love, freedom and truth
and God's Spirit.

The notion of taking a stand also suggest that the Church's
gestures and work are always historically and culturally contextualized. One takes a stand with respect to a specific set of circumstances, at a given time in a particular place. Moreover, although the stand will always be "for" the same "spirit," the particular stances will inevitably vary. In feudal times, it led Christians to oppose the lending of money for interest as dehumanizing. In a capitalist economy, Christians not only admit the mor-
ality of the practice but have found themselves engaged in it
rather extensively, in efforts to promote the humanization of society. In the face of Communist oppression, Catholics in Eastern
Europe have emphasized the separation between the religious
and political orders, while in the face of oppressive economic
structures many Latin American Catholics have stressed the
political character of faith. People who authentically take a
stand for Jesus' "spirit," although moved by the same Spirit are
nevertheless moved in a variety of different, sometimes quite
dramatically different, ways. Unity and uniformity are not the
same. A pluriformity of stances does not necessariy imply evil
compromise — in fact it often is demanded by a stand for Jesus'
"spirit" of love, freedom and truth.

Conceiving the Church as a people who take a stand includes the six models which Avery Dulles has so fruitfully investigated. Five of these are elaborated at length in his influential book, *Models of the Church*.[8] The Church, he observes, can be thought of as an *institution* which teaches, sanctifies and rules with the authority of Christ — an authority, of course, which authentically expresses love, service and truth, not domination. The Church can also be imagined as a *mystical community* — a solidarity and fellowship of love with God and neighbor through the Spirit of Christ. Alternately, the Church can be described as a *sacrament* — as the visible manifestation of grace in witness, worship and service. The *herald* model pictures the Church as those who proclaim and preach the Gospel of Jesus Christ. The *servant* model emphasizes the Church's mission to promote the justice and freedom to which God calls us.

In his book, Dulles scrutinizes the roots and implications of these images. He shows how each is typical of one theological perspective or another, and of one community of believers or another. It is not necessary to summarize that discussion here beyond suggesting some obvious examples: the influence of the institutional and sacramental model for Catholics, the appeal of the mystical community model to many Charismatics and Congregationalists, the herald model's significance for Evangelicals or the servant model's place in the thinking of groups like the Salvation Army or Latin American "base communities."

Dulles contends that each of the models has obvious advantages but also correlative liabilities. Although it is inevitable that one image or another will be focal in a particular theological perspective, he argues for the importance of balance and integration. An emphasis on the institutional character of the Church with which comes a clear sense of identity, stability and continuity must not be allowed to degenerate into a depersonalizing institutionalism. Care must be taken that the personally engaging, spontaneous and ecumenically promising community model not be understood in a way that reduces the Church's function merely to the promotion of human fellowship or in a way that would confuse the reality of faith with a feeling of fellowship. The sacramental model, so rich in its implications for Catholics, must not be developed in a way which leads to superstitious sacramentalism, the danger so feared by many in the Reformed tradition. The herald's emphasis on God's prophetic Word must not lose sight of the need to embody that word concretely in gestures of worship and service. Finally the servant model's focus on doing justice must not be stressed so exclusively that the Church comes to be conceived as just another humanitarian social agency. A valid and fruitful conception of the Church would have to integrate elements of each of these models.

Despite the popularity of his analysis, Dulles is quite aware that none of the models he identifies in his book, as a matter of fact, truly catches the contemporary imagination, at least of most Catholics. Nor do any of the models in practice seem to provide the balance necessary today either for effectively integrating each of the others' insights into people's conceptions of the Church, or for advancing the ecumenical efforts of a divided Christianity. His book *The Resilient Church* expressed that concern through a critique of both conservative and liberal excesses.[9] In a more recent essay, he comments on the need for a more effective image.

> The ineffectiveness of certain apostolates, I suspect, is closely linked with an inability on the part of Catholics to form an image of the Church into which they can plausibly fit what they think they ought to be doing. Some of the current images of the Church are repugnant; others are seemingly unrelated to daily experience. If we could fashion an inspiring and realistic image of the Church, we might be able to act confidently, and in such a way that our self-understanding would be reinforced by feedback from others.[10]

He then proposes the model of *discipleship* as one with a strong Biblical basis which offers a more integrative and ecumenically promising conception. Discipleship, he suggests, admits an institutional element. Indeed discipleship is an institution, but of a very personal sort. Discipleship calls to mind the bonds of fellowship and spontaneity of Jesus with his followers, but it also recalls the cost of following him and the responsibility which comes with that calling. The disciple is one who gives witness to Jesus in word, gesture and deed, and so incorporates the elements of herald, sacrament and servant.

The notion I have proposed of the Church (people who take a stand for the Spirit of love, freedom and truth fleshed out in Jesus) suggests a possibility for interpreting the meaning of discipleship in a more systematic and contemporary idiom. Moreover, it emphasizes the essential and necessary interconnection between the elements which are highlighted by each of Dulles' models. Indeed, if the Church is conceived as people who take a stand for Jesus' "spirit," it becomes clear that each of the these models if authentic must include the other. How, for example, could one effectively proclaim (herald) Jesus as God's Word without making that proclamation concrete in gestures (sacrament) and transformative deeds of love (servant) which seek to realize the solidarity of humanity with Jesus' Spirit (mystical community) and which entail some sort of structured embodiment in creeds, doctrines and a rule of life (institution)? Otherwise, the herald's proclamation would be empty words. Or how could one effectively promote the humanization of society (servant) without proclaiming in words (herald) and symbolizing in gestures (sacrament), which are focused and interpreted through creeds, doctrines and a rule of life (institution), that the basis and goal of human existence is solidarity with God's Spirit in Jesus (mystical community)? Otherwise, the basis and goal of our conversion and transformation would still be out of sight. Or how could one take an effective stand for human solidarity in love (mystical community) without gestures (sacrament), interpreted by words (herald) and specified through creeds, doctrines and a rule of life (institution), which disclose and communicate the Spirit of Jesus as the basis and goal of that community of love? Otherwise, the communion would be incomplete.

Each of the elements in these images is related to the other.

All are entailed if one is to take a stand for the "spirit" of Jesus. Each is involved in truly and effectively being his disciple. Moreover, there is good reason to be wary of "modeling" as a tool for achieving balance in one's conception of the Church, if the effect of that logic is to separate these dimensions and emphasize one over against the other, for example, stressing the servant model to counteract sacramentalism, the community model to counteract institutionalism, the herald model to counteract excessive activism and so forth. There is, indeed, a danger that one element or another may be overemphasized. Properly understood, however, these aspects of taking a stand for the "spirit" of Jesus are not at all contrary. Thus, opposing them in a way which suggests false dichotomies would be a dubious strategy for achieving theological balance.[11] In fact, there is not enough that service can do to concretely flesh out Jesus' transformative "spirit" of love, freedom and truth. Nor can there be too much human solidarity, too many gestures for embodying the grace of Jesus' "spirit," too many prophetic words calling us to his "spirit," or enough structures for adequately specifying the nature of that "spirit." The scandal of the hands and feet will be answered by nothing less than such an ongoing effort and stand of the whole person (head, heart, hands and feet) individually and collectively for the Spirit of love, freedom and truth fleshed out in Jesus.

Notes

1. See Juan Luis Segundo, *The Community Called Church*, trans. John Drury (Maryknoll, New York: Orbis Books, 1973), p. 56.

2. For a more technical argument for this position see Karl Rahner, *A New Christology*, trans. David Smith and Verdant Green (New York: The Seabury Press, 1980), pp. 18-31. For a discussion of his position and its development see Francis Schüssler Fiorenza, *Foundational Theology: Jesus and the Church* (New York: Crossroad, 1984), pp. 91-98 and Leo O'Donovan, "A Journey into Time: The Legacy of Karl Rahner's Last Years," *Theological Studies* 16 (December 1985) pp. 630-31.

3. Segundo, pp. 79-86.

4. Segundo, p. 81.

5. See in Karl Rahner's *Theological Investigations*, "The Word and the Eucharist," IV, pp. 253-86; "The Theology of the Symbol," IV, pp. 274-78; and "Personal and Sacramental Piety," II, p. 124. For a general overview, McBrien's *Catholicism* is most helpful.

6. See Juan Luis Segundo, *The Sacraments Today*, trans. John Drury (Maryknoll, New York: Orbis Books, 1974), pp. 68-75; and Bernard Cooke, *Sacraments & Sacramentality* (Mystic, Connecticut: Twenty-Third Publications, 1983).

7. Segundo, *The Sacraments Today*, p. 55.

8. Avery Dulles, S.J., *Models of the Church* (Garden City, New York: Doubleday & Company, Inc., 1974).

9. Avery Dulles, S.J., *The Resilient Church: The Necessity and Limits of Adaption* (Garden City, New York: Doubleday & Company, Inc., 1977).

10. Avery Dulles, S.J., "Imaging the Church for the 1980s," in his *A Church to Believe In: Discipleship and the Dynamics of Freedom* (New York: Crossroad, 1982), p. 3.

11. Hence, Dulles' elaboration of the discipleship model as an image of the Church offers a much more effective strategy than the one pursued in *The Resilient Church*; see my review essay "A Grammar for Dissent — In Response to *The Resilient Church*," *Living Light*, 15 (Fall 1978) pp. 428-33.

17. The Human Vector

It is now possible to characterize more explicitly the vector of human history as I believe the Christian understands it. First, that dynamism is divine as well as human. God is not beyond our reach. From the beginning, God has been reaching out and touching us in the love, freedom and truth fleshed out in the humanity of Jesus and in our solidarity with his "spirit." Because of this rootedness in the Spirit of God, human history can transcend its finitude and woundedness. Truth, freedom and love are thus genuine possibilities, not false hopes, idle dreams or fanciful projections. We can be transformed and converted from our inhumanity. Because of God's Spirit in Jesus, the vector of human history is saving and eschatological. It is a movement in God and to God because it is God's movement to us and in us.

On the other hand, this human vector is an historical reality. The salvation which Jesus' "spirit" promises is not complete. Our grasp and being- grasped by that "spirit" is provisional, partial and still ongoing. We are saved but still wounded. Our consciousness, freedom and love are historically embodied. They are fleshed out within the limits of a particular time and place, within the context of a specific history and culture, within the biases and sinfulness of wounded egos and social systems and so within a relativized and contextualized circle of faith. The provisionality and partiality of this faith of ours thus requires an ongoing hermeneutics of suspicion to allow truth and love a possibility for breaking into our circles and for breaking with and breaking from our circles' ideological bewitchment.

The provisionality and partiality of faith's circle requires, at the same time, a hermeneutics of engagement. If we are to be truly saved by the truth of Jesus, then our circle of faith must be moved by, grounded in and tested in the doing of love. To this extent the circle of faith must be socially and politically engaged. It must stand in the concrete for all that truly humanizes and against all that victimizes — not as another political party or program, but as a committed vision of humanity (a transformative praxis, as the liberation theologians would say) which takes its stand for Jesus' "spirit" of love, freedom and truth as the transcendent standard to which all human ventures are called and against which all are measured.

The provisionality, partiality and particularity of the circle of faith also means that it is fleshed out in a diversity of historical embodiments and expressions. One cannot live in Christ's "spirit," then, without critically, rigorously, faithfully and ecumenically attending to the Scriptures and to the history of the Church's life, doctrine, worship and saints. Christ's "spirit" of love, freedom and truth is not abstract, general or disembodied. It has a specific content, a concrete meaning and tangible history. It is necessary to be informed and formed by that specific history if people are to be truly touched by and transformed by its saving grace. The Protestant doctrine of Scripture's inerrancy and the Catholic conception of doctrinal infallibility are rooted in and expressions of this belief in the informative and formative character of Christ's "spirit" in history. God's truth really does reach us in Jesus' "spirit" and does really make binding demands on our consciences and commitments. Neither doctrine, however, should be understood in a fundamentalistic way which in affirming the eschatological and binding significance of Scripture and doctrine denies their historicity and provisionality. Even God, in Jesus, took on the limits of our temporality and particularity. Consequently, to be formed by the history of Christ's "spirit," to take that "spirit" seriously and truly be in dialogue with the Spirit requires a community which supports and nourishes historical research in faith and as an expression of faith, and which undertakes ecumenical dialogue with urgency, patience and humility. To be a people who stand for the "spirit" of Jesus, the Church must be a people who stand in his memory — a people who allow that memory to question their stance, test it and move it forward, not just academically but concretely in the world of commerce, politics and science.

Likewise, one cannot live within Christ's pluriform "spirit" without attending to the diversity of contemporary voices which speak to it and for it. Dialogue with these other voices is not something which one adds to faith as an improvement or further implication. Dialogue is intrinsic and essential to faith. Being human (that is to say, fleshing out what truth, freedom and love in the "spirit" of Jesus demands) is not limited to what we find incarnated within our own circles, but emerges in a variety of ways and diversity of contexts wherever his "spirit" is present — and often where we least expect it. To know the God to whom and by whom we are called, we must attend to those different voices. This is not just a question of translating an abstract truth which faith already possesses into new languages. Rather it is an ongoing process of being transformed and humanized by a truth which transcends us even as it is mediated concretely in the diversity of our humanity.

Generations of Christians, for example, did not see a contradiction between the "spirit" of Jesus and slavery. To be grasped by that contradiction is to recognize something new, is to recognize something not seen before about what it means to be human as Jesus was. When Jesus' own "spirit" is recognized in and as a black man, or when Jesus' own "spirit" is recognized in and as a woman, or in and as a "nobody" or in and as someone strange, it gives a content and meaning to human love, freedom and truth which goes beyond and even breaks with the conception of Jesus' humanity conceived only in the image of a white man. The more we recognize the extent of God's brotherhood and sisterhood with us in the many faces of Jesus' "spirit," the more we can recognize the concrete depth and breadth of God's unfathomably transcendent reality. The basis for diversity and dialogue, then, is not only the poverty of our wounded humanity, but also the richness of God's humanity fleshed out historically in the "spirit" of Jesus, in the "body" of Christ.

Nor are Christians the only people concerned about the meaning of humanity or its relation to God. Dialogue with Jews, Moslems, Buddhists, Hindus and all the other religious and secular traditions of humankind is important not only because the followers of Jesus have been called to take a stand for his "spirit" and so have something to say to those traditions, but because here too Christians can and must learn for themselves concretely what the content of Christ's "spirit" is. Just as the dialogue between the first Christians and Hellenistic culture led to a development of doctrine and practice, so the dialogues of our day must head towards the new understandings and different embodiments to which Christ's "spirit" calls humanity's future.

Finally, the historicity and embodied nature of humanity requires that faith must be in dialogue with the secular sciences. How can one take a stand for truth, freedom and love, if one does not understand what these are or how they function psychologically, socially, politically, economically, historically, culturally and even biologically, chemically and physically? Philosophy can no longer serve as the exclusive tool for breaking into faith's circle or for breaking out of our ideological circles. How does one humanely love one's enemy, for example, in a world of competing nuclear powers? What does it mean to be human in a world which can be genetically engineered? What in this context does it mean to be free and responsible? What are the differences between male and female, and what implications do these imply about one's conception of God? What actual role does freedom play in a capitalist, socialist or Marxist economic systems? Are there such things as economic and social rights? How distinguish neurotic guilt from a healthy recognition of personal sinfulness? The questions are relentless.

The vector about which we have been speaking is an ongoing task. Its path must be projected and fleshed out if the scandal of the hands and feet is to be addressed. It requires concrete action, engaged dialogue and "spirited" experiments in the worlds of politics, commerce and science and with other faiths. This vector calls for the participation of the whole "body" of

Christ, not just intellectuals, specialists or clerics. There is no denying that it is possible to miss the mark. There is no denying that the reality of this vector is hidden, obscure, even problematic. But, then, every theological anthropology is a human venture which requires risk, presumes faith and entrusts itself to a hope.

V. COMING FULL CIRCLE

18. Holding It Together:
The Vision and the Agenda

Recent decades have witnessed traumatic shifts and divisive polarizations within the Christian faith. It is not obvious that the circle into which we have been breaking holds together as coherently as I have suggested. Commentators have compared this situation to the swings of a pendulum back and forth from right to left, from conservative to liberal, from divine to human, from transcendence to immanence, from orthodoxy to orthopraxy, from spirituality to social activism, from ecclesiastical authority to personal charism, from archaism to accommodationism and so forth.[1] There can be no doubting, either, that such swings have had a deleterious effect. Certainly part of the reason why the Christian circle seems so bewitched is because of the conflict, confusion, disarray, disorientation and doubt which afflict so many within it. Conservatives, of course, blame it on an excessive and uncritical accommodation to modernity and secular humanism. Liberals blame it on a fundamentalistic orthodoxy which refuses to acknowledge the historicity of faith or its susceptibility to ideological captivity. Perhaps most eschew the excesses of both ends of the pendulum's arc, as do the signers of the 1975 "Hartford Appeal" for theological balance,[2] Avery Dulles,[3] Cardinal Ratzinger[4] or the editors and authors of the new publications *Center Journal* and *Catholicism in Crisis*. But even here there is considerable conflict. It turns out that one party's center is another's excess.

That is the difficulty with the pendulum as an image and with the agenda it suggests for restoring theological balance. Its remedy calls for countering an excessive swing in one direction with a good hard shove in the other. Thus, those on the right push for a renewed and more vigorous emphasis on the divine, on transcendence, on orthodoxy, on tradition, on inerrancy or infallibility, on spirituality and on ecclesiastical authority. Meanwhile, those who see imbalance in the other direction stress the human, this world, orthopraxis, political involvement, academic freedom and personal charism. All that pushing and shoving creates a lot of movement and tension, but it is not at all evident that it is a constructive strategy for holding the circle of faith together or for building up the "spirit" to which Jesus calls us. These remedies are ineffective because they oppose what should not be opposed and because the conception of a theological pendulum, in itself, does not show how the center is to be located or how opposite poles are to be reconciled.

Avery Dulles tells a story, as much fantasy as reality, which is helpful for illustrating this point.[5] He was preaching at a church and noticed a huge banner on the wall which proclaimed "God is other people." As the anecdote goes, Dulles took out a magic marker and put in the missing comma so that the banner would read "God is other, people." The gesture certainly would have been vivid and prophetic, but it also would have been quite incomplete. The Christian faith does not profess with Feuerbach that God is simply other people. When believers proclaim this as their faith, or say something more sophisticated which seems to imply the same thing, putting in commas is a necessary corrective. That gesture itself, however, could be a source of significant distortion. Although the phrase "God is other, people" is theoretically orthodox, while "God is other people" is not, the latter phrase despite its heretical implications, often expresses an existential appreciation of God's presence in our midst. To deny the phrase without bringing out this existential truth can be as misleading as it would be to deny God's otherness. As long as we argue over the comma, pushing it in and out, we force, or at least set up a framework that forces, people of good will and good conscience, people who are troubled and often out of touch with the transcendent dimension of spiritual life, to choose between one part of the truth and another. My point here is not to suggest that Dulles does this.[5] He does not. Rather the point of recounting the anecdote is to show that a different and more complete strategy is necessary to achieve theological balance. A different vision and agenda are required if such people are to see how the circle of faith holds together.

Quite obviously, the intent in the previous pages has been to break into the Christian circle in a way which would suggest the possibility for such a vision and agenda. The center and key of this approach has been the integration of the human and divine in Jesus. They are not opposed in him. He is not part divine and part human, but both *at once*. The Christian vision, at least ideally then, does not swing back and forth between the divine and human, but rather moves within the circle of divine/human solidarity in Jesus and in the solidarity of the "spirit" to which he calls us. Properly understood, theology and anthropology are not opposed, nor properly understood are God's immanence and transcendence, nor the Cross and Resurrection, nor orthodoxy and orthopraxis, nor historicity and eschatology, nor faith and reason, nor grace and freedom. This is not to deny that there can be a tension between these elements or that there can be false emphases which stand in need of correction. What it does suggest is the importance both of elaborating perspectives which show how these things come together and of working out agendas for the ongoing process of attending to this task.

Here in a concluding chapter, there can be no question of responding in detail to specific conservative and liberal arguments for correcting imbalance in one direction by countering with an opposite emphasis. It would be too difficult to avoid unfair caricatures of those positions. It is possible, however, to briefly recapitulate this book's own thesis and some of its implications for maintaining theological balance. Put most succinctly the thesis has been this: to be human is to be caught up in the saving circle of God's love. Within this saving circle, God as Father can be conceived as the distant horizon and mysterious ground of human existence. God as Son is one with our humanity and at the center of our history. God as Spirit is the historical vector through which the divine in person moves to us and in us, so that we can move in God and to God.

Because of this circular character in God's relation to us, the believer can coherently speak of Jesus ascending from our

humanity to God, as descending from God to us and as the point
of solidarity between God and ourselves. Indeed, each of those
ways of speaking is necessary to suggest the richness of God's
saving presence in the Incarnation, Cross and Resurrection.
This implies that no theology should be faulted for emphasizing
Jesus' humanity. His humanity cannot be emphasized enough,
so long as this is not done in a way which denies his divinity. It
is precisely through Jesus' being human to the utmost that God
reaches us, touches us, becomes one with us and thus frees us
from our inhumanity. Conversely, no theology should be
faulted for emphasizing Jesus' divinity. His divinity cannot be
emphasized enough, so long as this is not done in a way which
denies his humanity. Jesus truly communicates God to us because Jesus is God's own gesture — God's own self-expression
or realsymbol. Jesus is as much God·reaching humanity, as a
human who reaches God. He is not first one and then the other.
He is both at once.

Because of this solidarity or being-in-each-other of the divine and human in Jesus, it is possible, indeed necessary, to approach Christology both from below (by attending to Scripture
and to Jesus' humanity to discern the development from his
birth through his concrete life to his cross and resurrection) and
from above (by attending to the doctrine of Jesus' divinity to uncover its implications for understanding the unity of the divine
and human in him). Properly interpreted, each moment of this
divine/human solidarity (Jesus' birth, ministry, death, resurrection and sending of the Spirit) speaks of the whole and gets
its meaning from the whole. None of these moments and
neither the approach from below nor the approach from above
should be opposed to each other or emphasized against each
other. Rather, the corrective is to see their essential interrelation.

Likewise, the logic of the Christian faith requires that the
various manifestations of God's presence not be opposed to one
another. That presence is communicated as God's "spirit" sent
to the Church by Jesus, as God's "spirit" within humanity moving it toward solidarity with Jesus and as the personal indwell-

ing of God's "spirit" which opens the mind, frees the heart and empowers the love of those who yield to this holy presence's touch. There is no contradiction in asserting, on the one hand, that Jesus' and the Church which takes a stand for his "spirit" are necessary for salvation and, on the other hand, that there are people outside the Church who are saved and, indeed, who even have something positive to contribute to Jesus' "spirit" in the world.

So no theology should be faulted for highlighting the importance of the Church or for focusing on God's presence to the non-Christian, as long as the truth of either emphasis is not denied. The significance and irreplaceability of the Church cannot be stressed enough, nor can we stress enough the importance of respecting other circles of belief (religious or secular) and the urgency of genuine and open dialogue with them. Nor should the ecclesial presence of Christ's "spirit" be opposed to the "spirit's" personal presence to the individual. The institutional, communal, sacramental, prophetic, and servant dimensions are essentially interrelated and necessary in taking a stance for the "spirit" of Jesus. Authentic discipleship requires developing each as fully as possible. There is not enough that believers can do to flesh out Jesus' transformative "spirit" of love, freedom and truth. There can never be too much genuine community — with God or with one another. There can never be too many gestures or too many prophetic words calling us to, disclosing and celebrating this divine/human solidarity. Nor can there be enough structures for adequately specifying it. Once again, the corrective against imbalance is not polar opposition, but a mutual and proper interrelation which distinguishes a centering (or centripetal) tension which holds and pulls things together from a dichotomizing (or centrifugal) tension which thrusts them apart and puts things at odds with each other.

This circular relationship of the divine and human means, in turn, that revelation, grace, salvation, the Church and sacraments are at once transcendent, historical and eschatological. They are transcendent because they express humanity's reaching out towards God. They are historical and thus provisional, partial and ongoing because God's solidarity with humanity is fleshed out in the temporal and cultural contexts of human history. They are eschatological because despite and through their historicity they embody and reveal God's reaching out to us.

Here, again, there is a danger of polarizing emphases. It is tempting, for example, to counter the suggestion that Scripture's words are no more than historically relative human insights and hardly inerrant by denying Scripture's historicity altogether, or at least by so emphasizing the words' divine origin that their historicity is effectively rejected. An analogous denial of the historicity of the Church's teaching is the unfortunate outcome if one absolutizes doctrinal infallibility as a strategy for countering a wholesale relativization of doctrine. And, of course, there are the converse temptations to see an emphasis on the absolute inerrancy of the Bible or the absolute infallibility of all Church teaching as reason for denying altogether the revelatory character of Scripture and doctrine, or for so emphasizing their historicity that divine revelation is in effect undermined.

Once more, the corrective is not to be found in adjustments in one direction or the other which presuppose an opposition between the historical and eschatological, the temporal and eternal, the provisional and the infallible, faith and reason, or theology and science, but rather is to be found in a theological anthropology which focuses on the essential interrelation of the divine and human in history and through history. God's self is given to humanity in Jesus — in one who is human, in a divine gesture or realsymbol that is genuinely historical. God's "word" in Jesus does not abrogate history or circumvent it. God's word is mediated through human words.

So, for example, although the credibility of Christian faith certainly hinges on the historical reliability of the Gospel accounts, it does not hinge on the literal accuracy of all their details. Indeed, as we have seen, recognition of the historicity of this literature can be an immensely helpful step for focusing more clearly just what the "good news" was which the evangelists proclaimed. Likewise, one does not have to deny the historical relativity of the Genesis accounts of creation, or Moses' proclamation of the Law or the prophets' interpretation of it in order to acknowledge these as authentic revelations of God's relationship to humanity. Indeed, recognition of these stories' historical and literary contexts discloses more precisely what is distinctive about the biblical conception of God and humanity and clarifies what commends these testimonies to the believer as expressing a divine truth in human words — as speaking an eternal word in an historically mediated truth.

The same kind of reasons question the strategy of playing salvation's "other worldly" fulfillment against its "this worldly" manifestations or grace's supernatural character against human nature's woundedness. Theological balance requires an appreciation that salvation, although ultimately fulfilled in a definitive and complete union with God beyond history, is already a reality which touches us historically and concretely in this life through the "spirit" of Christ. On the one hand, it cannot be emphasized enough against humanity's idolatrous egoism that left to ourselves our humanity is wounded, our good will impotent, our language, self-understandings and social structures inextricably corrupted. Left to our own, we are sinners. But on the other hand, it cannot be emphasized enough that we are not left alone — that God has never left us alone. From the very beginning the "spirit," eventually triumphant in the Crucified and Risen Christ, has been extending God's reach to us so that our reach might be touched and transformed by a divine/human solidarity which opens the mind, frees the heart and empowers love. The real historical gestures and concrete historical sacraments of this divine/human solidarity are not only the signs of a salvation to come, but are essential moments within its coming in history. They are true vehicles of God's grace — truly gifts of his presence. Through the grace of God's "spirit" in Christ, we are not just sinners. We are being saved. We are graced. We are called to flesh out that grace concretely in our diverse worlds and cultures.

Such grace and revelation, which are at once transcendent, historical and eschatological, require a faith which engages the whole person — head, heart, hands and feet. Here too imbalance is a danger. The intellectual assent entailed in faith can be divorced from the conversion of the heart and the transformation of one's actions and world, just as the affective and activist dimensions of faith can be divorced from its intellectual moment. But these dimensions can no more authentically be emphasized over against each other, than orthodoxy and orthopraxis can be. One is really not possible without the other. Just as theology and anthropology come together for the Christian in Christology, as the Father and Son come together in the Spirit, as the transcendent and historical come together in the eschatological, so orthodoxy and orthopraxis must come together in a discipleship which engages the whole person.

This sort of discipleship, like the divine humanity it seeks, is not yet our achievement. It is a calling — an ongoing task in need of embodiment. It sets the agenda for the future. It requires a theology which attends at once to the difficulties of the head, the questions of the heart and the scandal of the hands and feet. It necessitates a thinking which at once is intelligible, credible and concretely transforming — a thinking which at once is coherent, historical and morally engaged. This agenda for holding things together thus requires an ongoing effort to break into the Christian circle and an ongoing effort to let the grace of that circle break in on us. The key is the correlation of theology and anthropology in Christ's "spirit," not the reduction or opposition of one to the other. The correlation, one might say to summarize, is a reflective and engaged participation in the charmed circle of the human and the divine to which God calls us in the Spirit of Jesus through our solidarity with one another.

Needless to say, what I have proposed here is but one very limited way of illustrating how the elements of this circle hold together. The aim has not been to elaborate a full-fledged systematic theology but only to suggest how a theology of the head, heart, hands and feet could help us break out of the spells of our charmed circles and privileged ghettos and so recognize what the Christian believes is the graced circle of God's saving Spirit of truth, freedom and love.

Notes

1. See for example Thomas C. Oden, *Agenda for Theology: Recovering Christian Roots* (New York: Harper & Row, 1979); and James Hitchcock's *Catholicism and Modernity: Confrontation or Capitulation* (New York: The Seabury Press, 1979).

2. See *Against the World for the World: The Hartford Appeal and the Future of American Religion,* ed. Peter L. Berger and Richard John Neuhaus (New York: The Seabury Press, 1976).

3. Avery Dulles, *The Resilient Church: The Necessity and Limits of Adaption* (Garden City, New York: Doubleday & Company, Inc., 1977).

4. Joseph Cardinal Ratzinger with Vittorio Messori, *The Ratzinger Report: An Exclusive Interview on the State of the Church,* trans. Salvator Attanasio and Graham Harrison (San Francisco: Ignatius Press, 1985).

5. See Richard Neuhaus, "The Hartford Debate," *Christianity and Crisis,* 35 (July 1975) p. 174.

Index